BUT YOU HAVE NOT OBEYED ME

BUT YOU HAVE NOT OBEYED ME

HE HAS NOT FORGOTTEN SERIES, BOOK 1

SONYA CONTRERAS

Bull Head Press

Copyright ©2018 by Sonya Contreras

All rights reserved.

No part of this book may be reproduced or transmitted in any form or by any means, electronic or mechanical, including photocopying, recording, or by any information storage and retrieval system without the written permission of the publisher, except where permitted by law.

All Scripture quotations are taken from Holy Bible, New International Version. Copyright © 1973, 1978, 1984 International Bible Society. Used by permission of Zondervan Bible Publishers.

But You Have Not Obeyed Me is a work of fiction. Although retelling the Scriptures' events as closely as possible, the real people, events, establishments, or locales are used fictitiously. All other elements of the novel are drawn from the author's imagination after careful research.

Published by Bull Head Press
Squaw Valley, California

Paperback ISBN: 978-0-9990009-6-0
eBook ISBN: 978-0-999000-7-7

Library of Congress Control Number: 2018906618

Cover Design by OliviabyDesign with Fiverr
Edited by Titania Porter

Printed in the United States of America.

❦ Created with Vellum

CONTENTS

Introduction — vii
Epigraph — ix

PART I
OTHNIEL

Chapter 1 — 3
Chapter 2 — 15
Chapter 3 — 23
Chapter 4 — 39
Chapter 5 — 45

PART II
EHUD

Chapter 6 — 51
Chapter 7 — 61
Chapter 8 — 69
Chapter 9 — 79

PART III
SHAMGAR

Chapter 10 — 91
Chapter 11 — 99

PART IV
DEBORAH AND BARAK

Chapter 12 — 111
Chapter 13 — 115
Chapter 14 — 133
Chapter 15 — 145
Chapter 16 — 161
Chapter 17 — 169

PART V
GIDEON

Chapter 18	185
Chapter 19	201
Chapter 20	211
Chapter 21	229
Chapter 22	237
Chapter 23	243
Chapter 24	251
Chapter 25	257
Chapter 26	263
Chapter 27	273

PART VI
ABIMELECH

Chapter 28	291
Chapter 29	305
Chapter 30	317
Chapter 31	321
Chapter 32	333
Summary Remarks	347
Bibliography	351
About the Author	359
There's More	361
Also by Sonya Contreras	363
Remember Me	365

Dear Reader,

Why study Judges?

Unlike Joshua, where the Israelites battled evil from without, Judges shows God's own people fighting sin within. The book doesn't soften their sin nor entice us to emulate it. Their sin brings their downfall. God delivers His people through judges, reminding them of His requirements and His faithfulness.

The more I researched how their addictive behavior caused by their worship led them farther from goodness, the more I could understand why God let them go. Their depravity was repulsive.

Their self-gratifying lifestyle resembles our own. So like today, where God's holiness is far from our own thoughts, and our choices bring addictive thought patterns that must be satiated to our own destruction.

Judges warns us of our peril as we live without God. Forgetting God brings ignorance of His Word. Without His Standard, man loses his anchor and finds pleasure in warped deeds. Man doesn't know he's lost until God, in His grace, brings oppression to show man his need. Man cries to God. God provides salvation.

In spite of the evil and oppression in Judges, it offers hope, not only to Israel who forgot, but to us, as we parallel their forgetfulness. We see evil growing. How bad can it get? Where is God?

God waits, as in the time of Judges, for us to remember Him. There is great comfort in Judges; not when we look at man who keeps forgetting and falling, but when we look to our great God Who does not forget.

He's still waiting for us to look to Him.

Sonya Contreras

I brought you up out of Egypt and led you into the land which I have sworn to your fathers; and I said, "I will never break My covenant with you, and as for you, you shall make no covenant with the inhabitants of this land; you shall tear down their altars."

But you have not obeyed Me;

What is this you have done? Therefore I also said, "I will not drive them out before you, but they will become as thorns in your sides and their gods will be a snare to you."

— JUDGES 2:1B-3

Then the sons of Israel did evil in the sight of the Lord . . . and they forsook the Lord . . . and followed other gods . . . And He sold them into the hands of their enemies . . . That they were severely distressed. Then the Lord raised up judges who delivered them from the hands of those who plundered them.

Yet they did not listen to their judges. . . .

But it came about when the judge died, that they would turn back and act more corruptly than their fathers.

— JUDGES 2:11-19

But you have not obeyed Me.

— JUDGES 6:10

PART I

OTHNIEL

JUDGES 3:1-11

This first story leaves a pit in my stomach. I prayed many times to remove it from the collection. But each time God's Spirit confirmed its place.

Israel's sin and rejection of God must be seen in order to see God's salvation and hope. Israel's sin, like our own, is not enticing or tempting, but reveals man's depravity, exposing it for what it is: a challenge against God.

Man must come to the end of himself before he looks to God. Even good people, when left to themselves, do not seek God. Only by seeing our peril and our depravity do we seek God for our salvation.

Yet, without God, man has no hope.

Read Othniel's story and weep at how far God's people had fallen.

Weep, too, for those today who still need to see God.

Some content of Othniel is unsuitable for children due to the nature of the sin. Use your own discretion.

CHAPTER 1

Ladonna turned to her servant. "If I had known then, what I know now, I never would have done it."

"Done what?"

"Married."

"But how could you have escaped, when your father had arranged it?"

"I would have killed myself first."

"Never that."

"Aren't we at the same place now?" She lifted the dagger. "Only I don't have the strength to finish the deed. Will you?"

The servant took the dagger from Ladonna's hand. Had they come so low as to want death over life? She stabbed her. She watched until Ladonna breathed her last. With that, the Jewish servant walked from the house and toward the caves. She did not hurry.

Her thoughts were not on today, but on many years ago.

She remembered a God Who was merciful, gracious, and forgiving, although jealous. Very jealous . . . and that, she laughed bitterly, was why her people were in trouble now.

When Joshua and the elders died, God's people forgot their God. It hadn't happened overnight. But it didn't take long for the Philistines to look over their walls and see Israelite beauties as perfect wives for their sons. Because the Philistines were a wealthy nation, respected by nations around them, they promised Israelites peace in the land, as well as a sea coast to serve their merchants. Alliances were made. Marriages arranged. Life settled comfortably for all concerned. It was for peace they changed. Wasn't peace what everyone wanted?

And prosperity. And comfort.

Only Israel had forgotten one thing. Their God was a jealous God and would share His glory with no other.

Ladonna paced in her guest chamber, looking over the grounds of her husband-to-be. His Philistine customs were foreign to her. Would she know what to do?

Her mother-in-law, Gardenia, entered the room without knocking.

Would she have no privacy? Ladonna didn't like it but forced a smile to her face.

Gardenia held a garment, draped over her arm. "I have your dress for tomorrow."

Ladonna shut her mouth against complaint. She would ask her father. He would allow her to wear her mother's dress. It had been passed down from her grandmother who had made it from Egyptian fabric given at the Exodus.

Gardenia spread out the dress on her bed. "Let's see it on you." She waited.

Ladonna walked to the bed. She fingered the rich silk. The skirt, narrower than what her people wore, although common among the Philistine women, accentuated elegant hips and slender legs. Ladonna blushed. Perhaps she could bring the fabric together across the front of the dress.

Gardenia waited, her lips pursed tightly, her eyes harsh.

Ladonna dressed in front of her, self-conscious of her attention. Once the dress was on, she pulled at the fabric, trying to conceal her front.

Gardenia eyed her exposed skin and smiled. "You have kept yourself hidden. Qadir will be pleased."

Ladonna could feel her face flush anew. She felt like a piece of meat bartered at the market.

Gardenia motioned for her to turn around. Then gestured to the window. "Walk to the window."

Ladonna did, but could only take tiny steps, making the journey a chore. Was Gardenia impatient by her slow progress?

When she turned, she glanced at Gardenia.

Gardenia was watching her, apparently enjoying Ladonna's movements.

Perhaps it was time to tell her about her own dress. "I have a dress—"

"This will do." Gardenia opened the dress more and gazed down inside. "The dress is worn like this. Don't tug on the material."

Ladonna felt like a scolded child. She licked her dry lips and tried again. "I already have a dress for tomorrow."

Gardenia stroked her hair away from her face and moved her hand down Ladonna's neck.

Ladonna stood stiffly, cringing. What was she doing? She could stand still no longer. She stepped away and turned to the window. She almost fell. She'd forgotten the little steps she must take to walk in this skirt.

Gardenia caught her by the shoulders and turned her around. She held Ladonna's arm firmly, not allowing her to move. "You will make Qadir proud." It was spoken more like a threat than a compliment. She tucked the dress back, exposing more skin.

Ladonna could only swallow. Her eyes burned with unshed tears. She felt exposed and used just standing before a woman. She couldn't wear this dress in public.

She blinked back tears and tried again. "I already have a dress for tomorrow."

Gardenia acted like she didn't hear. "Qadir sent you this." She retrieved a small box from a pocket in her dress. She handed it to Ladonna.

Ladonna stepped back and turned from Gardenia, uncomfortable with the way she made her feel. She sat on the edge of the bed. Opening the lid, she gasped at the emerald on a chain of fine gold. She lifted it out of the box. "It's beautiful."

Gardenia took it from her. "I'll put it on you."

Ladonna didn't want to be touched by her. This woman made her feel used, dirty somehow. But there was nothing she could do but bow her head as Gardenia placed the chain around her neck.

Gardenia followed the chain around her neck with her fingertip and held the emerald against Ladonna's skin.

Ladonna stepped back, only to find that Gardenia held fast to the necklace.

"This will make the gods proud."

Ladonna swallowed. She hated to ask so many questions. These gods were not her gods. Gardenia made her feel foolish, "Why would the gods be proud?"

Gardenia smiled. "Tomorrow you will see."

The day had been filled with wedding details. Ladonna had seen her father only at dinner. She wanted to speak to him. But he brushed her aside and drank more wine. She retired for the night exhausted, but wouldn't sleep until she spoke to her father about the dress. She listened for her father's footsteps outside her chamber. When she finally heard him, the moon had already risen. She tiptoed to his chamber door. "Abba?"

He opened the door, pulling his belt around his tunic as he did. He hiccupped.

Ladonna's heart sank. It was unusual for him to drink more than what he should. Would he listen? She must try. "Abba, I have a request."

Allowing her to enter, he sat on a chair by the window.

But You Have Not Obeyed Me

Ladonna knelt on the floor by his knee and held his hand. "Abba. I have mother's dress to wear tomorrow. But Gardenia insists I wear another."

He wiped her hair from her forehead and sighed deeply. "Ladonna, we must keep the peace. If you don't wear your mother's dress, who would know but you and I?"

Ladonna could feel her eyes fill with tears. "I miss her."

He leaned forward and held her face in both his hands. "I miss her, too. But you'll be making new traditions and learning your husband's customs. Didn't our people change when we lived in Egypt? You must bend or be broken."

Ladonna studied her father's face. He hadn't drunk enough to keep him from talking. "What if by bending, I forget who I am?"

Her abba sighed. "You cannot change who you are inside. No dress can do that. Please, Gardenia, at least until you are Qadir's."

She shifted on her knees. Her abba still didn't understand. She wasn't sure she did. But her feelings, in Gardenia's presence, made her feel exposed to evil. She wouldn't wear that dress. Could she wear her own and apologize later?

Her father held his head in his hands. "There's something you must know."

Ladonna didn't like his tone. Was it regret? He didn't seem as drunk now, as if the conversation had stirred in him an awareness of danger.

"You must please Qadir. It is for your welfare and mine."

She looked at him, startled. Why?

He raised his head and studied her. "I couldn't sell our skins to our own people. Everyone had plenty. No one needed them. I had no means to pay the Philistine's taxes. I borrowed from Qadir. He suggested I sell my skins to the Sea People. I did. When the ship sank, I lost it all. Qadir graciously suggested the marriage to clear my debt."

At her gasp, he continued, "Qadir helped me. He came when I needed him most."

Ladonna rose from her knees. She felt heat rise to her face. "Wouldn't our own people help you?"

He shook his head. "None of our neighbors had anything. That's why I shipped at Qadir's prompting."

"Of course." She pursed her lips trying not to say anything, but had to ask, "Did his ship really sink?"

Her father's voice broke, "Why would he lie?" He wore such a helpless look.

Her shoulders sagged. How could her father trust a Philistine? There was more to this than just taxes. She didn't trust Qadir. "Tell me about Qadir."

"He's a leader of his people. You will stand like a queen beside him." He nodded as he spoke.

Did he speak to convince her or himself? She shook her head. Gardenia would never allow that. Gardenia alone ruled as queen. Ladonna would be treated like a child, an ignorant child.

Their people had changed for peace. They were tired of fighting. They wanted comfort. They wanted rest. Wasn't peace what everyone wanted?

Her father smiled. "You're still my little girl. I wish your mother were here . . . to see you all grown and getting married." His voice petered out, and he stared out the window.

Ladonna rose to her feet.

He would not tell her any more about Qadir. It was as before when she had asked. He told just enough to give her a sense that something wasn't right. Now she felt it more strongly. If she didn't marry Qadir, her father would be destitute, and she with him. She kissed him on both cheeks. "Shalom, Abba. I'll see you tomorrow."

He tore his gaze from the window, as if his thoughts were painful. He attempted a smile. "Be at peace, my daughter."

She slipped from the room and hurried to her own chamber. Tomorrow would come. But would she find peace?

When morning came, Gardenia hovered over her. She commanded her to soak in a steamy, hot bath, smelling of lavender and mint, until she had shrunk to a raisin. Servants worked around her, preparing her hair and nails. She should feel spoiled with all this attention. But with each task, Ladonna's anxiety increased. Would she have no privacy? She must find a way to wear her mother's dress. She eyed the wooden chest that held it but couldn't open it without Gardenia watching.

Late in the day, the servants finally left her room. She sighed, relieved to be alone finally. She had worried the entire day, planning how not to wear Gardenia's dress.

She closed her eyes for just a moment. Her abba's conversation had tormented her far into the early morning hours.

When she opened them, Gardenia stood over her. She gasped and straightened. How could she have fallen asleep?

Gardenia studied her with approval and something more. Her eyes held a gleam that made Ladonna uncomfortable.

She heard her abba's words again, "Bend, so you don't break." She forced herself to smile. "Shalom."

Gardenia didn't acknowledge the greeting. She just motioned for her to stand. "It's time. Hurry."

Ladonna hesitated. Her insides twirled like a windswept sand eddy. She'd have no chance to wear her mother's dress. She dressed as a lump grew in her heart.

Bend or be broken.

She would do it for her abba.

But did her abba know what bending would cost her?

Qadir stood at the top of the temple stairs, waiting. He fidgeted, hearing the commotion of the people behind him. What could be taking Ladonna so long? He thought back to the day he had noticed her in the Jews' market. Even her homely tunic and coverings couldn't conceal her beauty. He had investigated her father's wealth and devised a way to make her his. Her dowry had been pittance, but having her beside him would bring many merchants his way without trouble. He had been pleased when Gardenia promised him more than he could imagine. He could hardly wait.

As a boy, Qadir had watched maidens climb the temple stairs to join their groom in front of the god of fertility. The crowds hindered him from getting too close, but he had seen enough to know his own wedding would guarantee an heir and the gods' blessing. The necklace, a charm of one of the gods, would seal their approval.

Now he waited for his bride. He watched her walk up the street to the temple's steps.

This would be a night to remember.

She climbed the many steps to stand beside him.

She didn't lift her face to his until she reached the top of the stairs.

Before them, Dagon, god of fertility, stood, ready to bless their union.

Qadir took a goblet from the table in front of the god and handed it to Ladonna. He reached for the second one. He gulped the contents, motioning her to do the same with hers.

She sipped.

Qadir nodded to her cup. Wine would help them perform what the gods expected. They must finish together to be blessed together. He motioned for another to refill his cup "You must drink it all, to enhance your ability to give to the gods."

She sipped again and coughed. "It's hard to swallow."

His eyebrows raised in surprise. He'd been drinking wine since he sat on his mother's knee. He gulped his second.

She still had not finished.

He motioned for five more fillings.

She hadn't finished hers.

He smiled and took her cup from her. As he finished it off, his hand trembled slightly.

She helped guide the cup to the table to set it down. He stood before the people and before his god and leered at Ladonna.

It was time.

But You Have Not Obeyed Me

The next morning, Ladonna woke on her bed, not knowing how she had gotten there. Her head felt disjointed, and her whole body was sore. She heard a pounding that must have come from the door. She couldn't rise to answer it.

Her father approached her bedside. "My precious, I'm so sorry. I had no idea."

Ladonna took in his sorrowful countenance and became afraid. "What is it, Abba?"

He mumbled and shook his head.

"Tell me."

"I should have listened about the dress. I didn't know their customs. My daughter, I'm sorry."

Ladonna took his hand in hers. "It's over, Abba. I didn't break for you. Are you pleased?"

He mumbled again but couldn't look into her face.

She noticed his red-rimmed eyes. "What is it?"

"Do you remember anything at the temple?"

Ladonna concentrated in spite of her aching head. "I couldn't drink the wine fast enough for Qadir." She studied her abba. "Is that what you mean?"

He looked at her with concern. "My sweet, innocent daughter. What have I done to you?"

She was frightened. What had happened? Why couldn't she remember?

He looked down from her searching eyes. "The drink made you do things you wouldn't do."

The door opened.

Gardenia strode to her side.

Ladonna rose on her elbow, trying to stop the spinning of her head. "Shalom."

"There will be no peace under this roof. For you have humiliated my son before the gods and the people."

Ladonna couldn't remember anything. What had she done to make her so angry? She remembered the drink. It was bitter. She couldn't swallow it. Was it more than wine? Qadir had finished it for her. "What have I done?" She looked to where her abba had stood.

He had vanished.

She felt deserted. Why hadn't he stayed?

Gardenia huffed. "What have you done? I'll tell you." She raised her voice, "You've humiliated my son."

Ladonna could feel her cheeks blush. As she concentrated on Gardenia's words, she remembered nothing. What had happened? She shook her head.

Gardenia spit in her face. "Don't deny your actions. Why did my son think marrying a Jew would make his life better? You allowed all the men to use you, yet my son was not the first. You are a dog and worthy of divorce."

Ladonna shook her head. Nothing made sense. Why couldn't she remember?

Her father would be ruined if she wasn't Qadir's wife. "What can I do to make it right?"

Gardenia stalked over to the window and gazed out.

Her silence made Ladonna tremble. She watched Gardenia's face. It turned from anger to resignation to a glimmer of a smile. Ladonna didn't like her anger, but she felt a foreboding with her smile. Her head throbbed more as she tried to guess what her mother-in-law was planning.

Gardenia walked to the bed. "I know of only one thing. Any child you have must be given to Molesch. He will make all things right.

Ladonna nodded in agreement. She didn't understand how she could be with child. She hadn't entered Qadir's tent, as was their Jewish marriage custom. Nor did she know who Molesch was, but if he was the father of the child, he should get him. All this seemed unreal, as if happening to someone else. What had been in that drink? She heard herself asking, "Does that mean I must serve him?"

Gardenia smiled. "Qadir would be pleased."

With her smile, Ladonna's heart sank. What had she suggested?

Gardenia left, not as she had arrived, but with a smile on her lips.

And Ladonna wondered who she had agreed to serve.

CHAPTER 2

Othniel oversaw his flocks in the hill country of Judah. The mountains tumbled toward the Great Sea. His sheep had thrived, and his wool was quality. But he was troubled. All his countrymen had done well. But he also knew they had expected more and had spent before they had sold their wool. The money hadn't come, nor could they pay their taxes. He had advised them of their folly. They hadn't listened.

They sold their wool to the Philistines, who lived just over the mountain range from their land. His people had followed the roads to their cities and found the Great Sea. They coveted the Philistines' coastline and thought they could impress them with their great supply of wool and hides. But the Philistines were only impressed with their daughters' beauty and their sons' strength. They bartered, not only for their wool, but also for their hearts.

Othniel shook his head. The Lord had not commanded them to destroy the Philistines when they entered the land. Othniel didn't understand why this wicked nation had been spared. Did God want to test His people and see if they would still remember Him?

They had not. Instead, they looked for comfort, wealth, and acceptance. They believed they had found it. But at what cost?

Cadman journeyed to the coast of Gaza where the Great Sea meets land. He brushed against the dagger hidden in the fold of his cloak. He had kept that and his sword close as he traveled across the Philistine land to reach the coast. He had pushed himself to reach Qadir before the other Israelite shepherds came to sell their wool.

He met Qadir to discuss his wool's shipment. His wool was stacked in front the ship that would carry it to the Great Sea people.

Qadir reviewed their contract, glossing over the details.

Cadman had him repeat the conditions. He wouldn't be caught gullible again.

Qadir rushed through his explanations.

Others interrupted him.

Cadman waited for them to finish. He worried about Ladonna. But he couldn't spend the night at Qadir's, no matter how much he wanted to see her. How could he face her after allowing her wedding? Did she remember what was done to her? He swallowed, unable to wait any longer, "How's Ladonna?"

Qadir smiled. "She waits to receive me until we know she is pure."

Cadman remembered the wedding ceremony. How could she not carry someone's child? He clenched his fists at his sides and took several breaths, working hard to contain his temper. "My daughter was pure for her wedding."

Qadir explained as if instructing a child. "But I wasn't first. It's our custom. If she's without child, all will be fine."

"And if she is with child?"

Qadir laughed. "Do not fret. If your shipment brings a good price, she'll be protected at my house. If not—" He shrugged.

Cadman hung onto his next words. What would he do to her if she was with child?

"She'll serve in the temple to pay for her impurity. Once your shipment sells, we can talk again about keeping her at my house."

Cadman swallowed. He spoke as if she were a pet to entertain him and discard when he was finished. What happened to cherishing her as his wife? Cadman hadn't considered the Philistine customs as different from his own, but this was his daughter. He shook his head. Her safety depended upon a good sale of his wool. He didn't doubt his skins were worth a good price, but he remembered his first shipment that sank in the sea.

Did he trust Qadir?

He had trusted Qadir with his daughter, and look where it gotten him! He'd seen enough at her wedding night to know what serving at the temple would do to her. He clenched his teeth in renewed anger over what had happened. Could he have stopped it?

He remembered his life with his wife. His life had been different then. Happy. Complete. But after his wife died, Cadman hadn't wanted to live.

Ladonna, though only two years old, had brought healing to his broken heart. He had poured his life into protecting her and providing for her.

She had rewarded him with hope.

When Qadir had approached him about his debt and taxes, Cadman hadn't wondered how Qadir had learned about his misfortune. He had blindly accepted his help. Why shouldn't he trust him? Didn't any neighbor help?

But when his first wool shipment failed to bring money, Qadir had instantly claimed Ladonna as his own. Cadman felt his first inklings of Qadir's deceit. But he hadn't wanted to consider it. Could he relinquish his only precious daughter to a man he couldn't trust?

The eve before Ladonna's wedding, he had drunk heavily, hoping to suppress his suspicions. But no amount of drink could remove his uneasiness.

He had confessed only a part of his problems to Ladonna on her wedding eve.

On her wedding day at the temple, Cadman realized he had not only lost her to a questionable husband, but to a corrupt people, and a god he didn't like.

Now his insides twisted with this added weight. For Ladonna's sake, he couldn't lose another shipment. This shipment *must* pay well. He shook his head to clear his thoughts, wishing again he could see Ladonna. Was she safe? The shame he'd brought on his daughter weighed on him. Did Ladonna even want to see him? He had fled when Gardenia had interrogated her after the wedding. He hadn't seen her since.

Cadman watched as Qadir strode from the docks. He walked like someone who owned the land he touched. Indeed, he owned more than Cadman wanted him to.

A sailor bumped into him as he hurried to load his wool.

Cadman stepped back from the dock's activity, watching his wool and skins being loaded onto the ship. He felt for his dagger. He must be alert to his own dangers. And watch his wool until it was safely on the ship.

He wiped his forehead with his cloak's sleeve. The cool sea breeze should have been refreshing after the journey through the mountains and the hot sand. But it did nothing to calm his unease.

Cadman thought of his own people when they had fought for their land. They had done what God commanded. He had been too young to fight, but not too young to remember their promise to obey.

He felt his cheeks flush. He'd forgotten God's Law when he entered an alliance with Qadir, a foreigner. He had only wanted to pay his taxes. And didn't he have to survive? That had led to giving his daughter to an idol worshiper. But again, shouldn't he pay his debts?

How quickly God was displaced by the need to survive.

But even as the thought came, another questioned it. How quickly survival became crucial when God was forgotten!

Cadman shook his head. This would be the last time he'd align himself with the Philistines, even for commerce. They should be battling them, not joining hands with them. How had he come to this?

The sun lowered behind the ship. The crimson colors outlined the timbers that held the sails. Cadman saw the sturdy beams and lines. Cadman nodded, reassured. This ship would make it.

The ship would leave with the tide in the early morn. His mission accomplished, he turned to find an inn for the night.

The captain's words stopped him. "Move the wool to the lowest deck."

His first mate hesitated. "But the water will damage it."

"So will throwing it in the middle of the sea but that's what you'll be doing."

Cadman remembered hearing his neighbors faring equally poorly with their wool on ships bound to the Sea People. Could so many ships carrying Israeli wool sink? He had wondered at the coincidence. Now he knew it to be their plan.

He stepped forward. He didn't feel bold, only angry and desperate. "Captain!"

The captain turned. When he saw Cadman, he scowled. Turning away, he ignored him.

"Captain." Cadman stepped forward. "I want my wool removed from the ship."

The captain laughed and shook his head. "Wool? What wool? All we carry is dung to be dumped in the bottom of the Great Sea."

Cadman reached the top of the gangplank in hurried strides. He pulled out the parchment from inside his cloak. "I have a signed statement of your receipt."

"Ai, do you? Then you also know once it rests on my ship, there's no removing it until the ship rests with the Sea People."

Cadman smiled, though his eyes still blazed. "Then it cannot be dumped in the bottom of the sea, can it?"

It was the captain's turn to smile. "And where do you think the Sea People are buried?"

Cadman swallowed. His temples pounded. He had asked Qadir about that clause, thinking it strange. Qadir had explained it was for Cadman's protection. He had believed him and been duped. He clenched the parchment in his fist.

The captain, after a moment of gloating, said, "Get off my ship. Your people belong where all dung finally lands; in the Sea."

Cadman hesitated only a moment, before seeing no choice but to leave. When he strode off the dock, he didn't stay at any inn that night, but started home. His anger spurred him.

What would happen to Ladonna at the temple?

He couldn't pay his debt with a shipment that never made harbor.

Qadir would demand payment.

Cadman must sell his sheep.

And warn his people the Philistines weren't to be trusted.

When Cadman reached his land, he didn't stop at his house, but continued to his neighbor's. He knocked on the door, although it was late.

Othniel answered, tying his cloak over his tunic. "Cadman, Shalom. Is everything all right?"

It had taken several days to return home, and his anger had turned to despair as he realized his calamity. "I have come from Gaza."

Othniel nodded, his face reflecting disapproval.

Cadman lowered his head, unable to meet Othniel's eyes. "I took my wool to the Sea People." He remembered Othniel's caution against partnership with people not the Lord's. "You were right."

Instead of Othniel gloating over Cadman's misfortune, Cadman was surprised to see Othniel lower his head.

"I'm sorry." He motioned Cadman inside. He poured him a drink.

Cadman drank the entire vessel and wiped his lips with the back of his hand. "They plan to dump it, like the first. I thought the first had been an accident. I am ruined."

"What of Ladonna?"

"This shipment was to pay for her release."

Othniel nodded. "It is a heavy price to pay."

Cadman swallowed a sob. "I sold my daughter to the enemy, not once but twice. I cannot ransom her. She will be sent to their temple."

Othniel rubbed Cadman's shoulder. "You now know the enemy. There are many of our brothers who do not see the enemy for who they are. That alone is cause to weep."

Othniel watched as his neighbors fell to the Philistine's deceit. Instead of heeding his caution, they thought themselves beyond danger.

They continued in their own ways, for they could save themselves. Or so they thought. They forgot from where their God had brought them. And by forgetting, their wickedness grew.

And God waited.

CHAPTER 3

Ladonna was with child. She kept her secret for as long as she could. She wasn't permitted to leave her room while she waited for her purity to be proven. She was treated well, but life was lonely. She watched others from her window and wondered at these people and their strange customs.

She remembered her people's customs. They held the marriage bed sacred for husband and wife. How could she follow God's law *and* obey her husband? And was she even his wife, when he could ignore her after the ceremony? How could she obey her abba's counsel "bend, and don't break"?

She hadn't seen her father since the wedding day. He had been her protector, her warrior, her provider, her everything since her mother's death when she was a toddler. She mourned the loss. Why didn't he come to see her? Did Qadir prevent it?

A servant entered the room, bringing her meal.

Ladonna always left the drink on the tray. She remembered how the drink had caused her to forget what she did. She would never touch another drop.

Gardenia came, her only visitor. Each time, she would stare into her face, as if she could read whether she was with child.

Ladonna would concentrate on nothing, lest she reveal her news.

Gardenia studied her form.

Ladonna shivered. She felt unclean by her look, like a leper she had once seen from a distance.

When Gardenia left, her spirit lingered, making Ladonna feel she was still watched.

Under God's Law, a woman desired to be married and have children. Children were cause to rejoice. They were a blessing.

This Philistine culture made blessings into curses. She dreaded this child growing within her. She cursed the day she had come to be with child.

How could a people turn such a blessing into something evil when God had pronounced it good?

If only she could confide in someone who could tell her what Gardenia was planning to do with her.

She watched each servant when they brought her meals.

They didn't look at her or speak to her. Was that by Gardenia's command? Wasn't everything in this house by her command?

One day, a new servant brought her meal.

She didn't look Philistine.

Ladonna whispered, conscious of Gardenia's ever-listening ears, "Are you one of our people?"

The servant looked up, her eyes widening. She nodded.

Ladonna lowered her voice. "Help me!"

The servant put down the tray, shaking her head.

Ladonna stepped forward and grabbed the woman's arm, not allowing her to leave. "What happens to me if I am with child? They said the child would be given to Molesch. Who is he?"

The servant's eyes widened. She backed toward the door.

Ladonna stopped her. "Tell me."

She broke from Ladonna's grasp and darted out the room.

L adonna planned as she paced her chamber. If having a child was what kept her from helping her father, then how could she eliminate the child?

But You Have Not Obeyed Me

There were herbs to make a baby slip out before its birth. Could she get those herbs?

She watched for the servant's return and was ready.

When she brought her meal, and placed the tray on the table, Ladonna grabbed her wrists.

The servant dropped the tray.

It clattered to the floor.

Dropping to her knees, the servant whispered as she returned the bread, meat, cheese, and fruit to the tray. "Molesch is a god. They sacrifice their children to him." Before Ladonna could respond, the servant rushed from the room.

Ladonna knelt by the tray. She repeated the message three times before the words registered. They kill their children for a god's pleasure? What kind of people were these?

She wouldn't be giving her child to the next man in line at the temple. She would be sacrificing her baby!

The more Ladonna considered, the more she wanted the herb. Wouldn't that be better than sacrificing her baby to the gods?

When the servant returned, Ladonna feigned being sick. The servant approached the bed alarmed. "Are you well?"

Ladonna grabbed her arm, not allowing her to go. "Bring me pennyroyal."

The servant paled. "It will cause the babe to leave you."

"If I must see my baby die by the gods, wouldn't it be better to have it die by my own hand?"

The servant shook her head and stopped struggling. "We've come a long way from the Law of our fathers."

"What is the Law but rules that do not help when life gets hard?"

The servant bowed lower. "The Law keeps life from getting hard."

Ladonna laughed, a hard, bitter laugh. "How could a Law do that?"

"As a small child, I listened to the Law given by our God. It protected us. But we no longer value His Law."

"We aren't protected by this Law."

The servant nodded. "Because we have forgotten the Law-Giver."

Ladonna shook her head. "I know nothing of this God, but I must have the herb."

The servant lowered her head. "I'll see what I can do."

The servant didn't return.

Had Gardenia caught her? She watched over everything, like a crow looking for the eyes of the dead to pick and eat.

Ladonna shuddered. She waited, paced, and watched for the return of the servant. She caught movement outside her window.

A gardener pruned a rosemary bush. The branches fell to the ground, lifeless. She felt like those branches. Each time a snip was made, part of her heart seemed to have died. Snip. Her mother was gone. Snip. Her abba. Snip. Her arranged wedding. Snip. Her husband. Snip. Soon her child. Did she have no say what happened to her? Snip. Snip. Snip.

She covered her face and collapsed on a chair by the window. Who could save her now?

Could her abba help? Wouldn't he have done so already, if he could? Why hadn't he visited? Was he allowed? Her thoughts whirled in circles. She tried to calm herself, to keep from panicking.

In this state of mind, she heard Gardenia enter as she always did, without knocking and in control.

Gardenia's eyes held a look of . . .what?

Ladonna backed away from her and placed her hand protectively on her growing baby.

Gardenia smiled, victoriously. "You *are* with child."

Ladonna dropped her hand, conscious she had given her baby's presence away. She backed against the wall and breathed deeply, trying not to look Gardenia in the eye.

Gardenia ripped her dress open.

Ladonna sucked in her breath. It was too late for the herb.

Gardenia laughed. "Molesch will be pleased. Qadir has been beside himself, waiting for your seclusion to end. He had almost convinced me there had been enough time to know you were his." She pushed on Ladonna's belly and laughed. "But I knew. You glow. You are not pure for Qadir."

Ladonna could only stand there motionless and tense as Gardenia handled her. Hadn't she learned from the wedding dress she couldn't argue with Gardenia? Ladonna lowered her head. "What does that mean?"

Gardenia seemed to find pleasure in telling her. "He is free from any obligation."

Ladonna licked her lips, trying to wet her dry mouth. "I am not his wife?"

Gardenia shrugged. "You never were."

"But where will I go?"

Gardenia smiled. "You are promised to the temple."

She didn't know what that meant, but if Gardenia was enthusiastic, it wasn't good for her. Ladonna wilted against the wall. "When?"

"Qadir will care for you until the child is ready for Molesch. After that, we'll see." She walked as if she floated.

Ladonna couldn't remember how long she had been confined to her room. Had it been four moons or five? How much time did she have?

When the servant came with her next meal, Ladonna was ready. Her insides were twisted in knots. She couldn't eat. But she would have answers.

The servant laid the tray down on the table, raising her eyes to meet Ladonna's.

Ladonna could no longer hold back her tears.

The Jewish servant spoke their people's language, using the endearing Jewish name for daughter.

Hearing her own language brought more tears. Ladonna thought of her father. How she missed him!

The servant held her as she cried. She soothed her with Hebrew words she hadn't heard in so long.

"What can I do?"

The servant shook her head. "Once promised to Molesch, you work the temples. Do you know what that means?"

Ladonna shook her head. She didn't want to know.

The woman swallowed. She whispered the words, as if that would soften the blow. "You become a temple prostitute."

Ladonna stared at her. Not only her child would be given to this god, but she would be also!

The servant looked at the door. "I must go. Do you have anyone who could help?"

Ladonna almost laughed with relief. Not all was lost. "My abba! Cadman, of the tribe of Judah." He would save her. But one thought kept troubling her: wouldn't he have helped already, if he could?

Cadman had returned to his land and flocks, but it did not bring the peace he normally found in caring for his herds. His debt to Qadir weighed heavily on his spirit. He had approached his neighbors, offering to sell his prize breeding bucks and even the ewes that always gave him twins. He must pay his debt and redeem his daughter. He would do anything to have her return.

But no one had silver. Everyone had too many animals. How could everyone have too much of a good thing?

Where could he earn silver to pay his debt and secure his daughter's future?

While watching his flocks, he saw a dust cloud in the distance. As it approached, a caravan became clearer.

He drank from his waterskin and adjusted his dagger as he watched its approach.

It was Qadir.

What did he want? Had something happened to Ladonna? He ran to meet the caravan. When it grew closer, he slowed his steps, licking his lips. His heart beat fiercely as he tried to still his breathing.

Qadir remained on his horse and peered over Cadman's flocks.

Cadman stepped toward him, rubbing his hands down his cloak, moving his hand closer to his dagger. Cadman remembered his wool, twice buried in the bottom of the Great Sea. He clenched and unclenched his fists and swallowed. "How is Ladonna?"

Qadir acted as if he hadn't heard. He directed his horse forward, almost on top of Cadman, scrutinizing his flocks.

Cadman repeated his question, now more urgent by his delay.

Qadir looked down at Cadman, as if finally acknowledging his existence. "Ladonna?" He paused as if in deep thought, "Oh, your daughter . . ." He let his words peter out.

Cadman watched the man. Why didn't he answer? Concern overtook him. "What have you done to her?"

Qadir shrugged. "I haven't seen her."

What did that mean? "Doesn't she live with you?"

"She wasn't pure."

"Pure?" Cadman almost spit. "How could any maiden be pure?"

Qadir spoke as if instructing a child. "She's with child."

Cadman felt like a rock had punched him. In their Jewish culture, men wanted children. They were a blessing from God. In this Philistine world, children were given to please the gods.

Qadir smiled, pleased by Cadman's reaction. "My mother has seen her. She lives at my house until the child is born. Then she will become the god's concern."

"She will live at the temple?" Cadman's heart sank. He had

seen enough at the wedding to know what the temple would do to her.

"Don't worry. I will see her there." Qadir smiled. His eyes shone with lust.

Cadman grabbed at the reins of Qadir's horse.

Qadir struck with his whip, his eyes black slits. He hissed through his teeth, "Do not touch my things."

Cadman felt the blood bead on his face and arms from the whipping. He wanted to scream that Ladonna wasn't his. But he had given her to this man.

"It's a pity to waste her on the gods."

Cadman chewed on his tongue, wanting instead to strangle Qadir.

Qadir leaned forward on his horse and lowered his voice, as if in confidence with Cadman. "I could help her, if I had your support."

Cadman would do anything to keep her from the temple. "What do you want?"

"If I had these flocks." He paused and looked over Cadman's shoulder at his flocks.

Cadman couldn't wait. "Would that keep her from the temple?"

Qadir shook his head, almost sadly. "No one can escape serving once they are promised to Molesch. But . . ." Again he hesitated. He lowered his voice even more. "I could make sure she had a special room in the temple."

Cadman didn't understand their customs, nor did he trust Qadir. But that sounded better than being exposed to any man. "What must I do?"

Qadir gestured to Cadman's flocks. "Give your flocks to me."

Cadman swallowed. He had been trying to sell the best of his flocks. How would he live if he sold them all. "All?" His question came out in a strangled choke.

Qadir shrugged. "How much do you love your daughter?"

Cadman remembered his wool on the ship. He had trusted this man with his daughter. He was unworthy. How could he trust him again? "Did you know the captain of the ship dumps my wool into the sea?"

Qadir's eyes widened, but then he seemed to reclaim his surprise. "You have proof?"

Cadman straightened his shoulders and looked Qadir in the face. "Your phrase in the contract about meeting the Sea People was very clever. I couldn't even take my own wool off your ship when I learned of your deception."

Qadir appeared genuinely concerned. "So sorry for your loss. Your loss becomes my loss, don't you see. For now, I don't get your payment." He glanced around as if at a loss for words. He pulled the reins to turn his horse away and nudged his horse to walk.

Cadman ran after him. "Wait. What about my daughter?"

Qadir shrugged. "You have no money. I have generously offered to take your flocks for your loss—"

Cadman forgot about Qadir's deception. He must save his daughter. "If I give you all my flocks, how will I live?"

Qadir stopped his horse. "You will be mine."

Cadman would lose his freedom? He hesitated. But, no, he wouldn't think of himself at a time like this. "My daughter would be free from the temple?"

Qadir didn't hesitate. "Yes."

"How will I know you've kept your word?"

Qadir's eyes grew dark, his face hard. "You doubt my word? After I've graciously waited for your daughter's dowry, not once but twice, and still haven't received it?"

Cadman's shoulders slumped. "What good is a dowry if you are not her husband?"

"What good is your daughter if she is not pure?"

They had come full circle. He couldn't argue with this man.

Qadir nodded to the flocks. "You'd care for the flocks, but you, and the flocks would be mine. I'd expect the same amount of wool as what you sent before."

Cadman felt his heart pounding. When he had given the dowry of skins and wool before, they had had years of abundance. He couldn't achieve that every time. "If I can't provide the same amount of wool, my daughter would be. . . ."

Qadir smiled. "By your service, you guarantee your daughter's peace of mind."

Cadman couldn't allow his daughter to go to the temple. He would sacrifice anything to prevent that. He'd promise Qadir his life to protect her. He nodded. Cadman had lost not only his flocks, but also his freedom, yet he still didn't know if he had helped his daughter.

Qadir nudged his horse to a walk. "ou and the flocks and your land would be mineI'll free your daughter from the temple, *after* her service is complete."

Cadman stumbled after him. "What do you mean, *after* her service is complete?"

Qadir reined his horse to stop and turned with an incredulous look. "She must pay for her lack of purity. That's what the gods expect."

Cadman nodded. What did that mean?

How had he sunk so low as to lose his flocks, daughter, and freedom to a Philistine?

Ladonna didn't realize how much she had put her hope in her father saving her until the servant, after many days, entered her room.

"I have news of your father."

Ladonna waited, unable to take a breath.

"He has become Qadir's slave."

"My abba?"

The servant bowed her head. "He bought your deliverance from the temple, once you've paid for your impurity."

"By becoming Qadir's slave?"

The servant nodded.

Ladonna wept. Her father loved his flocks, his land, his freedom. What would this do to him? How had one wrong decision led to such a mess?

As the time for the baby approached, Ladonna's fears increased. Her servant hadn't been able to find any herb that would help. When would they take her baby to the temple?

When the Jewish servant entered with her meal, Ladonna would not even glance up.

"You must eat, for you and your little one."

"Why, when we are both sacrificed to a god I don't like?"

The servant pursed her lips. "It is not a matter of pleasing their gods. It's a matter of survival. Their god's whims change with the wind. But your body needs food regardless."

Ladonna lifted a piece of bread to her lips and tasted it. "You make it sound like there is a purpose in eating."

"Your reason for life is not the gods. Have you forgotten our God?"

"He has forsaken us. He is not here in this Philistine land. He left me when my father sold me to Qadir."

"But you're still alive. Isn't that cause to rejoice?" the servant persisted.

"Alive? As a slave to this room? As captive to Gardenia's whims? What mercy is that?" She could not remember her father's face anymore. It had grown distant, like her mother's. What was family? These Philistines didn't have families. They had mothers who ruled. And sons who lied. And a culture that squelched even the desire for children.

Ladonna gave birth to a son.

When nothing was done toward taking him to the temple, Ladonna convinced herself that Gardenia had changed her plans.

Ladonna treasured the moments with her son as if they were her last. By loving him, she could live another day. In her little room, isolated from the world, she could forget the promises made to the gods.

Gardenia watched from a distance, questioning the servants who brought Ladonna's meals, waiting until her attachment was complete. The gift must mean everything from the giver. Then the sacrifice would truly be a sacrifice of heart, mind, and body. Gardenia smiled. She knew the tug of a baby on a heart.

She waited to make the gift more precious to the gods.

When the baby turned one year old, it was time.

Gardenia entered Ladonna's room.

Ladonna sat by the window, nursing as he slept in her arms. The gentle light of the afternoon sun filtered through the leaves of the tree outside her window and danced over her.

Ladonna was so engrossed in watching the baby, she didn't even notice when Gardenia entered.

Gardenia watched for a time then found Qadir. She barged into his study. "It's time."

Qadir looked up from his writing. His irritated expression showed he hated the interruption.

She didn't care. Her news would make him happy. "The child is ready."

He leaned back in his chair and stretched. He regarded his mother. "How old is the child?"

She took her time in answering. "A year tomorrow."

He nodded. "How does she look?"

"Like a goddess from another world."

He smiled. "I will see."

She laid her hand on his arm. "No. You will wait for the temple."

He cursed. "It's always the temple. When do the gods allow for my pleasure?"

She smiled smugly. "I'll take her tomorrow."

"No."

His sternness startled her. She stepped back.

Qadir gentled his voice, but his eyes still held strength. "I will take her."

She nodded. "I will make her ready."

The following day, Ladonna was surprised when Gardenia entered her chamber. It was the first time since the birth she had entered the room. She carried a silk garment.

Ladonna felt alarm. She looked at her son sleeping on her bed before she rose and met her. Fear choked her throat. Was it time for the temple? She had blocked the event from her mind, hoping the rest of the world had forgotten. Her time with her son had been too short.

Gardenia tossed the garment on the bed. "Put that on." She stood back to watch her dress.

The dress reminded Ladonna of her wedding day. She had become accustomed to the style of the open front. It made nursing easier. But she had lived with no one.

An unseen dread swelled from her toes to spread through her body. She closed her eyes and dressed. Was there some way she could escape with her son?

When she turned for Gardenia's inspection, Qadir stood inside her room, his eyes following her movements.

She felt her checks flush.

He smiled. "You are ready?"

Gardenia turned at his voice. "She will do."

"Shall we go?" He offered his arm.

Ladonna turned back to the bed. Her body grew cold, her fingers wouldn't move. How could she take her son?

Qadir grabbed the baby as if he were a package sold at market. He took her arm. "We must hurry."

The baby started to cry.

Qadir ignored him.

Ladonna clung to his arm to keep up with him. She inwardly cursed these people's styles that hindered her speed. How could she run when she couldn't even keep up with Qadir as he walked?

When Ladonna entered the hallway, after almost two years of being confined in her room, memories of the night before her wedding flooded over her. She had waited up for her abba, so she could speak to him about the wedding dress. She felt her cheeks flush. She slowed her pace.

Qadir glanced at her. He tapped her hand that still held his arm. "You'll be fine."

He almost seemed gentle with her.

She hurried to keep up with him.

As they entered the street, Ladonna felt like a stranger. She had watched the crowded streets from her chamber window, but the crowds and noise confused her. She glanced up once and saw a man looking at her.

His eyes held lust.

She lowered her eyes quickly and kept her face down. Her face flushed anew. She struggled to keep her feet moving. She couldn't run away, even if she could move in this dress, without her baby.

At the temple, Qadir finally stopped.

She caught her breath as she finally reached his side.

The baby wiggled and cried in his arms.

"Allow me." Ladonna took the baby from him. She held him against her heart.

The baby quieted immediately.

She kissed him on the head and cooed to him, in spite of her own pounding heart. Her attention on the baby kept her from noticing the priest until he stole the baby from her and walked to another room.

She started to follow. "I must see him."

Qadir smiled. "You will truly please the gods." He led her to the room where the priest had gone.

A towering statue burned red by the fire glowing inside. Flames flared through the god's arms that reached upward, beseeching a god for mercy. The flames leaped higher and higher.

Ladonna felt the heat as it reached heavenward, licking the fingertips of the statue.

The priest climbed a platform beside the statue. He raised her son in both arms over the god's outstretched arms.

She stepped forward and screamed to stop him.

Qadir held her.

She pounded against his chest, trying to make him let her go.

When the priest dropped her baby into the statue's outstretched arms, she heard the uptake of air before her baby's piercing wail filled the air for a moment. Then silence.

Ladonna stopped her fist, and fell against Qadir.

He embraced her.

She was hot, as if she had been burned. Her head throbbed from her own screaming. She wept.

Qadir carried her to a small temple room. "Drink this." He lifted it to her lips. "We will honor the sacrifice you have made and make the gods happy."

She drank without knowing it, numb beyond what any drink could do. She remembered nothing except that her child was gone.

When she awoke, she found herself in a small, windowless room with only a bed. Her clothes had been taken away and she lay without covers. She looked at the ceiling, seeing her son fall into the flames again. Her tears started to fall.

Qadir entered. "You're awake. Good."

She felt his eyes and blushed. She closed her eyes. She hoped if she closed her eyes, Qadir would go away.

He didn't.

When she opened them again, he was sitting beside her. His gaze made her cringe.

Her own voice surprised her. It sounded hollow, like it wasn't hers. "Where are my clothes?"

"They aren't needed here at the temple where you please the gods."

"I am cold."

He handed her another full vessel. "Drink this."

She accepted the vessel, gulping the contents. She forgot her vow never to touch wine again. She drank to forget, to dull her pain. She'd do anything to forget her baby's scream.

The liquid burned her throat and warmed her insides.

Qadir smiled. "You have learned. That is good." He stayed to partake of what she offered the gods.

Thus her life began at the temple, where she pleased the gods and the men who came to worship. And lost any hope of life.

CHAPTER 4

Cadman watched over the sheep and the goats in the hillside. It used to give him such peace and contentment to see them rest. Not anymore. The joy had been stolen when he became a slave to Qadir. Knowing he belonged to another made freedom unattainable. Yet more desired.

Cadman would have thanked God for what he had provided when his wife had lived. It seemed a long time ago. Now he could only bow his head and point to his tent.

Qadir dismounted and fingered the wool, testing its value. "Not good."

Cadman became flustered. "That's the best the rains have brought." He clenched his fists. He had told himself he would not respond angrily. It did not give him answers.

Qadir pointed to his flocks. "I must sell more to gain what the wool did not offer."

"But how will I supply the next amount of wool?"

Qadir shrugged. "That is not my concern." Qadir smiled then. "By the way, your daughter . . ."

Cadman looked at his face. His heart seemed to stop as he waited for his answer.

"She truly pleases the gods." Qadir smiled and shook his head. The lust on his face evident.

Cadman constrained himself from hitting the man. "When will she have finished serving the gods?"

Qadir looked at the piles of wool and skins. "Not for a long time, if you do not do better."

Cadman's frustration grew. What else could he give to save his daughter from her misery? How had he gotten into this mess?

Qadir watched him squirm. "There is one thing that may shorten her stay in the temple . . ."

Cadman stepped forward to hear.

Qadir looked around the hillside, where his flocks grew fat. "Your land."

Cadman swallowed. He had heard from other neighbors what temple life could do to a young girl. He had been surprised that Ladonna was still alive. If he could just get her away from the temple. He looked into Qadir's face. "You will take her out of the temple?"

Qadir nodded, the satisfaction evident on his face.

What else could Cadman do? He couldn't even look into Qadir's face. "Take it."

Cadman heard Qadir leave. But he could not raise his head to watch. His hatred grew not only for Qadir, but for himself.

Qadir returned to his city. Ladonna had paid for her impurity. He entered her temple room.

She didn't even know he was there. "It's time for you to return to my house. You have finished paying the price for your impurity."

She stood to leave. She would have left the way she was, but Qadir stopped her. "I have a cloak for you." He smiled. He walked her to his house. Now that she had been broken by the gods, she could respond to his needs. He could hardly wait.

As he entered his house, Gardenia greeted him. "Were the gods pleased with her?"

Qadir nodded.

Gardenia followed as Qadir led Ladonna to her former room. Any challenge was gone. In its place was an acceptance of anything. "The gods have done wonders with her!"

He took off her cloak and gestured to his mother. "She's ready for you."

Gardenia smiled.

Ladonna's eyes widened then glazed over.

Gardenia enjoyed what the gods had given to her as Qadir watched.

When the Jewish servant brought a tray of food for Ladonna, she gasped. "What have they done to you?"

Ladonna reached for the goblet that lay filled on the tray. "They have taken my body and trampled my soul."

"You must eat."

Ladonna laughed. "I must drink. Without drink, I cannot live."

"You will waste away to nothing." She shoved a piece of bread in her hand. "Eat."

Ladonna took a bite, but it tasted of sand. She took a gulp. It burned all the way down and settled her insides. She no longer had to sip the contents. She could gulp it and then wonder where it had gone. Ladonna's head seemed distant, uncompre-hending.

"The king of Mesopotamia has come to our land."

Ladonna shrugged. "It is no longer my father's land; it belongs to Qadir."

The servant continued, "They say our people are tormented by these people from Mesopotamia."

Ladonna leaned back against her chair. "I cannot conceive of any greater torment than what this people's wickedness has done to my soul. Where is God? Has He forgotten us?"

The servant shook her head. "We have forgotten Him."

"It's too late to remember Him now."

Ladonna sat on the chair beside the window, gazing but seeing nothing.

Qadir grabbed her shoulders. "I return to your father. I've heard Mesopotamia is overrunning Israel. I must see what has happened to my land."

Ladonna didn't respond, but continued to stare.

He shook her, trying to get her attention. "I'll take you and that Jewish servant you favor with me." He looked expectantly for her to respond.

She didn't.

"Perhaps I could make the old man fight harder, if he knew how I protected his daughter." Qadir laughed.

Her face revealed nothing.

They left for Israel.

She rode beside him.

He wondered out loud. "Many farms lay idle, and their workers gone. Should I have brought more soldiers?"

As they came closer to his land, he kicked his horse into a gallop. When they reached the house, it lay deserted. He dismounted and gestured to Ladonna to do the same. "The old man must be watching his flocks in the fields."

Qadir looked into Ladonna's face. "Do you know where I've brought you?" He expected recognition, praise for his thoughtfulness.

She gave none.

He voiced his frustrations. "Why don't you show me appreciation for bringing you to see your father? Aren't you happy to be home?"

She looked from his angry face to the house. The house looked as if it had been vacant for many moons. The roofing needed fixed. The door hung crookedly. The house looked as she felt: used up and wasted.

Qadir dismounted and stormed into the house.

Ladonna followed behind. When she entered the house, she gasped. Could her father still be alive?

Qadir glanced at her. It was the first time she had acknowledged anything since they left the city. "You stay here while I find him. He won't leave my service this easily!" Qadir stormed out.

When he was out of sight, she came to life. Running out the door, she ripped off the necklace Qadir had given her the eve of her wedding. She now knew the charm bound her to their gods and to their worship. She flung it as far as she could away from her. She breathed deeply, as if free for the first time in many years. She went to the saddlebags on the pack horse. After searching through its contents, she pulled out a dagger. She retraced her steps to the inside of her house.

Ladonna turned to her servant. "If I knew then, what I know now, I never would have done it."

"Done what?"

"Married." She said it with resignation.

"But how could you have escaped, when your father had arranged it?"

"I would have killed myself first."

"Never that."

"Aren't we at the same place now?" She lifted the dagger over her heart. "Only I haven't the strength to finish the deed. Will you?"

The servant hesitated. How could she take life?

Ladonna screamed, "Look at me! My life is not living. It is fulfilling their wicked lusts. Only death could save me."

The servant nodded. She took the dagger from Ladonna's hand and stabbed her, watching her breath stop. She stood, tears running down her face. "It's done. Your wish has been granted."

The Jewish servant walked out of the house and through the fields. She was in no hurry. She had nowhere to go.

She walked as one in a trance. Her thoughts not on today, but on many years ago.

She remembered a God Who was merciful, gracious, and forgiving, although jealous. Very jealous. He expected His people to love only Him. And that was why her people were in trouble now.

CHAPTER 5

Cadman knew the caves in the area and had hid, first when the king of Mesopotamia marched his soldiers through his land to the next city, and then when he saw Qadir's caravan approach-ing. He had lived in tents away from the house for some time, living off whatever the land would offer. His sheep and goats were gone. He had no way to survive, let alone pay Qadir.

He was finished being told what to do on his land in return for empty promises of salvation for his daughter. He had watched from a distance as Qadir searched for him. He wouldn't find him in all the caves on his land. He saw the clouds of dust that told of Qadir's departure. He rubbed his dirty hand down his torn tunic. He entered his house after the long absence, relieved the soldiers had not destroyed everything.

But when his eyes focused on the object on the floor, he fell to his knees and cried. His daughter had been returned to him.

Dead.

Cadman wept for the time he had lost. He repented to His God, Who knew great mercy, but also perfect holiness.

The years of Qadir's extortion were over. Qadir would have no cause to return.

After weeping more than he thought he could, he stumbled like a lost man to Othniel's land. This was the first time he had visited since that night long ago when he had returned from the city and unburdened his heart about his daughter.

Before, he had thought he was a broken man. Now, he went knowing he was.

Othniel had escaped the soldiers' looting. His house was tucked into a cliff, surrounded on three sides by the mountain. His door faced the road where he could see for miles.

Cadman looked around Othniel's land as he approached. It was an oasis in a desert. How had he been spared?

Before he reached the house, several dogs barked warnings. Othniel met him at the door. "Shalom."

"Be at peace." Cadman gestured to his orchards, heavy with fruit. "God has been good to you." He restrained himself from licking his lips.

Othniel opened the door and invited him inside. He gave him a vessel of wine.

It was the first Cadman had drunk in many moons. The taste was sweet. He licked his lips. Cadman couldn't help himself; he had to ask, "How did you keep it all?"

Othniel smiled. "Remember years ago, when we all had an abundance of wool and skins, and we couldn't sell what we had because the market was overstocked, but we needed to pay our taxes?"

Cadman nodded. That had started his poor choices.

Othniel continued. "While many went to the Philistines for their help, I went to the Lord. I almost starved those first few years. I'd see your plenty, wondering if I'd chosen right. But as our neighbors lost their lands, their flocks, and their lives to the Philistines, the Lord assured me, I had chosen wisely."

They were silent. Cadman thought of those years. They seemed like such hard years, but he had his land, his flocks, his freedom, and his daughter. He shook his head.

Othniel had remembered the Lord.

He had not. He had told his daughter, "Bend so you won't break." But now he saw how bending had broken him.

If he had stood for the Law, his daughter wouldn't be gone.

Othniel interrupted his thoughts. "How's Ladonna?"

Cadman swallowed. "I hid in the caves after the soldiers pillaged my land. I stayed hidden when I saw Qadir coming. When I returned, I found Ladonna in my house, dead."

"I'm sorry." Othniel leaned forward, resting his hand on Cadman's shoulder. "What will you do now?"

Cadman sighed. "What I should have done, many years ago."

"And that is . . ."

"Call upon the Name of the Lord."

Othniel's smile held sorrow. "Moses once said, 'You will not be afraid of the terror by night, or of the arrow that flies by day; of the pestilence that stalks in darkness, or of the destruction that lays waste at noon. . . . You will only look on with your eyes and see the recompense of the wicked."

Cadman looked away. "I've seen enough of the wicked, and the Lord has brought payment."

Othniel leaned forward and squeezed Cadman's shoulder. "Isn't it time for you to make the Lord your refuge?"

"I'm broken, trying to solve my own problems, forgetting His Laws, doing what I think is right."

"Did it work?"

Cadman swallowed. "My daughter's dead. I'm to blame."

"It's time to remember the Lord."

The Mesopotamians tormented the people of God for eight years. During that time, the people turned from their wickedness and remembered God. Othniel became their leader. He formed an army from those broken by their sin but seeking the Lord's favor. They hadn't seen the Lord's cloud or fire since they had entered their land. Nor had they felt the Lord's presence since Joshua and the elders had died. But now they knew the Lord's Spirit rested on Othniel. He had remembered God when all others had gone their own way.

Othniel didn't tell the men of their sin.

They fell under God's conviction by looking at their lost lands, possessions, and families.

God's ways were not always easy. Othniel had struggled, but he had obeyed God's principles and remembered His Laws. They had protected him from the wickedness that the others fell into as they looked for answers in themselves.

Othniel judged the people forty years and died faithful to the Words of the Lord.

PART II
EHUD
JUDGES 3:12-30

CHAPTER 6

Cache stood in the city's gates of Ir-hat-Temarim in the City of Palm Trees with the other city leaders. He leaned against the city gate and looked over the group to see the hills beyond the city. A piece of the gate fell off in his hands. He looked with disgust at the dried mortar and the crumbling wall. He threw the piece on the ground. He flaked off more mortar and threw it again in the center of their circle. His angry outburst startled the other city leaders over what could be wrong. He was the youngest, but they looked to him for leadership. Perhaps his brashness gave them confidence to trust him with things they secretly wished they could do. Or maybe the darkness they read in his eyes when he was crossed caused them to obey him. He didn't know, nor did he care.

He pointed to the pieces now that held their attention. "Look! These gates crumble. Yet they represent what our city is. These doors are supposed to be our defense. What kind of defense is that?" He picked another piece from the gate and tossed it at their feet in the middle of their circle. "The people are tired of remembering the glory of the past. We need a monument for today's people. Something they can be proud of."

Cache waited for Pearson to nod. Pearson, as one of the older leaders, swayed the group. Whatever he decided, they'd all agree.

After his nod, Cache looked around the group. "I propose we build a courtroom, rather than judging here in the streets for all to hear. Our courtroom would be a monument to our people's prosperity and power. We could cover one's embarrassment over being tried, especially when they're found innocent. It'd remove threats from our judgments. Visitors would praise our wealth, power, and people."

The oldest leader, Tadashi, leaned back on the hard bench. He stretched his arms over his head. He lived his name's meaning, "Correct." He hindered progress by making sure everything was correct.

Cache tilted his head in an accommodating gesture, expecting opposition.

Tadashi paused until he had everyone's attention. "How will we pay for it?"

Cache smiled. He had prepared for Tadashi's questions. "The harvest was good. The people will give to the priests, and the priests will share their abundance for the glory of our city. Isn't it a reflection on God's Name that our city's gates are run-down and we judge in the streets like villagers?"

The men nodded.

Tadashi pressed. "Why would the priests give what belongs to them?"

Cache smiled. "We would never take from their livelihood. The people will give extra to improve their city."

Pearson nodded; then smiled. "Brilliant."

Cache let out the breath he had held.

Others were nodding.

Cache waited for any further comments. When none came, he clapped his hands together. "I'll speak with the priests at once."

Pearson glanced around the room. "Any further business to discuss?" Hearing nothing, he rose from his chair. "Let's dis-miss."

As the men filed from their benches, each one stepped aside to commend Cache. Cache smiled, in spite of himself. He had found a way to the priests' money. Whoever held the money, held the power.

Eleazar, the High Priest who followed Aaron, had died long ago. Phinehas, his son, who had taken his place, also died. His successor and son, Abishua, did not love the law like his father, nor defend its truth to the people. By the time he passed the responsibilities on to his son, Bukki, he did not remember the Exodus of their people from Egypt, nor the desert lessons learned when their fathers had seen God. Bukki only knew the sacrifices were burdensome, but necessary to receive his livelihood.

The priests took turns with the morning and evening sacrifices. No one should perform the odious tasks all the time.

Bukki took off the high priest's breastplate. It contained gems and precious stones, twelve of them, representing the twelve sons of Jacob who had become the tribes of their nation. He caught the smell from many who had worn it before him. How could they wash it with the gems stitched into its breastplate? So the smell of unwashed bodies and sweat lingered as he hung it on the peg designed for it. He wrinkled his nose in disgust.

As he left the tent of sacrifice, the smell of blood and guts hung in the hot evening air. He held his breath until he was beyond the containers holding waste from the sacrifices. A cloud of flies rose as he walked by them.

The sin sacrifice demanded blood be sprinkled around the mercy seat with his finger. Other sacrifices required him to brush blood on his forehead and body. It made him sticky and smelly.

Fly bait.

He itched for a bath. He couldn't wait until he could bathe, not ceremoniously, but really wash the blood from his body.

He breathed a sigh of relief as he left the holy place. There were so many strict rules in the Law. His ancestors had been struck by fire from God for not following the Law. He didn't know if that could happen again.

That had been when God lived with the people.

God no longer did.

Still he didn't want to risk such a death. So he followed the letter of the law. But his heart certainly wasn't there.

He made a mental note to remind his son to remove the waste outside the city before dark or the flies and bees would be thick in the morning. He smacked one that chewed on him now.

The smoke from the incense only attracted them.

And the fires only made him hotter.

He sighed. He was tired of following a burdensome law. There must be more to life than killing animals for a God Who didn't notice.

He paused in the doorway of the Tabernacle before heading home.

Someone touched him on his shoulder. "Shalom."

Bukki jumped. He should have been paying more attention. When he saw who had spoken, he stepped back. Cache was not one who sought his sins to be removed. He was a man to be wary of. Still Bukki answered, "Be at peace."

Cache motioned inside the tent for the sacrifices. Their people had constructed the Tabernacle during their journey through the desert. Some said the construction followed the Lord's commands. "The heat makes sacrificing wearisome."

Bukki nodded, waiting for what Cache had come for. He slapped another fly which had left a welt on his arm.

"Tired from your duties at the temple?"

Bukki didn't know where this conversation was doing. What did Cache want? "I do what's expected of me."

Cache paused as if considering for the first time how he could help. "You're faithful in following the Law. I'd like to speak with you about your duties. Would you come for the evening meal?"

Bukki was tired. He longed for a bath. But once washed, he'd be refreshed and wishing for something besides priestly duties to entertain his thoughts. He was also curious about what Cache wanted from him. Why this sudden interest in what he did? Not many people cared how performing the sacrifices cost him. In spite of his initial hesitation, he asked, "What time?"

Cache smiled. "When the sun goes down. Would that give you enough time to refresh yourself?"

Bukki smiled for the first time all day.

Cache seemed to understand his duties. He looked forward to dinner. Perhaps someone could relieve his duties' boredom.

Bukki savored the beef as it fell from the bone and melted on his tongue. He couldn't remember the last time he had eaten so well. The people brought their sacrifices to the tent, but they didn't bring their choice meat. This meal of Cache's had been exceptionally high quality. Even the vegetables were fresh, not like those given by the people for the meal offering, a sacrifice to show the generosity of the people. He almost laughed out loud. The generous people brought mealy grain and vegetables that were unacceptable even for their animals. But *this* meal showed what a leader could attain.

He took another bite and let it dissolve on his tongue. He was concentrating on the flavor so much he didn't hear Cache speak until he noticed him looking at him. He shook his head. "What?"

Cache sipped from a wine vessel as he leaned back on his cushions. "The leaders have been discussing your difficulty."

Bukki raised his eyebrows in question. Why?

Cache continued. "The people don't respect your position. They live in elaborate houses yet worship in a tent. Why not build a temple for your services?"

Bukki could hardly believe his ears. If he had a building to do his duties, wouldn't the people respect him and give worthy gifts? "How would you propose it?"

Cache swallowed his drink, considering. "The people provide you with the tithe?"

Bukki nodded.

"You are paid enough?"

Bukki laughed. "Who doesn't think they deserve more?"

Cache smiled. "My words almost exactly to the counsel this very day. Require the people to give more."

Bukki could feel his eyes widen. Since when did the counsel care how he lived? He had eaten too much. He should be wary of this man. But his thoughts spun with hope and future wealth. He gulped his wine, trying to clear his thoughts. What could he do with more tithe?

Cache shrugged. "If the people were required to give more, we could build a temple that would better serve your needs." He hesitated, watching Bukki.

A temple would give the priests prestige and power. This was more than Bukki had even imagined. He smiled. "We'll do it."

Cache poured more wine in Bukki's vessel; then more in his own. He raised his vessel in salute. "Let it be done. To your wealth."

Cache oversaw the construction of the temple. He added elaborate rooms as judgment halls for the leaders. What better way to execute justice than to require sacrifices, once they were judged, to cover their trespasses?

He walked down the corridor, inspecting the builders' progress.

Bukki called after him, hastening to catch him.

Cache waited. "Shalom. How does the temple look?"

Bukki glowed. "It pleases me greatly. At first, the people were hesitant to part with their money, but as they saw how their worship would be improved, they gave."

"People do not easily part with things they think are theirs."

Bukki continued. "But as you showed, their worship would be more meaningful in a temple than in a simple tent." Bukki rubbed his hands down his tunic. "I'm a bit confused about this area over here." He led the way down a hall. He directed him into one of the big rooms and motioned to several side rooms. "What purpose do these rooms serve?"

Cache coughed. "These rooms will be used by the city leaders to execute justice." As he saw the scowl form on Bukki's face, Cache hastened, "When people are found guilty, they'll be required to give more to you. It will benefit the temple priests."

Bukki's scowl lifted. "Of course."

Cache squeezed his shoulder and smiled. Promises of wealth and prestige could always persuade men.

Cache left down another corridor. He had assumed Bukki had resumed his work and he was alone when he came to a hallway and entered another doorway. He pressed against the stone and entered a secret room. He'd included it in the design in case an emergency found him needing protection. He took from his cloak pocket a handful of candles and placed them in a vessel on a high shelf. He felt he wasn't alone.

He turned to find Bukki standing there.

He blew out a breath of anger, before recovering himself. Why hadn't he been more cautious? He smiled at Bukki. He must win him over to conceal his secret.

Bukki looked around the small room. "What purpose does this room serve?"

Cache put his arm around Bukki and led him from the room.

After leaving it, he carefully shut the door and studied the entrance again. There was no trace of the door's presence.

Bukki's eyes widened. "A secret room!"

Cache nodded, appeasing Bukki's curiosity without giving too many details. "A secret between you and me."

Bukki seemed confused. "What's it for?"

Cache led him away from the door and down the hall. "Only one city leader and one priest should know of its existence. It'll store the history of our people. If any danger comes to the city, it'll be protected."

Bukki nodded, "I'll place the scrolls there."

Cache caught himself before he asked what scrolls. He shook his head. "It would be better if you didn't enter the room again.

The secret will stay hidden and the scrolls will be safe. I'll put them in and we'll leave the room alone."

Bukki squeezed Cache's shoulder. "You've thought of everything."

Cache cringed at his touch. He touched others to enforce his authority, but didn't like to be touched himself. He stepped away from Bukki, trying to hide his disgust.

Bukki smiled. "I'm glad you trust me with such an honor." His voice carried.

Cache flinched inwardly and looked up and down the hallway for any listeners. He trusted no one.

He gestured to the altar room where Bukki would accept their people's offerings. "I have other things to attend to."

Bukki nodded. "Of course. I can't thank you enough for trusting me with—"

Cache hissed at him. Would the fool tell already? He must refocus him on other things to make him forget. He escorted Bukki into the altar room. "This room will give prestige to your priestly duties. You'll no longer be butchers, cutting and burning animals. You'll accept the people's gifts of meal and wine in the comfort of this temple." He pointed to an area where he'd brought cushions for himself to rest. "You can lounge here and enjoy the first-fruits of everyone's wine."

Bukki smiled. "That will please everyone."

Cache nodded and backed from the room. "Now, I do have other things to attend to."

Bukki started to follow him again, but a servant, carrying a case of wine, entered the room from another door.

Cache gestured for him to place it by the cushions. He had requested it for himself, but now he would distract Bukki with it. "It seems you'll be able to test the comfort of the room now."

Bukki looked from the servant to Cache. "May I?" He looked like a child unable to wait for feast day.

Cache pushed him toward the cushion. "It will give me great pleasure."

Bukki settled on the cushions and reached for one of the wine vessels.

Cache backed from the room and almost ran from his presence, hoping his secret was safe.

Some priests grumbled about sharing their tithe with the city leaders. Cache needed them to be united for his purposes. He sought their approval by bribes.

But they ignored his dinner invitations.

Cache knew other ways to persuade men.

Cache changed his cloak to an old, grimy one whose hood covered his face. He entered an inn where travelers lingered long over their cheap drinks and looked for the company of women to give pleasure. He surveyed the dark corners, for those who slept through the day, then sat at an empty table with a drink in his hand. He watched the door.

Another lone man entered, looked around the room. He spotted Cache. He wiped his hands nervously, shifting the dagger that could be seen through his thin cloak. Then, eyeing the second vessel in front of Cache on the table, he sat on the bench across from Cache.

Cache spoke without looking up. "You're late. Don't make me wait again."

The man nodded, hesitantly cupping the vessel in his shaking hands.

Cache lowered his voice. "Do you know Ethni and Malchijah?"

The man's eyes widened under the cloak's hood. "Priests from Gershon's line?"

Cache nodded. "Persuade them to share their tithe with the leaders." He flung a piece of silver on the table as he stood. "The rest will come when the task is completed."

"Should I come to your house when the job is complete?"

Cache met his gaze with cold power. "Never come to my house, Tobiah. I know where you live."

CHAPTER 7

After the construction of the temple, Cache again stood before the leaders. "Our cities are unsafe. We must protect our people."

Tadashi coughed and leaned forward.

Cache smiled, ready to refute Tadashi's condemnation of his plan.

Tadashi pointed his finger at Cache. "The priests especially live in fear."

Cache's smile disappeared, and he looked shocked. "Shouldn't they be the most protected? They live within our walls, in the center of the city, and pray to our God. And even they are afraid? The very reason why I propose we establish an army to patrol the city streets and bring justice; so the people can walk their streets in peace, unafraid of thieves and murderers."

Pearson nodded his head. "People are afraid to walk the streets."

The men around the circle nodded.

Tadashi again sat forward. "Who would be in charge of this army?"

Cache looked around the room, as if the idea had suddenly come to him. "Who else but the leaders of the city? We would direct their activities. Aren't we the ones who have to administer justice anyway? Why not catch the criminal before he does wrong and prevent it?"

They all agreed.

Cache hesitated. 'There's one minor thing that would hinder this . . . ."

He waited for someone else to suggest it. When no one did, he continued. "The army must be paid." He waited for suggestions. When none came, he added, as if hating to suggest it, "We could require more of the priests' tithe."

Pearson shrugged. "It is for the good of the city. Those who commit crimes will have to bring more sacrifices. And when crime decreases, there will be less sin sacrifices for the priests to offer, so they would be free to find other income."

Others nodded.

Pearson added. "Proceed."

Cache left the meeting, bouncing on his toes. He had gained power over the priests. He had control over who was tried. Now he would select rulers for his army.

When Bukki saw Cache approach him, he backed up. What did the man want now? He wanted to ask when the priests would get back their tithe. He had agreed willingly the first time to share, but the tithe hadn't covered all the expenses of the temple. The priests had to offer their own wealth to cover the difference. It still wasn't enough. And even with the completion of the temple, the city leaders still took the priests' tithe.

Cache ignored his hesitation, squeezing his shoulder. "Shalom."

Bukki cringed, gritting his teeth, "Be at peace."

Cache gestured to a side room. When Bukki stepped inside, Cache lowered his voice as if in conspiracy with him. "Don't the people respect you now?"

Bukki had to agree. More people came to the temple, increas-

But You Have Not Obeyed Me

ing his tithe, though not enough to cover the temple's building costs. But still he was leery of what Cache would demand next.

"People bring their wealth to the temple. Do you feel safe with that?" Before Bukki could respond, Cache continued, as if he already knew, "I don't. We need a guard at the temple's doors."

Bukki shifted uncomfortably, trying to decide how best to bring up the problem of money.

Cache smiled. It didn't reach his eyes. "You wouldn't want someone stealing from the Lord's wealth would you?"

Bukki felt Cache's cold look and shivered. He tried to look away, but Cache's gaze held him. He'd heard from Ethni and Malchijah about the threats to their families when they resisted giving their tithe to building the temple.

Ethni had one of his goats hung outside his door with a dagger left in its heart. He had decided his tithe could be shared.

Malchijah hadn't escaped so easily. He had found his son tied to a tree with a money bag around his neck. His tithe wasn't worth his son's life. He gave in.

Bukki swallowed and nodded. Guarding the temple's money would be good. Cache's suggestion of the temple's treasures reminded him of their secret.

As Cache started to leave, Bukki called him back, "Cache."

Cache turned back, his expression showing impatience.

Bukki lowered his voice. "I have something for you."

Cache replaced his impatient expression with resolution and followed Bukki to another room in the temple. Bukki pointed to a corner full of scrolls.

"What are those?"

Bukki responded, "The scrolls that we must take to the . . . well, the room, you know."

Cache gave him a blank stare.

Bukki reminded him, "The room where the treasure is to be kept . . . you know . . . between you and me."

Cache's face registered recognition.

Bukki smiled. "Do you want me to help move them?"

Cache shook his head. "I'll do it."

Bukki wiped his hand down his tunic. "They're our people's history."

"Of course." Cache gathered what scrolls he could carry. He left the room with them.

Bukki watched him go and wondered if Cache valued the scrolls as the treasures he said they were.

Cache returned home. With Bukki's approval to instill a guard at the temple, he could persuade the other priests. Things were going well.

As he entered his house, his son, Kadri brushed passed him. Cache grabbed his shoulder and made the boy face him. "Where are you going?"

Kadri pulled away from Cache's grasp. "Out."

"Don't use that tone with me. What are you doing?"

Kadri stepped farther back. He was as tall as his father, but not as heavily built. "Don't think you can control me like all your other victims."

Cache dropped his hand, but raised his voice, "Victims?"

Kadri swallowed as if he had said too much already. But he didn't stop. "Those special, elaborate meals you've given for Bukki and Pearson, to win them to your plan."

Cache smiled. "So my son eavesdrops on plans not meant for his ears."

Kadri shrugged. "When problems suddenly come to the priests' families after you want their money, it doesn't take good ears to see my father's hand behind it all."

Cache sucked in a breath. What else did he know?

Kadri turned to leave, but turned back. "Oh, and by the way, that mob you created over in the eastern part of town . . ."

Cache waited. He didn't want to appear too interested. What had happened with the unrest he had created for more revenue? How did Kadri know he had caused it?

"Your instigator, what's his name? Tobiah—" Kadri didn't wait for a response. His next words broke as he spoke, "He killed Rada."

Cache stepped back. How did he know about Tobiah? He gained control of his expression, "Rada; who's she?"

Kadri's face hardened, and he spit. "You think you control this city, the priests, the ruling leaders, the army you hope to build—but don't think you'll ever control me."

His son had been a calm, compliant child. Where had all this come from? What had caused this outburst? Cache couldn't allow this rebellion, especially when he was so close to ruling. Cache smacked him. "No son of mine will speak to me this way."

Kadri's face already showed red welts from the force of his blow. But instead of cowering and submitting, Kadri laughed.

How dare he? Cache hit him again.

Kadri's expression turned to stone. "Do you think a slap will make me cower? I'll see that you fail. When you feel a thorn in your side, it'll be me! And I won't go away. I will thwart your power." He turned and walked down the street.

How did Kadri know his plans? He must be more careful. Cache felt someone beside him.

His wife touched his arm. "Kadri was betrothed to Rada. Don't you remember?"

He pulled away from her touch and shook his head. When had his son become old enough to marry? Rada, his son's fiancé? She was just a girl. How could her death be such a loss?

His wife nodded toward their son's retreating back. "When your riot killed Rada, you brought a lion to life. He won't rest until he's worked his revenge."

Cache paced before the council. He had called this meeting to maintain their support. "The army has been selected with care. The temple's wealth must be guarded by men I trust." Cache coughed and corrected, "We trust." He looked at Pearson to see if his slip offended him. He didn't seem to notice. "The army practices outside the city walls. I've been pleased with their progress."

Tadashi stretched his legs in front of him. "The army's authority extends beyond keeping the peace."

Cache measured Tadashi's expression. He was tired of appeasing this cantankerous leader who always thwarted his plans. "When people plot against us, a soldier should take action."

Tadashi's gravelly voice irritated Cache. "We introduced the army for keeping peace in the streets, not stirring strife."

Cache looked at Pearson. Did he support him? Cache couldn't read his expression. "The people are discontent because they have nothing to do. What better way to keep them busy than to increase the army?"

"So we can fight ourselves?" Tadashi countered. "We will soon have more soldiers than citizens to support them!"

Cache needed the soldiers to coerce the people to pay more tithe.

The priests were finding ways to hide what they received, and he couldn't access it.

He needed the extra. He had started to build a new house fit for a king. Shouldn't it reflect the leader he was? He designed a room to hide what he was accruing. But the priests and people were hesitant to give what he demanded. The army encouraged them.

Pearson coughed. "The temple did elevate the people's worship. Yet it required more; so the army was beneficial for extracting what was needed."

His pause made Cache wary. So far he supported Cache, but he seemed to weigh his next words more carefully. Pearson took a sip from his vessel. "The people aren't peaceful. A city's peace reflects the people's ability to act responsibly. What makes people responsible?"

This wasn't a discussion Cache wanted. He redirected it back to his agenda. "If children don't obey parents, and citizens disregard city laws, what's a leader to do, but make them conform?"

Pearson shrugged. "But how do you create responsibility that comes from within?"

Tadashi nodded. "In the old days, we followed the Law of God."

Cache interjected, "We also stoned disobedient law-breakers."

Tadashi continued his interrupted thought, "We followed the Law, not out of compulsion, but out of love for God." He sighed. "Those days are gone."

Cache was weary of this discussion of the past and responsibility. He must have the army to do what he wanted. "Do we want to live in tents and wander through the wilderness again? Of course not! The army must enforce our desires."

Pearson shrugged. "Responsibility comes with personal accountability. How can we make people *own* the city?"

That was the last thing Cache wanted the people to do. He wanted to control the city by himself and tell the people what they should do. If they felt accountable, it would hinder their giving him the money he needed. He could feel his face flush as he tried to bring the conversation back under his control. "Should the people own anything? The riots in the city tell me the people can't handle what they already have. We must help them manage it."

Pearson shrugged. He wasn't emotionally involved in this discussion; he merely wished to speak of interesting issues. "Responsibility must be a heart issue. But how do you change hearts?"

Cache clenched his fists and exhaled deeply. Was anyone listening to him? He must control the people through force. Who cared about the peoples' hearts?

After the meeting, Tadashi hobbled over to Cache and touched his shoulder.

The council's discussion had frustrated Cache. How could he control the people without a bigger army? Cache plastered a smile on his face. "Shalom."

Tadashi looked into his face. "Is there peace in your home?"

Cache didn't like his inference. What did Tadashi know about his home? Cache clenched his fists as he remembered Kadri's disrespect. Nothing would hinder him from controlling the city; not even his own son. Cache shook his head and stepped away from Tadashi.

Tadashi questioned his authority.

He wouldn't be questioned—not by Kadri nor by Tadashi. He must be obeyed. He glared into Tadashi's face but said nothing.

Tadashi lowered his voice, "I caution you."

Cache didn't want instruction. Tadashi's condescending fatherly approach irritated Cache. He hadn't received support for a bigger army. Tadashi's comment about Kadri reminded him of another area lacking control. How much did Tadashi know? He waited for Tadashi to continue.

Tadashi continued. "It's lonely at the top."

Cache stared long at Tadashi. Did this man suspect his plans to gain the city? Was he threatening his power?

Tadashi's eyes held no malice. He warned without threat.

Cache smiled. Someone would always question a leader's authority. Tadashi was predictable. "Are you asking for a spot?"

Tadashi shoved his hands into his cloak's pockets and shrugged. "Only if I could be of value."

Cache could parry words with this man. Tadashi counselled by disagreement; he could provide insight about the people. Is that why he had known about his son? Tadashi could stab him in the back. But Cache couldn't find a better man to give the opposing side. Cache nodded. "I could use you." Inwardly he added, "for now."

CHAPTER 8

Eglon, King of Moab, looked to the west. He wanted the land and the people that lived on it. He sent messengers to Ammon and Amalek requesting their aid. He promised them the temple's riches. It was enough to entice their aid. They moved toward Israel and arrived at the City of the Palm Trees after marching through the night.

When the sentry at the top of the city wall looked toward the east that morning, he didn't see the green trees that hedged the Jordan River. He saw only sunlight glittering off countless soldiers' armor. As he raised his horn to his lips to sound the alarm, an archer released an arrow that caught in his throat and silenced him.

Eglon's army entered the gate without a fight. No city's army could match the strength of three countries coming against it.

Citizens awoke to the sound of marching in their streets. They weren't alarmed. Wasn't it Cache's army rising to torment them again? Instead of resisting when they saw it was foreign soldiers, they surrendered. What could another army do, that their own had not already done?

Little did they know.

After watching his father's strategies, Kadri made plans of his own. Kadri had spent the night at an inn. He paid for enough drinks to solicit help from any who would rise with him against his father's army. Weren't they tired of seeing their own people bullied in the streets?

His band of rebels heard the army approaching. Thinking only that it was his father's army, Kadri rose and boldly called for the others to join him. They streamed from the inn and stood their ground in the street, waiting for the army.

The marching feet echoed down the cobbled street. The new recruits looked to Kadri for confidence. He faced forward, readjusting his grip on his shovel. He swallowed as the sound came closer. His cause was just. He would hinder his father from controlling the city.

When the army turned the corner and marched toward them, Kadri could only stare.

This army wasn't his father's, who had terrorized their people. This one was disciplined, taller, even dressed alike, with an emblem on their shields and breastplates of a god he didn't know.

He looked down the line of those who stood with him. "Stand firm, my brothers. We fight for our people. And avenge those already slain."

They raised their meager make-shift weapons and watched as the soldiers with drawn swords advanced. Kadri wiped his damp hand down his tunic and re-gripped his shovel with renewed determination. He sought courage from the strength of its handle.

The distance between them lessened.

Licking his dry lips, Kadri swallowed the lump in his throat. How could he protect himself with a meager shovel against the thrust of a sword?

He had no more time to think before they were upon them.

He swung his shovel at the first soldier in front of him. He heard the clank as it glazed off the soldier's raised shield and felt the jar of its force. A sword pierced his exposed side. Instead of backing away, he adjusted his grip to swing at a closer distance. He hacked, back and forth, knocking a sword from one hand.

But You Have Not Obeyed Me

Gaining ground, he stumbled over those who had fallen. He could feel rather than see, his comrades by his side. But soon, he was surrounded by soldiers. He dropped his arm and hung his head.

Before a final blow was dealt him, their leader called for a halt.

Kadri breathed heavily, only now feeling the blood pouring from his side. He still held his shovel, now bloodied, its handle broken in half. He leaned on it to keep himself standing.

A leader stood over him, his sword drawn.

Kadri looked him in the eye. "I have one request."

The soldier looked interested. Requests wouldn't be granted; bribes might.

Kadri leaned heavily on the shovel handle. "I know where the leader of my people will hide."

The soldier's eyes widened, and he waited. He directed his soldiers to proceed down the street.

Kadri nodded to the commander's waterskin. He licked his lips in anticipation. "May I have a drink?"

The soldier took his time unfastening his waterskin before he dropped it before him..

Kadri dropped to his knees, barely able to keep from crumbling. His sudden feeling of weakness made it hard to sit.

The soldier kicked him in the face. "This better not be a trick."

Kadri faced him again, his nose bleeding, his cheek already swelling. He grabbed the waterskin and gulped several mouthfuls before handing it back and wiping his mouth with his hand. "The leader who controls our people . . ."

The soldier leaned forward to listen.

It required all Kadri's strength to finished his message.

The soldier drank from his waterskin, nodded, studying him.

Kadri watched the commander turn and walk down the street. Kadri's hand grabbed the shovel's handle in one last attempt to rise. His hand slipped. He bowed his head.

He hadn't become another casualty of Eglon, king of Moab's army, without fulfilling his vow.

When Eglon entered the city, Bukki, the high priest, hurried through the crowds in the streets to the temple. Breathing deeply, he climbed the temple's stairs. He brushed past the guards and entered the empty, quiet hallway. His sandals echoed as he ran to the corridor concealing the secret doorway. He grabbed one of the lit candles from the wall. Looking both ways to be sure no one noticed, he entered the secret room and pulled the door shut behind him. He heard nothing through the thick walls.

He leaned against the door to catch his breath, holding the candle in shaking hands. The candle's light cast an eerie glow around the small enclosed room.

He listened.

All was silent.

In that room, closed off from the rest of his city, from the rest of life, Bukki felt safe.

His heart returned to its normal beating.

His breath became regular.

But even in the safe confines of that room, Bukki could not escape God.

He paced, his candle giving only a small glow in front of him. He stumbled and knelt to examine what he had tripped over.

The scrolls.

Cache must have just thrown them into the room.

They were old writings that didn't mean much.

Now, with plenty of time and nothing to do, he stooped to inspect the parchments. He placed the candle on the ground and unrolled the first scroll. He settled on the cold, marble floor and read.

It was the history of his people.

He read how their God had delivered them out of slavery in Egypt, provided manna and water through a barren desert, and brought them to freedom in their own land.

He read of the sacrifices. He had obeyed the letter of the Law, doing the sacrifices commanded, but his heart hadn't been in it.

Now he saw them for the first time as an offering to this God Who had given them this land.

What emptiness in following rules without knowing the Rule Giver! It had been the Levite's responsibility to remind the people of Who this God was.

He became absorbed in the reading. Where had God gone? Why didn't He help His people now?

His candle flickered. He rose to search the room for more candles before it sputtered out. He remembered the shelf he'd watch Cache put something on. He remembered Cache leaving some in a vessel. It held more candles. He lit another just before the one he held sputtered out.

He returned to the scrolls, as if an invisible Hand called him to know more. He finished the first scroll, carefully rolling it up and replacing the covering to keep it protected. He carefully uncovered the next scroll with new respect and continued to read.

Reading about this God made him want to know Him more. He no longer felt the cold, hard floor. He no longer thought about the enemy fighting outside the walls of his room. He read to know this God.

He read, rising only when his candle was low and needed to be replaced. When he stood, his legs cramped from kneeling on the floor. He hurried to unroll the next scroll, finishing each one to start the next scroll.

He read of the blessings God had promised if His people would obey: sheep growing fat with lambs, cows full with milk, vines hanging with grapes. He read the Psalms of Moses: how he praised the God Who knew him, worshiped the God Who loved him, and yearned to be in God's presence.

But . . .

Bukki had to squint and lean forward to trace the writing with his finger to keep his place as the candle's fat sputtered. The God of Moses promised curses if they forgot Him in their plenty. Forgot Him.

Isn't that what he had done? He had obeyed outwardly, but his heart was far from pleasing God. Then as his tithe was taken away and he couldn't feed his family, he had begun cheating the people and stealing from God. How did he think God wouldn't see? Had he forgotten Who God was?

He stared beyond the circle of candlelight.

The darkness seemed to overshadow him.

He rested his head on his arms as he knelt on the floor of that airless, lightless room and repented of forgetting God.

When Cache heard the army running through the streets outside his house in the pre-dawn morning, he rushed to his window for confirmation. He would never command his army to loot and destroy *his* street. When he saw the soldiers and their swords and shields, he knew the army wasn't his. His city was invaded. He hurried down the marble stairs to the kitchen. Pushing aside hysterical servants, he entered his storehouse. Slamming the heavy door, he bolted it on the inside. The door was solid oak with steel plates reinforcing its heavy beams. Its hinges were forged for strength.

He felt his way down the dark, uneven stone stairway to the dirt floor. He traced the brick wall, seeing with his fingers to find a ledge high above his head. From inside a vessel there, he withdrew a candle and flint. He lit it and paused, breathing deeply, trying not to blow out the light. He had enough stores here to survive any siege. But he didn't linger here. The door at the top of the stairs was an invitation for soldiers to plunder.

He hurried to the corner of the room. He shoved aside crates and wooden boxes to reveal another door. He opened the door, placing the candle on a ledge under this door. He lowered himself through the hatch, and replaced the wooden crates and boxes partially over the door. When he was confident all the boards were returned to their places, he lowered his head and shut the door.

Darkness enveloped him.

He allowed his eyes to focus around the small room with the candle's meager light. He used the small circle of light to assure his safety. He sighed, smiling to himself. When he had re-built his house from the wealth acquired by his army, he had dug this room for this very purpose. He would wait and be safe.

When Bukki finally rose from his knees, the room was dark, his candle out. He felt his way in the dark to the wall and followed it to the door of the hidden room. Would it be safe to leave now?

He pushed the stone doorway open a handbreadth and lis-tened.

All was quiet.

He squeezed through the opening. He left it, the door still ajar. His feet echoed down the marble corridor.

He walked to the head of the stairs which overlooked the Tabernacle where all the sacrifices were made. The goats' skin walls had been slashed.

He stumbled down the stairs and pulled aside the goats' skin to see inside.

All of the golden instruments for sacrificing were gone. The candleholders and incense burners were stolen. Even the stone altar had been destroyed.

The destruction seemed even greater now that he had come to know the God for Whom the sacrifices were given.

He had read about the ark of the covenant, which contained the presence of God. That must still reside in Shechem. He hoped those people recognized the treasure they held in their midst.

He walked through the hallway in disbelief. The temple's riches were gone. It's beauty destroyed. When he reached the entryway, he stepped over the guard's bodies. Had no one survived?

He walked to the top of the stairs and studied the city street before him. He sheltered his eyes from the bright sunshine. How long had he stayed hidden in the room? A day? Two? He had no idea.

But in that time, his people had met with God's judgment.

Nothing moved.

He walked down the stairs. The only sound was his sandals on the marble stone. At the bottom of the stairs, he pulled his cloak more securely around him and retied his belt.

Something flapped in the light breeze.

He looked for the cause: it's lonely noise out of place in the eerie quietness of the city. As he stepped over the bodies of the fallen army, he found the source; one body lay contorted on his shield. The breeze fluttered his tunic to a rhythmic beat against his shield; its thumping loud against the silence of the street.

Bukki turned his head from the sight.

He stumbled through the empty streets.

Without thinking, he headed home. When he reached the doorway, he paused to prepare himself for what he might find. He pushed the hood of his cloak off and eased the door open.

The entire room was ransacked. The table and benches in the middle of the floor were turned over and cracked. Ashes from the kitchen fire were strewn across the floor. Jars used to hold barley and grain were broken in pieces on the floor.

He scanned the darkened corners of the room, gasping when he saw a huddled form in the corner. He dropped to his knees before his wife, brushing her hair from her face. "Karina!"

She wasn't cold. She lived!

She groaned in response to his touch. She swallowed, forcing her eyes open.

He stretched for a vessel within his reach on the floor. A swallow of water remained at the bottom. "Here." He lifted her head to help her drink.

After drinking, she closed her eyes again as if it caused too much pain. "The soldiers took everything."

He looked at the mantle over the fireplace, at the vessel where they kept their silver from the temple.

As if sensing his look, she shook her head. "It's gone. I cowered in the corner as they ransacked our home." A tear slid down her face.

Bukki noticed her arm, already bruising. He touched it gently.

She winced. "Our temple money was not enough for them."

He turned his attention back to her face. He didn't want to know what other payment they had extracted.

He dropped his head on his chest and wept.

If only he had taught the people the Law of God.

If only they had remembered God.

CHAPTER 9

Several days after the Moabite invasion, Cache was still hiding. He knew if he stayed where he was, he wouldn't be found. He had enough water and food in his vessels that he could survive until it was safe to return above ground and claim whatever survived as his own. His plan for power may have been delayed but it would not be thwarted. He grew confident even as he remained protected. Finally, he thought enough time had passed. He raised the floor of the storehouse and peered around.

It seemed lighter than he thought it should be. Maybe the storehouse door had been broken open and the storehouse raided by servants or soldiers. He lifted himself out of the hole. When he raised his legs to stand, he turned, sensing he was not alone.

A soldier sat comfortably with a wine bottle in his hand. "You have decided to return."

Cache studied the soldier. He was not one of his. His shoulders drooped. Why hadn't he stayed longer? "How did you know to find me here?"

The soldier smiled. "Your son sends this message, "Remember the thorn in your side."

This was more than a thorn. Cache remembered Kadri's interest in his new house. He had kept to himself after their fight.

Cache had underestimated Kadri's anger and thought he had forgotten. He hadn't.

He swore.

The soldier gestured with his sword for Cache to walk before him. He took him before the king of Moab.

Cache saw the king's riches and life of ease. He craved it even more.

Instead, he was sent to a dungeon where neither light nor warmth seeped into his cell or his heart. He lusted after what he couldn't have.

Instead of remembering the God of his people and seeking repentance, he grew bitter and angry at what he couldn't have. Bitterness ate him like a canker sore, shrinking him to a man with nothing, not even hope.

In that dungeon, he died, never seeing what glory God could again bring to His people.

But the Lord had more power than Cache or the king of Moab. He worked in His people, causing them to remember Him and turn from their wickedness. His desire for their repentance was stronger than Cache's passion for power. And He waited for it to come.

Those who remained from the destruction of the soldiers were broken. As the people returned to living, Eglon sent messengers demanding taxes.

The people groaned under the bondage. Their lives were nothing but slavery and survival. The sons of Israel served Eglon, King of Moab, eighteen years.

Bukki could offer no sacrifices for the people without instruments. Without sacrifices, he had no livelihood. He worked beside the other citizens for enough to stave off starvation.

As he farmed outside the city, he told of what he had read in the parchments hidden in the temple. He retold the stories of how their God had brought them out of slavery.

But You Have Not Obeyed Me

Most people stared, unable to fathom a God Who would care for them.

For some, their eyes would light up at his words; but then the reality of their own survival would return, and the light would die.

Bukki told the stories over and over.

But as the days melted into years, and as the rulers of Moab oppressed them more, even Bukki's hopes started to die. How could they become God's people again, chosen and set apart for Him?

One evening, Bukki returned to the city after working his barley fields. He stumbled under the yoke around his neck. It had once been worn by two oxen, who had carried it with ease. No ox helped him. He had butchered it to feed his starving family. Now he dragged the plow.

Bukki's skin was coated in fine dust. No rains had fallen. How would the barley seed sprout if God did not send rain soon?

Someone grabbed his shoulder.

It startled Bukki out of his drudgery.

"Shalom."

Usually no one spoke. They worked side-by-side, oblivious to those around them.

Bukki was pulled out of his thoughts by the words. He recognized the man.

He collected the taxes taken to the king of Moab.

Bukki was glad he hadn't smiled. He had paid his taxes, barely, but he knew many of his neighbors couldn't scrape enough together to satisfy Eglon's demands. He spoke warily, "Be at peace."

The man still held his shoulder.

Bukki stepped away, causing the man to drop his hand. Would he demand more taxes? Bukki had nothing more to give.

The man looked into his eyes, licking his dusty lips. "They say you have read the words of Moses."

Bukki let out the breath he was holding. The man didn't want more taxes from him. But still he was wary. "I have."

His eyes looked hungry but not just for food. Even after plowing all day in the heat, he seemed eager. "What does it say?"

Bukki motioned for them to step off the road and sit under the tree. The king's spies listened everywhere for any uprising. He didn't trust anyone these days.

He leaned against the trunk and closed his eyes, feeling the parchment again between his fingers, as if he were reading it in the dark. "Moses spoke of our people in slavery in Egypt. But God delivered them."

The other man squatted before him, expectant. "How?"

"God sent plagues."

"Plagues?"

"He turned water to blood, killed their cows with disease, sent darkness."

"Darkness? How could that plague a person?"

Before this man who searched to know truth, Bukki became excited to share what he'd read. Finally, someone wanted to hear. "The darkness could be felt for three days." He continued sharing what he had read, even after the sun had set and the city gates would soon close. He gestured to him. "Come to my house. Eat with me. I'll tell you more."

The man extended his arm. "I am Ehud, son of Gera, from the tribe of Benjamin."

Bukki took his arm and squeezed his shoulder, "Bukki, from the tribe of Levi."

Bukki shared through dinner and into the night of what he had read from God's Scrolls. They talked of what God had done for their people and what they should do now.

When the stars started to shine and the moon had risen overhead, Ehud rose and hugged Bukki. "You have introduced me to our people's God. I feel like I've found a lost Friend. We will talk again." Ehud's eyes burned with a desire to know this God.

Bukki could hardly hold his enthusiasm. His plowing for the

morning was lighter, his burden less, because he had found someone else who desired his God.

Ehud brought more men to Bukki. They were hungry to know this God Who worked miracles. They were willing to do whatever He wanted, if only He would relieve their bondage.

By the time barley was harvested, the people of the city had come as a group to call on the name of the Lord for His deliverance. They didn't know how He would do it, but they knew they couldn't survive without His aid.

It was time for taxes to be delivered to the king. Ehud gathered the meager sacks that held the people's harvest. The rains had not come, nor were the barley heads full.

Ehud attached his waterskin to his belt

He picked up the oat cakes his wife had made for him as he glanced one more time into their house. "Shalom."

"You have your waterskin?"

He pulled back his cloak and tugged at his belt where the waterskin hung.

She hugged him, pressing against his sword. "You won't lose that to the king when you enter his presence?"

Ehud smiled. "They do not expect anyone from our city to own a sword. They have long since been taken."

She looked at him with worried eyes. "What will they do to you if they find it?"

Ehud laughed, squeezing her tighter. "They do not expect it, so they will not find it. Our God is with us."

She tried to smile, but her eyes still held his. She stroked his beard. "Why do you trust this God Who leaves His people to struggle like animals for a bit of food?"

"He waits for His people to seek Him."

"And what will happen when we do?"

Ehud stood straighter. "We will fall to our knees and strive to do nothing but please Him." His eyes gleamed with a light not his own.

"That makes a difference?"

Ehud looked beyond his wife to the wall behind her as he thought about the past. "Knowing God makes all the difference."

She shook her head. She didn't understand, but she wouldn't question him.

He wished he could explain it to her. These were heart issues, not understood by logic, only by the longing of a heart seeking God. He prayed her heart would seek God soon.

He must go.

Outside his door, he studied the wagon that held the city's offerings. It was far from what the king expected.

He would journey to the city of Gilgal, where the king lived part of the time to maintain his control over the Israelites.

His wife stepped outside and hugged him. "You will come home?"

"As God wills."

She released her hold on him and stepped back. "Why do you believe this God Who has done nothing for us?"

Ehud raised her chin to make her look at him again. "Our God will deliver us. He has given me peace."

She nodded. "And if He does not?"

"If He does not deliver us, then we will all perish. But that will be as He desires."

When Ehud entered Gilgal, the soldiers led him through the streets to the palace of Eglon, king of Moab. Ehud adjusted his cloak, reassuring himself that his two-edged sword was still in position and the bulge didn't show.

Ehud stood outside the king's chamber in the dimly lit hallway, waiting to be received. His insides jumped and skittered at his plan. God's people were broken. They were listening to God. And Ehud was ready to do anything God directed.

But You Have Not Obeyed Me

The massive door of the king's chamber swung open. A servant gestured for him to enter.

He followed the servant into the room.

He blinked. It took several moments before Ehud's eyes adjusted to the bright light streaming through the windows. When he could see, he struggled to distinguish the king's body resting on the mound of cushions.

The king's eyes were like raisins concealed in dough that rose around them. His neck escaped from his tunic in layers of flabs of flesh. His body rolled in deposits of fat.

Ehud couldn't help contrasting his own people with this king: their bodies gaunt from hunger, their faces shrunk, and their strength wasted.

He bowed to the floor before this wad of flesh and swallowed the disgust and anger that rose within him. He extended a sack toward the king. "I bring you our city's taxes from the barley harvest." His own people starved, living each day as though it may be their last, while this man thrived in such stupor he wouldn't even raise his head to acknowledge their hard earned taxes.

As he spoke, servants brought in the remaining bags of barley from the wagon.

The king didn't even reach to take the sack. Instead, he gestured for a servant to take it.

The servant emptied its contents on a table before the king.

The king squinted at the mound. The effort seemed too great for him. "The heads are skinny."

Ehud raised on his knee, praying silently that his sword wouldn't clatter on the tile floor. "Our people strive under the hot sun and wait for the rains that don't come. Many of our people perish without food." He waited for the king's response.

The king waved for a servant to gather the grain back into the sack again. He dismissed him with a nod.

Ehud rose to his feet. The sword bumped against his thigh. He felt the Lord's prompting as he considered how to complete his plan.

The king's servants and soldiers surrounded him.

Ehud couldn't carry out his plan in their presence. He must find a way to be alone with the king.

He watched all the soldiers who had escorted him turn to leave. "O king, I have a secret message for you."

The king eyed him. "Keep silent." Then motioned for the soldiers to leave.

With great difficulty and help from several servants, the king rose from his cushions. After he gained his balance, he swished them away with a hand gesture. When all had left the room, he walked through a side doorway.

Ehud followed him.

The door led to a stairway.

The king labored up to a door at the top.

When Ehud stepped through the door, he walked out onto the roof. The brightness of the sun blinded him after the dark stairway. Heat rose from the marble flooring as the sun's rays radiated from it.

The king turned and gestured for him to speak.

Ehud reached with his left hand to where his sword rested at his side. He thrust the sword into the king, pushing against him until the man's fat covered the handle and he could push no deeper. He sliced upward.

The king's eyes bulged. A grunt and sigh escaped the king as he fell against Ehud. His insides began slipping out.

Ehud stumbled under the king's weight. He struggled to draw out his sword, but couldn't. He pushed the king off of him and wiped his bloody hands on the king's silk tunic.

Ehud looked around the rooftop.

He was alone.

He ran down the stairs, his feet echoing on the tile. When he reached the bottom of the stairs, he locked the chamber door from the inside and pulled the door shut. Re-entering the room where he had paid the tribute, he glanced around nervously. No one remained.

He gulped from the king's vessel by the cushions the king had recently occupied.

The wine was good.

He felt refreshed.

Then he re-entered the hallway, shutting the door behind him. The soldiers waited for him.

"The king has dismissed me."

They nodded and led him to the palace gate.

He left the palace, trying not to look back, nor wipe his hand down his side. He couldn't remove the stickiness from his hands.

When he was no longer within sight of the palace, he ran through the city streets. He passed by their temple and its idols. He kept his head down and hurried beyond them, out through the city gates.

Once he had left the city's wall far behind him, he stopped to breathe deeply; then set out at a steady trot towards Seirath.

Ehud didn't have much time after leaving the city. When he reached Seirath and the hill country of Ephraim, he blew his trumpet. Would the men come, or had they forgotten what the call meant?

When he saw shadows hiding behind boulders, he called for the men to come and stand tall.

With great hesitation, they studied this man who had dared to blow the trumpet commanding battle. They shifted from one foot to another, unsure whether to oppose or help this man. "What's the meaning of this war cry? Do you want our families killed?"

Ehud lowered the trumpet. "The king of Moab is dead."

The men stared unbelieving. "Dead?"

"How do you know?"

"God has delivered us from the hands of the Moabites today. Take heart. Trust God. Listen. We must hold Jordan's fords, and not allow the Moabite army to cross. Our God has given us the victory."

When he finished, they ran to their homes for picks, shovels, bull whips, and farm implements to fight against the soldiers who would come. They gathered at the ford of Jordan.

As the Moabite soldiers crossed the waters, God's people waited and challenged them.

The rolling waters subdued their charge.

Israel defended their position.

The men of Moab were defeated by Israel's God that day.

And Israel had peace for eighty years.

PART III
SHAMGAR
JUDGES 3:31

After him came Shamgar the son of Anath, who struck down six hundred Philistines with an oxgoad; and he also saved Israel.

CHAPTER 10

The peace of Israel did not last long before they forgot why they had peace. They looked at what other people were allowed and wanted it. Why should they struggle under the sacrifices and rules of God when their neighbors prospered without rules?

Instead of standing for the Lord, they knelt before the desires of their own heart.

Instead of believing the One True God, they embraced what they deemed important.

Instead of living separate unto Him, they joined hands with the Philistines. They found the Philistines' hand held a sword.

But it was too late to turn to God. The Philistines' sword had pierced deep into their sides before they realized it. They didn't see it happening because they were too busy pleasing their bodies, satisfying their souls, and deadening their hearts to the living God.

But God did not forget them.

The barley harvest had passed, and with it the rains. It had been a good season. Enough rains to bring the barley to thick, plump heads; enough to feed his family, had the Philistines not stolen it from his hand as he threshed it from the stalks.

Now, Shamgar looked over his harvested field. All that was left for his ox to nibble were the few stubbles of stalks. But he had no seed for the next planting. The Philistines had taken all and left nothing for his future.

He laughed bitterly. His future held nothing but toil for a Philistine's wealth. He grunted in disdain. He could barely look at a Philistine without anger burning within him and pouring into his hands the desire to strangle their throats.

Shamgar looked up from his thoughts to find his ox waiting for him to direct her to where she would eat that day. He tapped her on the ear with the point of his ox goard.

It was enough to make her pick up her feet and walk.

He had once had two oxen, Clip and Clop. The thought brought a smile to his face. His daughter Abby had named them for their steady stride as they trudged through the hard packed ground, creating a deep furrow to plant the seed.

Abby followed behind him, stumbling over the big clods of dirt. She kept up, not only with her faltering steps, but with her constant chatter. "Clip, Clop, don't you hear it, Abba?" But she wouldn't wait for his answer, she would be on to the next question. "Do their feet ever get tired? They have four, you know? Or does having four feet help them rest between each step? But they have so much more weight to carry. Does being big make you get tired faster?" She would pause.

He could feel her look at him, making sure he listened. If he didn't nod, she would repeat it.

He learned to nod, even if he didn't hear all she said. How could anyone keep up with all those words? If she waited longer than normal, he would know to ask her to repeat it.

She really wanted his answer.

His little shadow.

Sometimes when he would pause in the hot sun and wipe sweat from his face with his arm, he would glance back at the house. His wife would be outside the door, straining to make sure his little shadow was safe.

He would wave.

He couldn't see her smile, but he would know it was there, as she waved back and turned back to the house to do her work.

He'd fling his ox goad with its sharp, pointed end at Clop's ear and nipped it just enough to encourage Clop to lead. "Get up."

Abby would repeat his command.

He would flip his wrist with such speed that the ox goad would touch Clip's ear, without warning.

The oxen would then start. As if they waited for her spoken command before they felt they needed to obey.

At a pause in the chatter, he glanced back to see Abby had fallen. "Whoa." He paused the oxen, even though it would take more goading to move them again.

They didn't wait for the second command to stop, but obeyed instantly.

He grunted at their selective hearing.

He lifted Abby to her feet and brushed off the dirt from her tunic. "All better?"

She looked into his eyes, tears already forming. "Abba, my knees are in the way, and my legs don't want to stand."

He bowed his head to cover his smile. He touched her knees. "Looks like they need a rest."

Her tears stopped pooling. "Do you think Clip could hold me?"

He studied the ox, waiting, almost bored. It was the same question every day. He gave the same response, "His knees don't look in the way."

"But does his legs want to stand?"

He would appear to study their legs. "No, they want to walk." And he swung her high in the air.

She squealed. Her loose hair from her braid flying behind her.

He put her on Clip's back where she held with her knees and bounced. Her eyes had lost their tears, and her smile covered her face.

He took his waterskin from his belt and offered it to her.

She pushed her dark hair back from her face, sipping and returning the water skin. She breathed deeply. "Thank you, Abba."

He gulped long and hard from the water skin before placing the stopper back on the top. "That's good water." He offered to her again.

She shook her head.

He looked again to reassure himself that she was situated. "Ready?"

She sat as if she were a queen ruling her world. She nodded.

He turned back to the oxen, and commanded, "Get up."

The oxen paused, waiting.

She spoke, "Get up."

They moved.

She did rule his world.

They were a pair.

He didn't plow without her behind him.

Nor would she leave his side, except when he had to plow past the time when her eyes grew sleepy and her legs couldn't keep up.

But that was before.

In those days, when the sun had set and the oxen were fed and watered, Shamgar would carry Abby into the house. When he entered the house, smells of seasoned stew and flatbread greeted him. He met his wife's eyes and smiled.

She arranged the pallet beside their bed for him to lay Abby on.

He removed his soil-covered tunic, washed at the basin by the door, and put on the clean tunic that hung on a peg by the water.

He then turned to the table, where a feast awaited him.

His wife sat across from him. The table was set for just him. "Aren't hungry?"

She shook her head. "I couldn't wait. I ate while I cooked."

He'd nod, bow his head and bless the God Who had provided their food. He was hungry; hadn't eaten since the morning meal.

She had taken flatbread to the field for Abby to eat, so her "insides didn't fall apart," as Abby would explain. He waited to sit and enjoy his meal.

He ate. His abba use to say, "It's a man's reward for working."

He enjoyed eating. His abba would also say, "we get more pleasure from eating when we thank God."

He filled his flatbread with just the right amount of meat, vegetables, and soft cheese to make each mouthful taste it all.

When he was about to take his first bite, his wife grabbed his hand, and brought it to her lips, and sampled it.

His eyebrows rose as he watched her chew, her eyes closed, her face smiling in spite of her mouthful.

When she opened her eyes again, he still watched her.

She laughed. "Sorry, you make it look so much better than mine."

He offered her another bite.

She shook her head, her cheeks blushing. "No, you eat. I did already."

"So you said." He took his first bite. He didn't just sample the meal, he filled his mouth, savoring every time he chewed. He swallowed and took another bite. "That's good."

She smiled and watched him eat.

The sun had set for the day. There was nothing more that a farmer must do.

They slept, rewarded by a sleep they had earned.

Life couldn't get any more complete.

Maybe Shamgar should have seen the signs. His people did not go to the Tabernacle any more for sacrifices. As a boy, his father Anath made the journey once a year to offer sacrifices. They lived too far to make the journey more often. They had land to plow, harvests to take in, animals to tend. One year his abba had returned, his shoulders more stooped than from a long day behind the plow. "They do not sacrifice to God anymore."

His mother gasped. "What sacrifice do they make?"

Anath shrugged. "Some god I didn't know. I won't return."

Shamgar remember his stern look, his jaw hard, his shoulders thrown back. He could read that sign of his abba; he wouldn't budge.

Not only did his people not worship the God that knew them, but Shamgar should have also seen that God's people didn't consider His laws important enough to follow.

As a farmer, they were to let the ground rest the seventh year. God blessed His people with extra on the sixth year, so they weren't in want. His abba found plenty to keep his boys busy during that year of rest; much of it had to do with making sure God's Law was known in their hearts. He would say, "Rest for your body; work your mind."

Then the following year, when they would again lift yoke to their oxen, they would have renewed vigor and something new to meditate on when the day was long in the sun and the mind could concentrate on the words they had learned from the Law the year before.

But not all abbas were like his. Many didn't rest their land. They had bigger houses to build, and larger barns to store their harvest. Wasn't God blessing with more children?

Anath shook his head. "We forget too soon. In seven years we don't return to our God."

Shamgar saw the signs but still didn't see the results.

He loved farming. He loved the land. The rains came. The planting. The after rains, bringing barley, wheat, flax, chick peas—all thick, green, and full. Harvest. Rest. The rhythm of life.

Shamgar married. He had his land. He had his wife. He had contentment. He found what God meant when the "two shall become one." He felt united in body, mind, and heart.

It was enough.

Then God gave him a daughter. At first Shamgar felt a pang of disappointment. Who would farm his land when he grew old? Who would inherit his life's work?

But as little Abby grew, she wrapped him around her little

finger and held him close to her heart. She reminded him that life was more than rhythm. It certainly had more words in a day than he had ever thought by himself.

Life was good.

But still Shamgar didn't read the signs of his people and their ungratefulness to their God. He was absorbed with his life.

Until they were no more signs of what was coming.

It just came.

CHAPTER 11

When it came, no one expected it.
    But they should have.
Hadn't their God told them to remember?
Remember what?
They had forgotten.
They had forgotten their worship belonged only to God.
They had forgotten His Law expected compliance.
They had forgotten His blessings came only through obedience.
When they had forgotten it all, the Philistines came.
They brought their own kind of worship. It brought man to his knees. Women to be his dog. And children to be his sacrifice.
They brought their own law: whatever pleased them.
They brought their own blessing: cruelty that showed contempt for their Maker and death to their fellow man.
They showed no mercy.

When they left, all was destroyed. The land was wasted of crops, of people, of hope.
But Shamgar remembered. He would not forget.

He looked across his dirt. No crops. The wind sent eddies of whirlwinds that tossed the scraps of leaves in circles of hopelessness.

Clip was all he had left of his oxen. Her once broad shoulders had narrowed with age and hunger. If she had been worth any meat, the Philistines would have butchered her.

Shamgar kept her. Not for any purpose except that she represented another time. He blocked his mind from reliving those days. But his heart wouldn't stop the flood of memories. His life had passed from good to nothing.

Why must he survive when his wife was gone? Why must he live when Abby no longer followed as the shadow of his life?

Abby had been struck by an arrow as he goaded his oxen. Her chatter had stopped and he had looked back, wondering why. He saw the arrow piercing through her little body. Her expression of surprise, then pain as she couldn't take a breath. He had grabbed her off the ox and ran for the protection of the house.

He stumbled over furrows, recently plowed, crushing her body against his own, willing her to breathe.

He glanced back once to see one of his oxen down thrashing on the ground. He didn't turn around again.

When he reached his house, he discovered the Philistines had already found his wife. Her body mutilated after she was stripped and molested.

Shamgar couldn't register all that his wife had gone through, as his daughter coughed up blood and struggled with each breath. When she lay still, he listened, his head against her chest, hoping for some faint rasping struggle for air.

Nothing.

The silence was the beginning of an ache that no noise could fill.

He then turned to his wife. He groaned over her torture. His groan turned to a piercing yell, "Not her." He numbly yanked a blanket from their bed, wrapped her body, and held her against his chest and sobbed.

They were gone.

But You Have Not Obeyed Me

The tears he shed were not for them. They had gone where no tears could touch The tears were for him.

He had lost a lot.

The good life was gone. In its place was an emptiness that nothing could fill.

He buried his wife and Abby behind the house, where he could look out the window and see their mounds. The two side by side made his heart ache like it was ripped apart and fed to the buzzards.

They would not die in vain.

The Philistines had come. They left nothing but destruction. They knew how to lower a man to bondage: take all he valued. What was left to fight for?

After Shamgar buried his wife and daughter, he gave away the meat of his dead ox to his neighbor and asked him to care for his remaining ox. He followed the destruction of the Philistines from farm to farm, village to village. He didn't know what he would do when he found them, but he knew the anger burning within him would not diminish until he did.

He didn't find them.

He found only looted ruins. Everything valuable was taken, as well as anything that could be used as a weapon.

God's people were left defenseless against the brutal Philistines who promised they would return for what they thought was theirs at harvest time.

Shamgar would wait.

And be ready.

He returned to his own house for fall planting. He brought his ox home from the neighbors. He couldn't look at the house. He focused on his ox and the barn.

The ox hurried into the barn as if she knew she was home. Once inside, she stopped and peered into the darkness.

Shamgar laid his hand on Clip's back and swallowed, trying to form the words without his voice breaking, "Clop's gone, Old Girl. Gone."

She glanced at him, shoulders drooped, seeming to understand.

He led her to her stall, unlatched her harness and threw her a handful of grass, growing by the barn door. She forgot her loss in the grass before her.

He carried buckets of water from the spring to a tub inside her stall.

He puttered in the barn, not wanting to face the empty house. Too many memories. He swallowed hard and looked for something else to do in the barn. There was nothing.

The day had darkened.

With heavy steps, he crossed the path to the house, the overgrown weeds showing its disuse. Just as Clip did at the barn, he stood at the open doorway of the house, looking for his wife's face.

She wouldn't be there, but still he looked, even in the corners' shadows.

It was as he had left it. Empty of life, love, laughter. The loss weighed greater than when he had searched for the Philistines. Then he had moved to keep the memories from catching him. Here, there was nothing but memories. Memories and silence that slapped him in the face and reminded him of the hole in his heart.

Grass wouldn't calm him, nor would drinking all the water in the spring. He shook his head. He had not eaten all day, but he wouldn't eat now. The table sat as he had left it from the last day she was here. His place set for the evening meal. The dust lay thick on the dishes, but he wouldn't touch them. Eating held no pleasure; neither did life.

He sprawled on the dirt floor before the cold hearth rather than sleep in the bed shared with his wife. Morning would come, and with it no answer to the pain in his heart and the anger in his spirit.

But You Have Not Obeyed Me

Day followed day. Shamgar's life as a farmer fell into a routine. He couldn't walk to the field without thinking of Abby stumbling behind him. He'd glance back to grab her hand as he pushed Clip to the field. She wouldn't be there. Now the rhythm of farming, what he had once loved, became dust in his throat, choking him so he couldn't breathe. In his pain, he whipped his ox goard at the air, as if he could fight the Philistines who had brought him such pain. But as he walked his land, back and forth, making each furrow, he found solace in the rhythm of the land. The stabbing pain of grief mellowed to the dull ache of loneliness as he did the next thing. He plowed. He sowed. He waited for the rains.

The Psalm of Moses his abba had made him recite years ago came to mind. "He who dwells in the shelter of the Most High will abide in the shadow of the Almighty. I will say to the Lord, 'My refuge and my fortress, my God, in whom I trust.' For it is He who delivers."

His grief healed as his thoughts turned toward the God of all comfort. The anger that so consumed him began to melt away, but not all of it. He still remembered the vow he had made.

Because the rains did not come in time, Shamgar's fall crop of wheat didn't sprout. He watched his land grow weeds scattered with a few sparse plants of stunted wheat.

Clip ate those.

Nothing would take away his own hunger.

He wouldn't consider butchering Clip to curb his hunger, although many of his neighbors had butchered their own oxen. It seemed Clip had earned her place in his heart, reminding him of his little shadow.

But without the harvest, nothing showed for his plowing, sowing, and worrying.

Where was God?

What about His promise that this would be their land?

Most his people knew nothing of God's Law or His promises. He had learned from his abba the stories of their deliverance from slavery. But were they just stories?

Who could believe a God would care for him?

Shamgar had brought Clip to the barn for the night and had hauled the water to her stall. He paused at the barn's door, looking toward the setting sun.

Across his empty fields, he saw a dust cloud.

He fingered the ox goad, just inside the doorway. He didn't need it for Clip. She walked willingly to graze in the morning and home to water at night. Almost like without Clop, there was nothing to live for. He understood that feeling.

The dust cloud emerged as a group of Philistines, come to take more.

He glanced back inside the barn door once more reassuring himself that Clip was out of sight.

She chewed her grass in the dark corner.

The Philistines would not take her.

Not if he could help it.

But they destroyed everything they didn't want for themselves whenever they came.

He glanced at his house, remembering his vow. He breathed deeply, his jaw set hard, his shoulders thrown back, his mind focused.

If he could have seen his reflection in a pool of water, he would have seen the image of his abba the day he had returned from the Temple and promised never to return to worship the false gods. He would not be moved.

Nor would Shamgar. He would do what he promised.

He waited, his hand gripping his ox goad, his gaze fixed on the road that led to his house and the Philistines' approach.

He did not feel restless nor afraid, but remembered what they had done to his family. And what he had planned for this day.

His land was at the cross-roads around the hills to the west. Their group of six hundred split. Some moved to the left; others to the right toward his neighbors.

Only a handful walked through his empty field toward him. They were on foot, looking over his field as if they already owned it. They were in no hurry. They studied his house, as if they had missed something the first time they had come.

When the one in the lead noticed him standing in the barn doorway, he changed his direction and walked over to stand before Shamgar. His confident smile showed a row of white teeth. His cloak held dust from traveling far. He appraised Shamgar from his feet to his head. When he was finished, he gestured to the barn. "What's in there?"

Shamgar shrugged. "Nothing you'd value."

The man stepped closer. "I'll be the judge of that." He pushed passed him and walked to the back of the barn.

He laughed when he found the ox.

Shamgar followed him, still holding his ox goad.

The man removed his dagger from his sheath and pierced Clip's throat.

"No!" Shamgar stepped forward, but it was too late to stop him.

Clip looked up. Her gaze locked on Shamgar's. Her knees buckled and she fell, convulsing on her bed of dried grass.

Shamgar watched in stunned silence. Although expecting cruelty, he hadn't been prepared for its quickness. It took several moments to register what had just happened.

Shamgar had planned to protect Clip. There had been no time.

He was normally a patient man. As a farmer, didn't he wait many moons for the harvest?

But today, he wasn't patient. Within him surged an anger that boiled. He glared at the one still gloating over his kill. He licked his dust-covered, dry lips and wiped his forehead with his arm.

The man towered before him, grinning.

What could he fight with? His people had nothing. No swords. Not even metal to make swords. Everything had been stolen from them. Where was their God?

As if to answer, the Philistine wiped his knife on the hide of the ox. "Your God is nothing."

If God were here now, what would He want from Shamgar?

Shamgar shifted his feet. He leaned against his ox goad. He would need it no more. A farmer without oxen isn't a farmer at all, is he? He swallowed.

This heathen challenged, not him, but his God.

Shamgar shifted again. He glanced at the Philistine then at his ox goard. It was a farmer's tool, but a weapon if he must defend the Name of his God. He was skilled in hitting his oxen at just the right bit of flesh to make them move.

Now he whipped it through the air.

It snapped the air as it flew with speed.

When the tip of it hit the Philistine's flesh, Shamgar saw his eyes widened in surprise. Did he expect no fight?

Shamgar struck out again and again with his ox goad.

The Philistine sank to his knees, covering his face with his arms.

When Shamgar's anger was spent, he looked at the man before him.

He would rise no more.

Shamgar took the man's dagger from its sheath,

Shamgar had killed over an ox.

No, he had killed a man who had blasphemed God's Name. His anger was right. In fact, his anger still swelled like a savage beast, needing a target.

With a worried glance, he looked for the other Philistines. He could see their outlines in his house as they destroyed what they wanted.

Shamgar ran.

Not away from the Philistines who tormented God's people, but toward those dogs who thought they could tell God's people what to do.

When he entered his house, the Philistines didn't even turn to acknowledge him.

Shamgar paused to catch his breath before he struck out with his ox goad. His aim ran true and the Philistine fell to the ground, but not before grunting in surprise.

But You Have Not Obeyed Me

Shamgar cleared his house of the dogs of the Philistines. He wished he had been able to do that the first time they had come. Wouldn't things be different now?

Shamgar ran to his neighbors and continued his battle for right. This was his people he defended. This was for his God Who would deliver them. He moved from his neighbor's to the next as one possessed. Not by his own spirit of revenge, but by a Spirit not his own. God gave him strength to fight. The reason was just.

When Shamgar returned home, his heart glowed with passion. Although he hadn't slept, he wasn't tired, almost like when he would return from a long day behind an ox and sit with his wife to eat. Shamgar ate like he hadn't eaten since—his wife died. Before he ate to stay alive. Tonight, he ate for a mission. He scooped the barley mash into his mouth. Filling his mouth, he chewed, enjoying it.

After swallowing, he stretched his arms over his head and wiggled his toes as he pushed his legs in front of him.

"Deliverance has come to Israel."

He heard a commotion at his door. "Shamgar!"

Before he opened the door, he touched the ox goad he'd placed inside the door frame. He opened the door to a group of his neighbors.

One neighbor stepped forward and hugged him. "Shamgar. Thank you."

Shamgar shook his head. "It wasn't me."

"We all saw you. By our count, you killed over six hundred Philistines. You saved Israel today."

Shamgar shook his head. "The Lord of Abraham delivered us. He gave me strength to do it."

The neighbor shook his head. "We no longer know this God of Abraham. We have lived for ourselves too long. How do we find this God Who gave you strength?"

Shamgar wiped his mouth with the back of his hand. Where

did he begin to tell his people of their God? He told of their history, of their deliverance from Egypt, of their journey to their own land and the battles God had already fought.

The men listened, thirsty to hear of this God they had forgotten.

He told of the required sacrifices that covered their sins and of the sacrifices of their firstfruits to God who gave it.

They shook their heads. "We have nothing to give. We have no harvest."

Shamgar looked beyond the men to his own field of dirt and stubble luminated by the moon. Shamgar saw the faces of his neighbors, waiting for him to tell them what to do. He shook his head. "We didn't remember. God promised bountiful harvests if we had just obeyed."

"What can we do now?"

"He waits for your sacrifices. He waits for your prayers."

The neighbors looked back the way they had come, toward Shiloh where they had once offered their sacrifices. "You help us look to Him."

"God has not forgotten. He only waits for repentance." Shamgar nodded. "He alone is worthy."

God saved Israel from the Philistines using a simple farmer with an ox goad and a passion for his God.

PART IV
DEBORAH AND BARAK
JUDGES 4-5

CHAPTER 12

A nd the sons of Israel again did evil in the sight of the Lord. Jabin II looked over his city walls and studied the countryside beyond. His father's dynasty had been crushed when Joshua's desert people had waged a campaign against his country. In defense, his father had formed a coalition of twenty kings to fight against Israel.

Jabin II remembered listening at the door of their council meeting. His father had called for the destruction of this desert people. Afterwards, the group of leaders had led the way to the temple, ordering a night of praise to the gods for the victory they would have. The night had grown long. Although only a child, Jabin II had crept back to the castle in the night, exhausted from watching.

He had been too young to appreciate the dancing, but the images had stayed in his mind and now that he was grown, he emulated his father's worship to the gods of fertility with much pleasure. Jabin II couldn't hold back his smile just thinking about it.

As his father had led the armies from his city toward the desert people, Jabin II had followed, watching from a distant hillside.

When his father's men tried to mow these desert people down with chariots, he had held his breath, anticipating victory. Instead, the strong horses, trained for battle, couldn't pull the chariots. His father after whipping his horses and going nowhere, left his chariot and mounted an unharnessed horse. He rode through camp, bringing order to his troops.

Jabin II had lost sight of his father.

He watched their victory seemingly so sure, become defeat and death to his father, his city, and his people. The final blow was when he saw smoke billowing like a black, hovering cloud where his city had stood.

The city had burned for days. Its ashes sifted through the air and coated his clothes. The smoke's smell lingered for months afterward, especially after the dew in the morning or a rain shower.

He remembered living in caves, hiding like some dog, as these desert people searched for strays to destroy.

These desert people had conquered the land but not its people. They were in a hurry to settle the land and find comfort.

Their great military leader, Joshua, died. Their high priest, the old man that led in sacrifices after their victory, died. Other leaders died.

Those who remained were a proud people, who thought they could do anything they pleased. They soon forgot the teachings of their former leaders who had led them to victory.

And so Jabin II had waited. He recruited remnants of his former city, and he remembered. He vowed to live again like before.

He rebuilt the city, repairing the walls on its former ashes. It had been a good fortress. It was now. He looked over the countryside surrounding the walls of his city. The hill made a strong defense, unapproachable from all sides. Guards stood posted, able to see any approaching army.

He could only be attacked by being drawn away from the city onto the plains below.

But now these desert people must be shown *he* alone could do what he pleased. They must satisfy him.

Jabin II strode on the city wall, studying the plains where his soldiers trained. He turned to his general, Sisera. "The Israelites have taken our choice lands for farming."

Sisera's armor clanked as he followed beside him. He didn't hide the anger contorting his face.

Jabin shielded his eyes from the sun, glittering off the rows of iron chariots waiting for a command. He had remade the chariots that had made his father famous. "How many chariots do we have?"

Before Sisera could respond, the flag signaled. Sisera paused, watching as the chariots started in unison across the plains. They moved with a driving purpose of destruction. They could crush bodies fallen on the battle field. Nothing could penetrate their forces.

Even from this distance, Jabin could hear the thundering horse hooves. The wall beneath his feet vibrated with their power.

Sisera smiled. "Nine hundred, Sire."

Jabin turned his back on the soldiers. "It's time the Israelites remember this is *my* land." He faced Sisera, staring into his eyes. "Need I say more?"

Sisera's eyes shone in anticipation of Jabin's request. "No, Sire, nothing more need be said."

Jabin smiled for the first time. "Good."

Jabin II ruled with a fist that showed no mercy.

He ran through Israel's fields, ripe with harvest, as if the wheat were sand under his feet. When he finished, it *was* like sand. Then he required payment for the wheat destroyed by his own chariots.

The people of God cried to Jabin for mercy.

But he refused to hear.

He thought only of the destruction they had brought to his own life.

And so the suffering of God's people began.

In the months and years that followed, Jabin's spy system kept him informed of what happened in his land.

Jabin II couldn't keep back a smile as he settled back on his couch, surveying his chamber. On his window hung heavy silks from Egypt. On the wall hung his armor, sword and shield, forged from a mighty metal by Egypt's skilled craftsmen. Even the gems that sparkled on his rings came from Egypt's mines.

But he had never fought Egypt. Egypt wasn't even a power to be considered, now that the desert people had destroyed it and brought with them the wealth of her land. He threw his head back and laughed. Egypt's wealth had been handed to him.

He "traded" well on the roads from here to Shiloh, where the Israelites had sacrificed to their God. Much could happen on their journey. In fact, his entire army was armed by the "trade" he had found on these paths.

He questioned Sisera now as he stood before him, "What wealth do you bring?"

Sisera stood before him now. His hand resting on his sword's sheath. His face held the arrogance that comes through uncontested power. The marks on his sword and his hardened, uncompromising features spoke of cruelty. "The Israelites don't journey to Shiloh to sacrifice anymore."

Jabin flipped his hand in a gesture of disgust. "They have nothing of value." He had grown bored with their meager offerings and disgusted with their pittance of taxes. They no longer had weapons, not even a dagger to protect their families. "How long have these people dirtied my feet with their presence?"

Sisera shrugged. "Twenty years."

Jabin sat taller. "You have served me well."

Sisera stood taller. He had presented all the riches of this desert people to the king.

They had nothing more to offer.

Jabin shifted on his cushions and reached to pluck some grapes from a bowl on a table before him. He threw one into his mouth. "They're a stupid people who offer nothing of value. They aren't even worth the thought I've given."

But the people of God mattered to Someone, and He had not forgotten.

CHAPTER 13

The sun had already set over the mountains outside her window, but Deborah hadn't had the time to notice. She lit another candle and placed it on the table so she could see by it. The dishes of the evening meal had been cleaned by the sand outside her doorway, the water vessel filled for the early morning chores. She pushed her dark hair from her face with the back of her hand; then moved the treadle with her foot again. Her hands were already twirling the fine goats' hair into a soft, thick thread. She didn't need to see her fingers; she could feel the thickness and know they twisted evenly, but she must see when she selected the goat's hair at her feet from the basket. She could feel the best hair, but she must also select the same color. These strands would form the wicks for burning the lamps at the temple in Shiloh, and they must be the best.

Barak leaned over and kissed her on the cheek. "You will be up late?"

Deborah nodded, not pausing in her spinning. "I could do nothing today. I now must make enough wicks."

Barak sat beside her on the bench. "You did not do nothing today."

Deborah shrugged.

Barak continued, watching her fingers as they flew, twisting and adding hair to the rhythm of her feet that kept the wheel turning. "Many men came to speak to you."

Deborah sighed. "They don't go to the tabernacle to hear the Words of God. If they did, they wouldn't need to talk to me."

Barak rested his hand on her leg as she worked the treadle. "The priests don't read God's Word anymore. They've forgotten their promise to God to remember Him."

Deborah stopped her feet. The silence in the room seemed strong after the wheel's constant humming. "So why do they come to me?"

Barak took her hand in his. "Our people don't remember God until they're in trouble."

Deborah sighed. "They've neglected God's Word for years, and now, they finally realize it?"

Barak brought her hand to his lips and kissed it. "You are tired. This can wait. Come to bed. Tomorrow will be another day."

Deborah sighed, but finished spinning the goat hair in her hand.

"Besides, I can't add any more to the cart. We've had a good harvest. The olive oil is excellent."

Deborah took the candle and started down the hall to their bedchamber. "Why do we give the priests our best oil and wicks, when they do not honor God?"

She knew Moses had commanded their people to give their tithe to the tribe of Levi, assigned as their priests. The tithe was ten percent of their earnings. This way, the Levites would have the means to spend their time teaching the people the Law. But what were they to do when the priests no longer taught the Law?

Even in the dark hallway under the candle's flickering flame, Barak's eyes sparkled with passion. His voice was stern, "We obey even if no one else does."

Ignoring Barak's sternness, Deborah asked, "Do we honor God, when we give our best to those who use it wrongly?"

"Do we disobey because others don't obey?"

His question silenced her. She didn't like what he meant. How could she tell others what God's Word said, if she didn't obey?

But You Have Not Obeyed Me

But should she be teaching men what they should be learning from the priests and teaching their own families? She sighed and dropped her head.

This had all started when she had gone to the gates of their village with a message from Barak.

The leaders sat in a circle discussing problems.

Although custom dictated women didn't speak to men in public, Deborah had waited respectfully until one court case had been decided; then she addressed Adonai, their leader. "Barak takes the oil and wicks to the temple, should any others want to include their tithe." She had looked around the circle of men.

Custom didn't allow men to look a woman directly in the eye, but Adonai blatantly looked her in the eye, challenging her request. "No tithe is expected when taxes take it."

Deborah had only gone to relay Barak's message, but she couldn't allow this untruth. Before she could stop herself, she blurted, "So a heathen leader dictates what you give to God?"

Adonai's mouth wouldn't even close. He stood and strutted around the circle of men. After he seemed to regain his composure, Adonai looked around the circle of leaders. Rather than shock and criticism that this woman questioned him, they seemed to be agreeing with her, nodding their heads.

Adonai licked his lips, rethinking his response. His voice rose attracting others to gather and listen, "When the people have nothing to give, how can they pay their tithe?"

Deborah didn't pause. "The tithe, according to Moses, is our first-fruits, given before we eat and pay our taxes."

Adonai stepped forward, now angry. Everyone knew by the size of his house, the biggest in the village, he avoided taxes and tithe. This women dared to challenge his dedication to God! He glanced at the growing crowd, conscious she was humiliating him before others. "Do you know the mind of God that *you correct me?*"

Deborah didn't flinch. She didn't even notice the crowd that waited for her answer. Instead she challenged him. "By not giving your tithe, you show your heart. You have forgotten God."

Adonai couldn't speak. He glanced at his peers. They didn't

tithe, they skimped on their taxes, yet they didn't defend him. Yet to be accused of forgetting God? Who was this woman?

She didn't wait for a response, but turned to walk home. She felt embarrassed she had corrected a man. When she arrived home, she told Barak what she had done.

He laughed.

She could feel her cheeks flush as red as crimson, as if she were standing before the leaders again. "Why do you laugh?"

"Because that's what you do to me."

The impact of what she had done to their village leaders fell on her. She started to cry. "I don't respect you?"

Barak wrapped his arms around her and placed his head on the top of her head as she leaned against him. "You give me honor. But sometimes I need to be corrected. You're not bashful about telling me."

"Only when you'll be hurt." Her voice lowered as she sniffed.

Barak's voice became serious. "You tell our people how they can stop hurting."

Deborah pulled away from his arms to search his face. "Why don't they see their actions will bring harm?"

"You see what others don't."

She buried her head back into his chest. "I don't want to see what others do wrong."

Barak rubbed her back. "You don't have a choice. God has given you a gift. You must share what He gives with the people who ask."

"Even to men?"

Barak hugged her tightly. "If the men listen and obey, then our people will remember God. Don't you want that?"

Deborah pulled away, wiping her face. "I'm not sure."

He wiped a tear from her face. "Just share what God has given you."

After that confrontation in the gates, men came to her. At first, they came secretly at night, embarrassed to be bringing their questions to a woman. But as more men sought her counsel, Barak suggested she judge under the palm tree between Ramah and Bethel.

The men came.

And Deborah told God's Words.

So her days were filled with the people's needs. But she must hear and obey God's Words to share it accurately with those who came to her. She sighed.

Barak shrugged again. "Tomorrow I must take our olive oil and wicks to the Tabernacle, and you must tell men what the Lord says. But tonight, you must rest."

After Barak returned from taking the tithe to the priests in Shiloh, he prepared to take their taxes to Jabin II, King of Hezron.

Deborah watched him fill his saddle bags with the oil that would be their payment. "How do you expect to keep the payment, when the army is so willing to take it from any traveler?" She knew her argument fell on stubborn ears.

Barak was from Kedesh-naphtali, close to Hezron. "If I don't, the army will come to our village."

"Aren't there others in the village who are not so valuable?" She swallowed further objections when his jaw clamped in that stubborn position of his. She handed him a loaf of bread. "I don't have a good feeling about you going."

Barak paused, taking the bread and looked into her face. "I must protect you."

She laughed. "Am I in danger here?"

Barak laid the bread on top of his bag, dropped the cover over it, and pulled the string closed. "You are a leader in this village. People come to you from other villages. The king can't help but know that, with all his spies. If they come here, you will be hurt."

She felt the strength leave her. She hadn't thought of *that* danger. Barak's words left her speechless. When she found the courage to look into his face, she saw his love. What words could she say to refute that? Her shoulders slumped in defeat.

He dropped the bag and wrapped his arms around her. "No one else has as much to lose as I do. That," he raised her chin to look into her eyes, "is why I go."

She sighed heavily, sinking further into his chest.

When he broke from her, he picked up his bags and went to the door. At the doorway, he paused and turned back. "I love you."

She nodded, swallowing the lump in her throat. Tears formed in her eyes. She blinked to keep them from spilling before he saw. She wouldn't call him back. This was something he must do. She loved him for it, but she also feared for him.

She watched until he was out of sight. Then the tears came without restraint.

Her feeling of dread kept her from eating and sleeping. Instead, she reminded God they needed His help.

Several days later, before Deborah could expect Barak to return from delivering the taxes to the king, Deborah worked with her household in the olive grove. It was still early morning; the sun's rays had just peaked over the mountains.

They spread cloths beneath the olive trees and beat the limbs.

They had already hand picked the better olives for the tabernacle oil. Now she and her servants gleaned from the groves for their own use.

The harvest would be good this year. The cooler temperatures had allowed the olives to ripen slowly and they were big.

Their gleaning should provide enough to last until the next year's harvest. How much would they be able to keep from the pillaging army?

Harvests fluctuated. Next year, because they beat the trees to extract the harvest this year, the damaged limbs wouldn't produce as much.

The king demanded high taxes, even without a good harvest.

But You Have Not Obeyed Me

She wiped the sweat from her forehead with her tunic sleeve. Even the coolness of the morning didn't help.

She worried about Barak. Had he reached the king yet? The feeling of doom hadn't left her. If anything, it had increased. Swinging a stick should help keep her mind busy.

She was wrong.

She swung the stick again, trying to refocus on the task at hand. She wanted to finish this grove by noon. Then she'd judge in the afternoon, *if* she could concentrate. She beat the trees with renewed effort.

The morning was half gone when she heard a startled cry down the row. She paused as horses barreled down the row, trampling the harvested olives and knocking down servants.

Deborah gave a startled gasp as she stepped out from under the tree limb. She held her stick, raising it to shield her if they would continue their path. She waited.

The lead horseman stopped in front of her.

The others remained behind him, pulling their horses to an abrupt stop.

The horses pranced and fidgeted, crushing the olives under their hooves.

She looked briefly at the olives, now unusable even for oil, then glanced back at the man before her.

By the emblem on his helmet, she knew him to be Jabin's general, Sisera. His armor reflected the sun's rays.

She shielded her eyes as the sun silhouetted his face, making it difficult to see. But she wasn't blind to his arrogant sneer.

Deborah bit her tongue to keep from accusing him of stealing his armor from her people. Her hand holding her stick shook, not from fear, but anger. She pushed it into the ground to keep from jabbing him. She took a few deep breaths.

He was a long way from his city. What did he want here? Barak's concern of a few days before came back. She was a leader of their village.

He misread her deep breaths for fear and laughed. "Your husband is Barak."

Now, she felt fear. Why would this man know her husband? "Aye."

"He hesitated to give us his goods."

Deborah's knees felt weak. She leaned on the stick to keep from crumbling on the ground. Should she believe him? She stepped to the side so she could see his face without the sun in her eyes. "Why? Tell me."

"Barak cursed our gods as if they do not exist, proclaiming his own as the only God."

That sounded like Barak. His words reminded Deborah of where her strength lay. She stood taller and returned Sisera's look. "He is."

The general snorted. "Your God is weak and allows His people to wallow in the mud. He is nothing."

She could not defend her people. They hadn't remembered Him. Sisera's cruelty should have reminded them of God. It had been twenty years of torment. Were they ready to turn to God? "You touch His people only because He allows it. If He did not, you would be like Egypt, gone without a trace."

His dark eyes blazed before he lashed out with his horse-whip, snapping the air once with a loud crack. It was a hands-breath from her face.

She jumped. That had been close.

He laughed and whipped his wrist again, this time striking her across the chest. The whip slashed her tunic, ripping her skin.

She felt the sting of the whip; then her blood dripping through the cloth. She stepped back, drawing her tunic closed.

The general rested his hand back on his pommel. He leaned forward on his horse as if in conspiracy with her. "Your husband. . ." He allowed his words to hang in the air. Then his eyebrows raised in resignation, and he shook his head.

Her voice wavered, "What have you done to him?"

He smiled as he sat straighter. "Let's just say, he won't threaten me for a long time."

She tightened her hold on the stick, trying not to give him any satisfaction by her response. She swallowed her angry response and studied the general.

He seemed too cocky.

Something wasn't right.

Was he seeking information? Why would she know anything?

She loosened her grasp on her stick, moving her hand up and down on it. The movement caught the general's gaze.

Sisera nudged his horse almost on top of her.

The horse snorted in her face.

She turned her head but wouldn't step back.

"What did your God tell you?"

Deborah smiled. For mocking her God, he certainly was worried about what He would do. Why would Sisera ask her? Was the Lord telling her people to do something?

She shrugged. "Obey Him."

He repeated, "What did He tell *you* to do?"

She laughed now. "It's for His people to do. Would you obey if you knew?"

His eyes blazed. His jaw clenched.

He didn't like to be questioned. He made people cower before his questions.

She had not.

He fingered his whip handle and studied her for several moments. He sighed. "I heard you are different. And now I see it with my own eyes. Most would be babbling nonsense and telling me their entire life story by now. As if I would give them mercy. But you. . ."

She waited. She didn't know how she found the strength to speak, but it had to be God's Spirit. "What is there to tell? Your power is short-lived, and God will rule forever."

He tightened his hold on his whip and started lashing at her. "No one speaks to me as if I'm nothing. And no one ignores our gods."

She covered her head with her arm as she fell to the ground. She said no more.

For no apparent reason, he stopped and pulled roughly on his reins, turning his horse. "You have not heard the last of me." He took several steps away. Then turned back, "But Barak may have."

Deborah gasped. What did that mean?

He smiled at her response. He studied her as if she was wine to be tasted, licking his lips; then shook his head. He turned again to retreat down the row of olive trees.

Those with him pulled their horses aside to allow him to pass before following him.

Deborah watched them depart. When she could no longer see them, she leaned against her stick and struggled to her feet.

Did Barak still live?

Deborah had stood without fear in front of Sisera, but now that he was out of sight, she trembled. She was afraid, not only for Barak, but for herself. Her knees wobbled, and she fell against the tree.

Naomi, her servant, dropped her stick and grabbed her. "You're pale as the moon's light. Sit. Let me get you a drink."

Deborah sat and rested her head in her hands. Now that the intensity was over, she felt her wounds. Her tunic was wet from blood.

She took the dipper with shaking hands and drank deeply, as if by drinking she could forget what had just happened. "Thank you, Naomi."

Naomi, although a servant, was more like family. "Let me help you to the house to treat your wounds. Don't worry about the olives."

Deborah nodded. Her trembling had stopped, leaving a helpless feeling. She felt relieved someone was telling her what to do.

Naomi bustled around her, cleaning her wounds. She humped, "Only an animal attacks women."

Deborah heard but didn't respond. It felt good just to sit and rest.

But You Have Not Obeyed Me

But her mind raced. Where was Barak? He could be lying on the side of the road, dead.

When Naomi finished, she patted Deborah on the hand. "Rest."

Deborah shook her head. Sitting had only given her time to decide what she should do. "I must find Barak." She stood, motivated by her resolve. She pushed the table to the side of the room, rolled up the rug, and pulled on a latch concealed where the table had been. The trap door opened, revealing a stairway.

Barak had dug the lower storage room, saying it may save them from starving once King Jabin had stolen all he could find.

"Deborah, let me get what you need."

Deborah smiled at Naomi. "I don't even know what I need."

"Rest a bit first."

The smile left Deborah's face. Naomi's mothering was usually endearing to her; but today, she was annoyed. Didn't anyone sense the urgency to find Barak? "I must know how Barak is!"

Naomi nodded, wringing her hands, not knowing how else to stop her.

Deborah lit a candle by the cook fire; then descended the stone steps of the cellar. The coolness touched her feet and then reached her head as she descended. It revived her. She paused a moment at the bottom to steady the candle and decide what she needed.

She dusted off a wine vessel. It would ease Barak's pain; help him rest and heal. She sighed. What would he need?

She grabbed dried figs and dates, bundling them in a cloth. She took a block of cheese, not quite cured, before ascending back to the main room. She was relieved Naomi had left. Maybe she'd gone to finish gleaning, although she doubted it.

After closing the trap door and returning the rug and table, she stuffed the food in her saddle bags.

She sensed someone watching her and looked up.

Lazor stood at the door.

Naomi must have gotten him. If Deborah wouldn't listen to her, Naomi knew she must listen to Lazor.

Deborah sighed.

He was their servant and foreman since she could remember. He was more father than servant to her.

She didn't like his expression. Deborah read disapproval in his eyes. "I must know if Barak lives."

"Sisera is still on the road."

Deborah pulled the string to close the bag. "Do I wait and do nothing? Barak needs me." Her voice cracked.

He touched her arm, steadying her. "Barak knows where to find refuge. He won't get better worrying about you. I'll go."

Deborah bit her lip, keeping the tears back while she studied his face. "It'll be days before you can send word—"

Lazor closed the saddle bags. "You are needed here. And Barak wouldn't forgive me if something happened to you."

Deborah didn't want to go. Her confrontation with Sisera had frightened her. She still felt weak. But neither did she want to stay. She must know how Barak was. She hesitated. "I couldn't forgive myself if I let you go."

He shook his head. "Pshaw. You must judge. You need someone who doesn't look threatening or wealthy. Someone who knows where to hide along the way. I'll find Barak. And send word."

Deborah tucked the cheese in the saddlebag and retightened the straps. "Pshaw yourself. Judging? Why do I do it? No one changes. The people don't acknowledge God."

Lazor shook his head. "The people are finished being tormented by Sisera. This last act against Barak will turn the people. Enough is enough. Barak is a leader, not only here at Bethel, but also in the north, Kedesh-naphtali. God will use this to unite His people to remember Him."

Deborah covered his hand with her own. "You remind me of what Barak tells me. He keeps my focus on what God wants me to do, not what everyone else is doing."

Lazor held her hands. "Few are faithful."

Tears pooled in her eyes. "I wonder if we're the only ones."

Lazor pushed her hair from her face and left his hand on her face. "Abraham left his family to follow God. He didn't know where God would lead him. But he was faithful. We must be faithful where we are placed."

"You make it sound so simple."

Lazor laughed. "Simple, but not easy. Nor is it acceptable to others. But we don't please others; we please God."

A tear slipped unbidden down her cheek. She wanted to obey. She wanted to be faithful. But she also wanted to know Barak was fine. Could she live without him? Could she allow Lazor to risk danger to find Barak? What would it cost if she didn't heed his words? She swallowed. She must let Lazor go. And she must stay behind to do what she knew God had told her to do.

She looked around the house walls. They constricted her. She breathed deeply, trying to make her resolution match what she should do.

She stepped away from Lazor and removed a brick from the fireplace, withdrawing a small knife. She handed it to Lazor. "Take this. You'll need some weapon to defend yourself against thieves."

He smiled. "A paring knife against a sword and a whip?"

Deborah hung her head at the contrast. "How will you defend yourself?"

"Contain cruelty? You can't. You eliminate it. If left, it grows and controls everything around it. Moses told us, 'God is our refuge in times of trouble.' He will protect me."

Deborah fingered the knife's edge. "What will happen to our people if this cruelty grows? We can't take any more."

Lazor pulled his cloak over his tunic and tied his belt, slipping the knife in his pocket. "Our people must suffer before they see God."

"But they have fallen so low."

He lifted her chin to look into her eyes. "Too low for God to lift them?"

Deborah couldn't look into his face, but lowered her eyes. "No. but . . ."

"God prepares His people. God prepares Sisera for His ends. God prepares you through this time of waiting for news of Barak."

She nodded.

Lazor smiled. "Be faithful. God has not forgotten His people. Nor has He forgotten you."

As Deborah waited for news of Barak, she kept herself busy. The olives were gleaned, washed, and pressed. The oil was extracted, strained, and then hidden in the cellar.

She was tired of hiding. She was weary of feeling oppressed. She didn't even have a decent knife to prune the olive trees. They had let the sprouts of the new shoots grow around the older limbs. How could they hope for another good harvest without pruning and caring for the trees?

Anything resembling a weapon had been taken from them. No one had tools. Her people were slaves to this king who knew not God. They lived like animals struggling to survive.

When would they rise again and live like the people of the Most High God?

How could they when they were beaten into the ground at every turn?

Hope had been crushed.

She watched the road to the north as she gathered her dried laundry or went to get water. On her lips was a constant prayer to keep Barak and Lazor safe. Nighttime was hard. She burned her candles long into the night, spinning thread, weaving cloth, looking at the stars as she prayed for peace for her people, and for Barak's return.

One day, long after the sun had set, she sat at the table before her soup. Judging had been long. She was tired.

Naomi touched her back.

Deborah jumped. She must have dozed.

Naomi hovered over her. "You'll sleep better in bed."

Deborah yawned and sat up. "I'm awake now."

"There's enough time for everything without you trying to do it all today."

Deborah returned her dishes to the pan by the door to be washed in the morning. "Time stands still when he's not here."

Naomi nodded. ""You can't make him come back any sooner by wearing yourself to nothing."

"My mind imagines why it takes so long to hear."

"You must make your mind obey."

Deborah laughed. "That's harder than making a child obey."

Naomi shook her head. "With your wisdom for others, I'd think you could tell yourself the folly of killing yourself by overworking before your time. You'll end up an old woman like me. Rest. Wait. And talk to God."

"That's what I've been doing."

Naomi tutted. "There's no rest, when you don't eat and sleep."

Deborah hugged her servant. "I'll go to bed now. But that doesn't mean I'll be able to sleep."

Naomi humped. "That's a start."

The day finally came that Lazor returned.

Deborah ran down the road to meet him. She could barely keep the tears from her voice, "Barak?"

Lazor hugged her. "Barak lives."

"But he couldn't come home?"

Lazor's smile faded. "He's with his family in Kedesh-naphtali. It was closer. He must heal."

Deborah's enthusiasm faded. The distance seemed longer. "He can't come home to heal?"

Lazor shook his head. His hand still rested on her shoulder. "Barak needs to heal. He will heal better without your worry."

More men came to Deborah for counsel. They weren't fighting each other, as was the usual case, but were angry about their struggle to survive. They remembered enough of the good times to realize their life could be better.

Her judging changed from instructing them of the Laws they

disobeyed to reminding them of God's faithfulness when His people called upon Him.

Was He preparing them for deliverance?

She was beginning to feel hope that her people would turn to God.

Ira, her brother, stood waiting beyond the line of men to be judged. He lived in another village to the north.

Why would he be here? Her insides felt knotted and tight. She excused herself and walked over to him. "What is it?"

"We are leaving for the wilderness. I've come to say goodbye."

When the army had gallivanted through his village, the people hid behind closed doors. Several weeks ago, caught unaware, his daughter had been scrounging on the outskirts of the village for herbs to help fill their family's hunger.

The soldiers found her. When their fun was over, she was dead.

"My wife's afraid to leave the house, even for water. The children stay inside."

Deborah studied his face. When had his gentle, carefree look been replaced with such defeat? His helplessness to protect his family tore at his manhood. His shoulders bowed under the burden. But even in that brokenness, there seemed a hardness. To be without hope was one thing. To be hard, angry, and . . . what was it? Vengeful?

Many families had crossed the Jordan to live in the wilderness, hoping to find food and safety from the soldiers.

She could find no words of comfort. She couldn't even think of reasons for him to stay. She nodded, understanding. She hugged him and watched him plod away. What had happened to the confident man she had known growing up?

When she could no longer see him, she shook herself and returned to hear the waiting men.

Somehow she struggled through the rest of the afternoon, before stumbling home.

That evening, she sat at the table before a bowl of soup. She sipped without tasting it.

Naomi hovered over her. "You eat like you hate my cooking."

But You Have Not Obeyed Me

Deborah shook her head. "Eating seems such a waste without Barak." She pushed her bowl away, dropping her face in her hands. "Our people work so hard to survive. . . ." She stared but didn't see. "Ira came to see me."

Naomi sat on the bench beside her. "When they lost their daughter, he changed."

"How can he help but change? Suffering makes you lean *on* God, or run *from* God. You must choose. When Ira forgot God's goodness in the midst of man's rebellion against that goodness, he gave up his healing. He is becoming like those who hurt him. That hardness eats at him until there's nothing left."

"Did you tell him?"

Deborah shook her head. "Sometimes, confronting only makes the hardness stronger. He'd be more accountable for that truth." She wiped a tear from her face. "All I could do was watch him go."

When would the suffering end and they be safe?

How could they be safe without seeking God?

CHAPTER 14

Lazor again went to see how Barak healed. When he arrived at Barak's father's house, Barak rose from his bed. He limped into the main room of their house to receive any news with the others.

His mother offered Lazor a drink.

He sat at the bench by the table, slowing his breathing. He removed his hood. "It's a long way."

Barak waited, biting his tongue to keep from asking him to hurry. He knew it was a long way. How was Deborah?

When the servant finished his drink and wiped his mouth with the back of his hand, he sat back against the table and stretched out his legs in front of him.

Barak could no longer wait. "What news do you bring?"

Lazor smiled. "Good news. And bad news."

Barak paced in front of him, heedless of his pain and unable to wait.

"The people are ready to acknowledge God as their deliverer." He paused and took another gulp of the water in his vessel.

Barak paused in his pacing. That was good news. But that didn't warrant Deborah sending a messenger to tell him. "And the bad news?'

Lazor choked on his water as he gulped wrong. He turned his

head to cough into his cloak. When he finished, he said, "Deborah followed me."

Barak stared at him. "Followed you. What do you mean?"

"She sent me to deliver that message. I should have considered why she thought it was so urgent that I deliver it. When I was too far along to turn back, I noticed someone following me. At first I was afraid it was soldiers using a different tactic to waylay travelers. But this traveler camped close to me, yet not close enough for me to see him. In the morning, I would again see someone on the switchbacks following me, but far enough behind to not to be recognized."

Barak sighed. How could she expose herself to such danger? What was she thinking? "Why did you think it was Deborah?"

Lazor laughed. "She caught up with me and made me run the rest of the way."

Barak stood before the servant, unable to understand. "Then where is she?"

"I'm here." She spoke from the doorway. She stood uncertain.

Barak turned to see her. What was she thinking? "Why did you come?" His voice rose. He was unable to conceal his anger. "Don't you realize how dangerous these roads are, especially for a lone traveler and a woman?"

Deborah stepped away from Barak. Her look of confusion and hurt could not be mistaken. "I stayed as close to Lazor as I dared."

Barak turned away from her. "You shouldn't have come."

The silence in the room could be felt.

Deborah swallowed and sat on the bench beside Lazor. "Don't be angry with Lazor."

"I'm not." Barak paused for emphasis. What was she thinking? She had risked her life to come; then expected him to happy she had? He wasn't angry at her either. He was—what was he? Frustrated he couldn't protect his own wife. He hadn't defended himself. Look at his own condition! He glanced at her now.

Her chin trembled as if she was struggling not to cry.

He had hurt her. He raised his arms toward her.

She flew into them, crying. "I'm sorry. I had to come."

He hugged her tight, in spite of his wounds' pain. He brought her head against his chest and kissed the top of it. "It's good to have you here."

But he wondered if her discernment would be his undoing.

Deborah and Barak were in the small chamber off the back of the kitchen. It was the first time they were alone since she had arrived. Barak sat down heavily on the small bed, covered with goat skins and padded with wheat chaff. He leaned against the back of the mud and stone wall and sighed. "It's good to have you here."

Deborah sat beside him and leaned on his shoulder, his arm around her neck. "How are you healing?"

He laughed, more a grunt than from humor. It gave him time to answer, without too many questions. How could he tell her healing must come to his mind first? His body may be recuperating, but his mind would never be the same. How could the faith he had known since childhood be gone? He had always reminded Deborah of Who God is. He had obeyed when the other men lost focus. But now—he didn't even want to think about God. He couldn't even trust Him. How could his faith be stripped from him by just one event? He didn't know how to put his feelings into words, nor did he have energy to try.

He shrugged. But didn't look at her. He felt her gaze, like he was exposed, and she already knew. He cringed.

Instead of answering, he pulled her to him with an intensity of one who hung to life by one thin cord. Even as he held her, the dam of tears held back during his long weeks of healing broke.

Deborah lay on his chest until he had no more tears to weep. She didn't speak, only waited.

He fell asleep with his arm around her, exhausted, and slept better than he had for many nights.

When he woke, the moon's rays shone through the cracks of the door. He lay on his back, covered with a goat skin and stretched out on the bed. He propped his arms behind his head and surveyed the darkened room.

Deborah lay on a pile of skins on the floor by his side. The room was a servant's quarters, adjacent to the kitchen where duties would be close at hand. He was glad for the privacy.

He shook his head. The earlier tears hadn't released anything but the pent up feelings of his inadequacies. Where was his faith? The question that really plagued him was, "Where is God?" He had confronted Sisera about his weak, non-existent gods . . .but where was his own?

At his stirring, Deborah woke and sat. "You're awake?"

He grunted.

She rose from the floor and crept to squeeze beside him. "You are warm." She put her hand on his forehead. "Feverish." After touching his brow, she asked, "Need a drink?"

He shrugged. "Stay."

"I'm not crowding you?"

"Never." He brought her closer to his side and tucked the goat skin around her, removing it from his own hot body.

They lay in comfortable silence.

"I feel like I'm the one who must heal." Deborah swallowed before she could continue. "I came here with the Lord's words to tell you. But I don't want to." Her voice broke and she swallowed again.

He squeezed her against him. His bandage shifted, and he felt pain, but ignored it. It felt good just to hold her again. What words of the Lord would she have for him? He could do nothing. Could she read his heart and feel his lost faith? He swallowed hard. His throat was sore. He wiped his head.

She pulled away from him and went to the door where there was a vessel of water. She brought the dipper to the bed. "Sit up. You're too hot not to be thirsty."

He obeyed, shifting his back to lean against the bedding. He drank it all.

She dipped more, sipping some before returning the dipper to the vessel.

But You Have Not Obeyed Me

When she returned to the bed, she sat by him. She seemed to be working up her courage to speak.

He waited. He didn't want to hear.

Deborah began in a monotone, like she was reading it from a scroll. "God's people are broken. My brother left with his family."

"Where will they go?"

"Where all families are running, to the caves and wilderness across the Jordan River, as if that would keep them safe.

"God's people are ready to be delivered. But are they ready for the fight?"

Barak interrupted. "I'm not."

Deborah looked at him.

"Why do you look at me like that?"

"That's not the man I know."

He grunted. "What would the man you know do?"

"He would take the bull by the horns and ride it until he was dead."

He sighed. "I am dead."

Deborah leaned away from him and squinted at his face.

He would not meet her eyes.

"Look at me, Barak."

He shook his head. She would be able to see his doubts. Know his fear. Feel disdain. He wouldn't confirm what she probably already knew. He thought she might continue to probe.

She didn't. She looked away.

His response ripped a chasm between them. Made him feel isolated. But he didn't want her too close.

After several long moments of silence, she spoke, "Initially, I wanted to know you were safe and healing. It seemed such an urgent thing for me to know. I sent Lazor with haste.

"After he left, the Lord pressed on me to speak to you."

Normally, Barak would be just as excited as she over the words of the Lord. He enjoyed seeing her enthusiasm bubble from within. He watched her eyes shine like two diamonds in the black sea. This time, he turned away. He didn't want to hear.

Deborah seemed not to notice. "As Lazor rushed, so did I. I

didn't know if it was out of fear of what could happen or excitement of what was going to happen, but I kept with him. Toward the journey's end, he slowed for me to catch him. I welcomed his company. But not his rebuke. I had to see you. Now I know why."

Barak took a shallow breath, preparing for her words. They must spill out of her or she would burst. He wasn't ready. He took another breath, bracing his arm over the bandage around his chest. His ribs were slow to heal.

Deborah felt his movement and brushed a lock of hair away from his forehead. "You're hot." She brought another dipper of water for him to drink. "Little sips, not gulps."

He sipped. He had missed her. His mother cared, but Deborah knew him.

She took the empty dipper and held it in her hand as she looked out the window. "The Lord God of Israel has told you to march to Mount Tabor and take ten thousand men from Naphtali and Zebulun. God will draw out Sisera. He will give Sisera into your hand."

Barak laughed not from mirth but from unbelief. He laughed so hard he had to put his arm around the bandages on his ribs. "You shouldn't make me laugh. My ribs . . . ouch . . . oy."

Deborah sat and watched him. "You must heal before you can lead the Lord's army, but as you heal, you can gather the men to fight. That will take time. But we now have hope. Deliverance is coming."

Barak shook his head. Did she know how much he must heal? Could God give him a faith that clung to Him even when all others forgot?

He felt nothing but hollowness that ate at him even when he tried to rest. Could God deliver him from that? He shook his head.

Before he'd have had no reason to doubt; now he had every reason not to believe.

But You Have Not Obeyed Me

In the days following, Deborah felt distance from Barak, like he had pulled away from her. It was nothing he said, just a feeling. He wouldn't look her in the eye, even when he spoke to her. He seemed to want to talk, but then say something trivial. She wanted to confront him about what was wrong, but wasn't sure she could face it. She hesitated to talk about what the Lord had said to do, because she felt resistance. She didn't know how long she could stay but she didn't want to leave before whatever hung between them was gone.

She was washing clothes by the well. The cooler temperatures of the mountains made the season changes more noticeable. Even the olive trees were missing from this region, where they received more rains and colder weather.

She rubbed her hands together to warm them before stirring the water to clean Barak's tunic. Maybe the fresh smell of his clothes dried in the sun would encourage him. She doubted it. She was tired of trying to make him smile. This melancholy was not like him. She was the one who questioned, who hesitated, who doubted. He had always been the one to reassure.

But now, he questioned. Not out loud to her, but in his heart. She could feel it. His eyes held a haunted look, like he was cut adrift from the shore and lost at sea.

She wanted to shake him, to tell him he knew his anchor. His God was bigger than Sisera. Fear was ruling his spirit.

But shaking wouldn't bring him back. She knew it. And felt helpless.

This confrontation with Sisera had been more than a contest of control. It had been a test of the Evil One to break Barak from his source of strength. He must get rooted again in the Lord.

But she couldn't do it for him. That was the hardest thing for Deborah. She pled to the Lord for Barak's deliverance from his doubts.

Several months after Deborah had arrived, she was changing the dressing on Barak's wounds. Whenever she looked at the sword wounds, she winced at how close they had come to his heart. Sisera had not only cut him up, but had kicked him after he was down. "You will scar. But they're closing well."

Their conversations had become trite. The gulf between them had grown.

Deborah sighed. "I'll be leaving with Lazor tomorrow to return to Bethany."

He looked up, startled.

She didn't know what to say. He had healed in body mostly, but he was still broken in spirit. She closed her eyes to keep the tears from spilling and took a deep breath.

"I don't want you to go." He said it with such force.

Over the past weeks, he had become quiet, withdrawn, sullen. Deborah didn't even know this man anymore. She didn't like it.

He repeated, this time almost pleading. He grabbed her hand and held it. "Don't go."

She blinked back tears. He was not a man to beg for anything. "Barak, what is it? What's between us? Is it because I came? Have I done something—"

He shook his head and laid his hand on her arm. "You've done nothing."

She swallowed her tears. "Then what is it?"

He sighed and looked down.

His voice was not more than a whisper, she had to lean forward to hear him.

"When Sisera met me on the road, I stood strong for the Lord, even as he sliced me with his sword and kicked me. I even rebuked him for his empty gods and told of our one and only God."

Deborah laughed. "I know."

He stopped his story. "How did you know?"

"He told me."

Barak's face changed to horror. "He told you?"

"Shortly after you left, he came to our olive groves and told me of your beating. He didn't tell if you lived. That's why I sent Lazor to find you."

Barak shook his head. "Lazor didn't tell me." Barak studied her with an intensity that made her nervous. "What did Sisera do to you?"

Deborah shivered. She didn't like to remember. She squared her shoulders, like she had done the day Sisera had confronted her. "I told him our God was the only God, just as you had told him."

Barak watched her. His eyes seemed to pierce into her very being. "Did he touch you?"

Deborah shrugged. "With his whip." She saw his expression of pain. "It healed. The Lord gave mercy."

"I was not there."

Deborah didn't understand his response. Of course he wasn't there. He was delivering the oil to the king for their taxes.

He repeated it as if he could have changed history. "Sisera beat me, whipped me, even sliced me with his sword. I could barely move. But I could still spit in his face and tell him our God would get vengeance.

"Sisera laughed. He cursed our God. He said control belonged to him. He threatened to find you. He told me in detail what he would do to you. It was then I broke. I begged for his mercy. I begged for his protection for you." Barak's voice broke.

The silence that hung between them was only filled with his sobs.

It was a long time before either spoke.

When Deborah did, her voice, although quiet, seemed loud after the silence. "You were strong before the enemy. You proclaimed God—so much so that he spoke in fear of your words. He wanted to know what this God would do to him. I laughed at him."

Barak shook his head. "But I begged for his mercy. He has no mercy."

Deborah squeezed his arm. "But God heard your plea. God showed me mercy."

Barak pulled away. "I didn't trust."

"You trusted when it was your own body he sliced and cut. You remained faithful.

"It's harder to trust when it's out of your control. You wanted to protect me. You couldn't. That was for God to do. Isn't that what you tell me? You couldn't protect me. But God did.

"Your faith, Barak, isn't destroyed by this meeting with Sisera. It's made stronger.

"You only think your faith is gone, because you look to your faith, and not to the God Who gives you your faith.

"Focus on God. Your faith is still rooted in Him. Your faith has roots that go deep: deep where they hold to what is true, what is right, what is good—even in the midst of this evil. Even if Sisera had touched me and killed me, God is still good. You know that. You do.

"But your desire to control, by demanding to protect me when you can't, makes you forget God alone controls. You just obey." She pushed his hair from his forehead and smiled. She was repeating his words.

He nodded slowly at first, then with more assurance. He smiled, took her in his arms and hugged her. "It's out of my control, but not God's."

His words, though few, spoken from his heart, brought tears to her eyes.

Her husband's faith was focused again. This was the man she knew. He would heal now.

Her heart lightened. She laughed, almost giddily.

God would make everything right.

It was early morning the day after. Barak closed the bag with bread and cheese. Words didn't seem adequate to express the loss he already felt as Deborah prepared to leave.

She tucked a vessel of olive oil into her sack and smiled. "For blisters. Even though I shouldn't have to run to keep up with Lazor this time." She laughed.

He didn't. "I wish you wouldn't leave."

Deborah sighed. It was hard to know how much she should submit and how much she should help him be strong. "Are you telling me not to go?"

He sighed. "No."

"Then I must go. You are gaining your strength. You must go to Naphtali and Zebulun to recruit men. Inspire them with the Lord's words." She pointed to his heart. "Men will follow you because you follow God. He's in control."

Barak nodded. He must remind himself of God's control, especially with Deborah leaving. "When I recruit the men . . . we must have weapons."

"God will show you." Deborah smiled.

"When you walk the roads, Sisera will be there."

Deborah's chin came up in that stubborn way she had when he knew she wouldn't relent. "So will God."

"When we are ready to go into battle—"

"God will still be with you."

Barak nodded. His voice was no more than a whisper. "But I want you there."

Deborah started. "What?"

"When I go into battle, I want you there."

Deborah seemed flustered. "I can't fight."

Barak's voice was not pleading, but resigned. "Neither can my men."

"*Your* men?" Deborah smiled. "That sound like you are taking control again. Won't they be God's men?"

Barak smiled. "I'm God's man. They will fight under me."

Deborah nodded. "Then I'm not needed."

Barak's smile disappeared. "I must see you are safe. Sometimes God shows His care by visual reminders. I need you here when we fight. Then I know you're safe and no harm will come to you."

Deborah hugged him. "God is in control."

Barak rested his head on her hair. "God will remind me."

"Then why must I be here for the battle?"

Barak paused. He wasn't sure if he could explain. "In the heat of battle, God may be there. But I need His reassurance that He protects you."

Deborah stepped back from him. She studied his eyes for a long moment. She seemed resigned when she nodded. "I'll be there."

He smiled and squeezed her tighter.

She spoke with more force, "But, the victory will not go to you."

Barak shrugged. "I don't care for credit. I want you safe."

Deborah's soft features seemed to harden. "The victory will go to a woman."

Barak shook his head. "As long as *my* woman is safe."

He felt her shoulders slump under his embrace.

"You can be so stubborn. Don't you even care you won't get the credit?"

Barak shrugged, hiding his smile. Deborah was easily frustrated when she was passionate about something.

"Focus on God. He will deliver us."

Barak did smile. "Yes, He will. With you by my side."

She sighed in resignation. "Indeed, He will."

CHAPTER 15

Barak had healed, and with his healing, he had gained a greater focus on his Deliverer. He didn't try to have *more* faith, he focused on the God Who was the object of his faith. He continued to trust God for Deborah's protection, even though he couldn't be there to protect her. He hadn't returned home, but instead had headed north into the territories of Naphtali and Zebulun, going to the villages and towns to recruit an army.

The rains would come soon. This was no time for fighting, but his mission was clear, and he would obey.

Barak looked over the crowd of men gathered before him. All of them had that same defeated, depressed expression. How could he inspire them to fight? "Aren't you tired of living like servants in our Land promised to us by the Creator of the world?"

None answered. Their blank stares mirrored their lack of heart.

Barak squared his shoulders. "Remember the stories of our deliverance from Egypt? God destroyed Egypt when our people left. He gave manna and water in the desert. Look at your feet. Even our sandals didn't wear out."

Many of the men didn't even have sandals to protect them from the hot sands or the rough, dry ground.

"Do you remember battles with those who lived here? God promised victory. And gave it." He looked around the group.

One man, hunched in the back, kept his head hidden within his cloak's hood. He wouldn't meet Barak's gaze. But he seemed to miss nothing. He carried a staff, as if he had journeyed from the mountains.

No one traveled anymore, unless they were in the king's service. Was he the king's spy?

What could he report to the king? That a lone man told about their history? That a group of destitute men were unwilling to even consider fighting?

No one had committed to follow him, let alone fight a battle.

The other men listened as if they were tales of old, made up for children.

How could he convince them God would help them too?

Barak had already been through several towns, receiving the same hopeless response.

They had no purpose, no dream. No one dared to fight the king. Their families would be killed.

What else could he say? He looked at the sky, where the clouds piled on top of each other over the mountains. The rainy season was coming. At least the time of drought would be over. But when would the time of trouble be over for his people?

He was frustrated with their apathy, disheartened by their listless response. "You give your harvest to a man who doesn't know our God! He treats you like slaves, as he depends on you for his food!

"Look at his palace. His windows are covered with the silks *we* brought from Egypt.

"Look at his table. It's spread with *your* food while your children go hungry.

"Look at his army. They keep *you* prisoners in your own house!

"God gave us this Land. He gave victory over the giants that lived here. He broke down the walls of Jericho. He fought the south with wasps. He stopped iron chariots from running over His people."

Heads began to nod.

It encouraged Barak.

But You Have Not Obeyed Me

Barak didn't know why he did it, but he took off his cloak and opened his tunic to show his sword wounds.

Several gasped.

He whispered making them step closer to him. "These are the marks of Sisera, general of Jabin's army. Do you want this to happen to your family?

"We must prepare for God to deliver us!"

From the back of the crowd the man Barak had noticed earlier shouted, "But the king has iron chariots, swords, whips and daggers. We have no weapons."

Another shouted, "If we had the weapons, would we know how to use them?"

Their people had forgotten the skill of war. They had grown complacent and sought comfort. In their well-being, they forgot evil doesn't stay away by itself.

God had commanded them to do battle, to be skilled in fighting to guard against evil.

Now their forgetfulness kept them from doing what they should do.

Hadn't Barak asked Deborah the same thing? She'd said God would give him the answer. Barak tapped his walking stick a few times. "What is in your hand?" Barak laughed at the answer. "Do you have a stick long enough to gouge out an eye before they come at you with their sword?

"Do you have a sling to protect your sheep? Use it to hit our enemy.

"Do you have an ox goad to direct your beast? Use it to lash the enemy's flesh.

"What is in your hand? Use it for the Lord."

Barak could see hope awakening in their faces.

Some nodded.

They were beginning to believe.

He directed them to the One Who could give deliverance. "We have sinned. We've forsaken the Lord, Who delivered us when we came to our Land. We must renew our covenant to serve Him. Then God will use what's in our hands for what He wills."

A voice from the crowd shouted, "God is our Deliverer!"

Others picked up the words. The chanting grew.

Barak smiled. Yes, God would indeed be their Deliverer. And He was building His army.

King Jabin shoved the bowl away from him. "Return this. It's cold."

A servant hovered around him, taking the soup and bowing. "Sorry, Sire. I'll return with hotter."

He knocked it from the servant's hands. The soup dumped over the servant, and the vessel clattered to the floor, splintering into pieces. "How can you return with hotter, when it's not even warm?"

The servant stood, soup dripping from his nose and chin. He bowed. "Yes, Sire. I mean, no Sire."

King Jabin grabbed his wine vessel and swallowed the contents in one gulp.

Another servant stepped beside him to refill it.

A messenger arrived, tiptoeing through the cracked pieces scattered across the floor, and bowed before Jabin.

Why couldn't he eat a meal without interruption? Jabin's tone dripped disgust. "What is it?" He filled his mouth with drink.

The messenger raised his head to speak. "Sire, the people of the Land . . . they rise against you."

Jabin choked on his drink. "Against me?"

The messenger bowed as wine sprayed over him. "They gather on Mount Tabor."

Jabin laughed. "An army of what?" He turned to a servant behind him. "Call Sisera."

He slammed his empty vessel down on the table.

A servant refilled it.

"I'm finished." He waved his hand over the second bowl of untouched soup.

A servant hurried to remove the uneaten food before him.

But You Have Not Obeyed Me

He tapped his foot as he waited for Sisera. He studied his wine vessel as if that was the most important thing in his kingdom. He slowly swallowed the richly-flavored liquid.

Sisera burst through the doorway; then gingerly picked his way through the broken pieces to bow before Jabin.

Jabin leaned back against his cushions and studied Sisera. Had he grown soft in his dealings with this people? "The desert people have gathered on Mount Tabor."

Sisera nodded.

Jabin waited for Sisera to explain.

Sisera stood before him silent. His shoulders thrust back in confidence and conceit.

Jabin chewed on the inside of his mouth. The people were controlled because of Sisera's cruelty. Jabin's spies often reported on Sisera's murderous raids. "What do you plan to do about it?"

Sisera smiled, but his eyes showed a hardness that made Jabin shiver. They were dark pools of evil, waiting for the next victim. "We will mow them down with our iron chariots as dirt before a plow. What our chariots don't destroy, our swords will. They will not survive."

Jabin studied his general's face. Sisera could have been talking about mice in a field instead of men under his rule. Jabin smiled. His kingdom was in good hands. "When?"

Sisera shrugged. "They don't have supplies to stay long. If we wait, they'll go home. I want to catch as many as I can. I'll bring my men from the south, north and east." Sisera shrugged again, glancing out the window as if he were already bored. "We will fight in seven days' time."

Jabin nodded, resting his chin on his hands. "So be it."

Sisera strode from the king's presence. Who did these people think they were to rise against him? Hadn't he crushed them? Didn't they grovel at his feet? He had heard of their gatherings. Didn't his spies keep him informed before even the king knew? But he hadn't considered them a threat. Now that the king knew, he would have to waste his time in the northern region, during the rainy season, instead of enjoying his spoils in comfort.

Sisera reached his chamber and flung his sword down beside him as he leaned against his cushions. He stretched his legs, put his arms behind his head, and lay back.

He was not a man to underestimate an enemy. But there wasn't much to consider. They had no weapons nor battle training. The valley, where they gathered, was wide enough for his chariots to run ten abreast. He'd mow them down like he was plowing a field.

Why did they think they could win? What did they have?

He called his spies into his chamber. They had already told of men rallied in the northern villages. How many would gather?

He drank from his vessel as his spies filed before him. "What news do you have?"

None spoke.

He had trained them not to waste his time on worthless news. But with their silence, Sisera's anger grew. "What do you know about the rebels who gather?"

One man ventured, his eyebrows raised in question. "They gather on the hills of Mount Tabor."

Sisera spat in his face. "Even the king knows that." He leaned into the spy's face. "How many?"

The man shrugged and looked at the others, finally volunteering, "Ten thousand?"

Sisera turned away to conceal his surprise. That was a number worth considering. "How did they find so many?"

Another spy stuttered, "A man went from village to village."

Sisera interrupted, pointing in his face "You told me the men were too afraid to unite."

The messenger swallowed. "The men started hoping—"

"Hoping?" When a people had hope, they had purpose. When they had purpose, they could unite. Sisera's voice rose. "Hoping for what?"

The messenger shrank behind the other men. "This man showed his wounds and spoke of protecting their women."

Sisera paced. Normally when he tormented a traveler, they would beg for mercy before he even drew his sword. But with that man . . . he couldn't forget him. He had challenged him in the name of his God with nothing to defend himself, even as he fell in a bloody mess. It was only when Sisera had threatened his wife that the man had begged for mercy. His words had tormented him ever since. But how could he still live?

Sisera pointed to one man, "What was that leader's name?" He hated to even speak of him.

The man hesitantly spoke, "Barak."

Sisera stopped before the man. He touched his sword's scabbard and realized his sword lay on the cushions behind him. He adjusted his belt instead. "And you didn't think *that* was important enough to tell me? Now they have ten thousand angry men. That's a mob!"

The spy tried not to meet his gaze, but Sisera waited until he raised his head. The spy's face was pale; his lips trembled.

Sisera paced as the spies fidgeted in front of him. "What could they fight with?"

Another shrugged. "Whatever is in their hand?"

Sisera stopped his pacing. "We fight a mob with what they hold in their hand?"

The speaker shrugged in response. "That was what the man said."

Sisera stepped before the spy who had spoken. "Do you know how they protect their sheep?"

The man shook his head, looking down.

Sisera spoke slowly as if addressing a child. "They stop lions with a stone from a slingshot."

Sisera looked at his spies in disgust. Their news, though not devastating, was worth considering. He turned from them and sat, waving for them to leave.

He heard them scurry from the room.

He should have pressed Barak's wife for what their God would do. She had stood against him, not even bowing before him. Not only would he learn what her God planned, but he would find great pleasure in forcing her to his needs.

He smiled.

He felt he wasn't alone and looked up.

One spy remained.

Must he repeat himself? He spoke slowly, not even trying to conceal his anger. "You were dismissed."

"I have more news."

He sighed. His patience was already spent asking the right questions for these imbeciles to provide news. "What is it?"

The man licked his lips. "These people believe their stories of how they came into this land when their God favored them."

Sisera hated when he had to lead them to say the next word, "And . . ."

"They truly believe their God will deliver them."

Barak. It had to be the same man. He had never seen such faith. He was to blame for this new-found faith. He had instilled in the men a hope in their God. Sisera had been impressed, enough to seek out Barak's wife.

When confronted, she had not wavered, until he mentioned her husband. What was it that bound this couple together in faith toward this God? If he could use that to build his army, he would have a formidable bond.

He heard a cough and looked up.

He had forgotten the spy's presence. He waved. "Leave."

The man ran from his presence.

Sisera would have laughed under normal situations. But today, Barak and his wife and the men who believed this God pierced his confidence and left a hint of doubt about his own success.

He called for his sergeants. "Tell my men to meet at Harosheth-hagoyim. Prepare the chariots and horses. Call the footmen to order. We'll move out in two days."

They nodded and left.

He paced again. Then laughed. No god could win against his power and might. Hadn't he proven that daily by making these people grovel before him? Even with their God's help, he had nothing to fear. He shoved the trickle of doubt deeper and stomped out to watch his footmen train. Now *that* was power.

After two days, Sisera, dressed in his armor, called for his chariot. He stepped into his chariot, his shield bearer standing before him, and led his army through the city streets. The cheers of the people sounded as if they'd already returned from battle victorious. He nodded to King Jabin II as he stood on his balcony watching his army leave for battle. Victory was sure.

He had nothing to fear from this God, nor from the people who had remembered their God. He pushed back his shoulders and stood straighter.

He glanced at his sergeant in the chariot by his side and nodded. He pointed with his sword. "Forward!"

Once outside the city, he led his army south, following the Sea of Galilee. He looked at the 900 iron chariots in perfect formation behind him. Their horses displayed the finest horseflesh this side of the Great Sea. His riders were arrayed in the finest Egyptian armor. He smiled. Armor acquired from the very people they now fought.

Behind his chariot marched footmen, disciplined and well trained. His men were taller than this people they fought, taller by at least a cubit.

In the distance he saw dark storm clouds, but here sunlight glittered off their armors. The rainy season was coming; not a good time to fight. He pushed the thought away.

They traveled by road, around mountains and through valleys to reach Mount Tabor. The marching of many men shook the ground behind them. Leather harnesses creaked. Iron wheels rolled, leaving a trail behind them.

Anticipating the battle, Sisera felt exhilarated. He was confident. His men were ready. Victory was his.

A small doubt stabbed him when Barak's image came to mind,

but he pushed it down, remembering all the other men who had cowered before him. They would cower again and not live to stand before him to question his right to rule. He demanded nothing less than total victory.

They had almost reached their rendezvous when the clouds they had seen in the distance now loomed over them. Rain started to fall. Because it was the beginning of the rainy season, the roads hadn't become rutted yet by their wheels. They continued to move quickly.

But his footmen slowed their progress. They now marched through puddles on dirt too hard for the water to penetrate. Their legs splattered by dust now turned wet. Mud caked their boots, adding weight to their already full load.

As the rains fell, Sisera remembered why he never instigated battle during the rainy season. It was wet and cold. The rain weighed down his armor and dripped off his helmet, trickling down his neck. He shook it off like a dog.

It continued to drip, drip, drip.

When would they reach camp?

His attention was diverted by a tent, pitched off the main road under the shelter of several trees. Wasn't that a certain Kenite's tent? Heber by name. Sisera had stopped at his tent before on his way to report to the king.

Heber, although a descendant of the father-in-law of Moses, had bartered peace with Jabin II. He paid heavily for that peace so he could maintain an independence. Sisera suspected that independence bordered on rebellion. But since Heber gave freely of his flocks and provided meals for Sisera on his trips to report to the king, Sisera had allowed that touch of insurgence.

And Sisera remembered Heber's wife.

She was beautiful.

Sisera wanted her.

Heber was old. How could he satisfy such a young wife?

Heber's tent would be warm, dry, and inviting. The day was half over. Heber would be with his flocks. He wasn't expected home until well after dark.

Sisera would get dry at Heber's tent and wait until the storm broke, while his sergeants pitched camp and built a fire.

He commanded the sergeant at his side, "Lead the men ahead. Make camp." He nodded toward Heber's tent. "I'll come later."

The sergeant followed his glance, his eyes widening; then nodded.

After his men moved on, Sisera turned his chariot toward Heber's tent. Sisera licked his lips in anticipation of his visit. He adjusted his reins and cracked his whip over the horses' heads.

They leaped into a gallop. Their legs pulled as one, their strength defying the storm.

He felt like he was flying across the open land. He kept them galloping until he reached the tent door, yanking the reins to bring them to a sudden stop.

When the mud settled, he stepped from his chariot. He could feel eyes upon him.

Her dark, long-lashed eyes on him.

He threw his shoulders back and swaggered toward the tent.

She watched him from the doorway. Her eyes darted from Sisera to inside the tent. "My master isn't home."

Culture should have prompted Sisera to wait outside the tent for Heber. But he wasn't here for what was proper. He pushed passed her and entered the tent.

A fire burned in the center, warming the air where he stood. He blinked to adjust to the haze from the fire's smoke.

He noticed with satisfaction the absence of servants.

Heber's wife stepped inside the tent. The opening closed behind her.

He stepped toward her, watching her. He smiled, licking his lips in anticipation.

A noise behind him caused him to turn.

Heber stood in a back doorway, his rod in his hand.

Sisera felt the blood leave his face.

No tent had two doorways! Where had he come from? Why was he home?

He swallowed, angry at the interruption.

Sisera turned to Heber's wife for an explanation.

His wife looked from Sisera to Heber. After a moment's hesitation, she ran to Heber, embracing him, appearing relieved he had come.

No one had spoken yet.

Heber encircled her waist, his other arm still held his rod. He studied the general's face. Then turned to his wife. "Jael, you are safe?"

"Master, I'm glad you arrived. The rain brought the general."

Heber nodded, hesitantly releasing her from his embrace.

She stepped away from him and moved toward the cook fire to make flatbread.

Heber nodded to Sisera's armor. "You go to battle?"

Sisera breathed deeply. The woman had excused his presence. He couldn't kill Heber outright, not with the king's promised protection. But neither could he forget Jael. He let out a breath and nodded. "These people rise against the king."

Nothing more was said through the simple meal of flatbread and lamb seasoned with rosemary, sage, and mint.

Heber seemed preoccupied.

Sisera choked down the meal. He hadn't been hungry for food. But the wine was good. And he tried to drink enough to forget what he couldn't have.

He glanced several times at Jael, appraising her, yet feeling cheated.

She didn't return his look, but kept her eyes down.

Her coyness only made him want her more.

Sisera watched Heber in frustration. He wasn't returning to his flocks today.

After eating, Heber rose and glanced out the tent doorway. "Looks like the rains have stopped." The obvious hint, against custom, irritated Sisera. There was nothing more for Sisera to do here, yet.

Sisera stood and adjusted his armor and sword. He resented not getting what he thought he owned. He left. But Sisera would long remember that meal and Jael's manner that invoked an invitation for him to come back soon.

After Sisera left, Heber fingered his vessel of wine. He swallowed, slowly savoring the mellow flavor. He was a Kenite, but separate from his people. He liked the freedom of roaming where the grass was good for his flocks. That's why he had pitched his tent in the oaks of Zaanannim near Kedesh. But with his independence, he lived in danger from those who envied his wealth. That was why he had sought peace with the king. His flock would be protected and his wealth would stay his.

That morning while watching his flocks, he had noticed men gathering in Kedesh. In alarm, he had hurried home to make sure all was well. He hadn't liked what he had found in his tent. But neither was he sure how loyal Jael was. He remembered Sisera's visits before. Jael had been nervous, different when he had come. Was she attracted to Sisera?

He felt his age now, comparing Sisera's strength and power with his own. He was not a young man. But had he not provided enough for Jael?

Jael rose when he had finished his meal and brought more wine for him. She sat at his feet, quieter than usual.

He turned the ringlets of her hair around his finger absentmindedly. "What is it?"

"What made you come home early?"

Heber hesitated, without accusation. "You are disappointed?"

She retrieved a small knife from her tunic pocket and held it out to him. "I was relieved. I had only this."

"You would have used it?"

She shrugged as if she spoke of a meal she must make. "He was asking for it."

Heber laughed then, and brought her to his side in a hug. He had no reason to doubt her loyalty. "You are my precious jewel."

Jael leaned against him. "How can the people win the battle?"

He looked at her keenly. Her deference toward the people of the land concerned him. "The battle is not ours. We remain protected by the king's promise of peace."

She lowered her face and patted his leg. "Not when his general declares ownership where he chooses."

They were quiet for a moment.

"Our people are intertwined with this people. They fight in the name of their God. Aren't we descendants of Moses's father-in-law? Their suffering is our suffering."

Heber shrugged. "Should we war against tyranny when we could lose all?"

Jael raised her face to study her husband. "Do we sacrifice what is right so we may keep what is loaned to us?"

Heber could feel his face flush. He valued his wealth. All of it. He had worked hard for it. It was hard to remember everything was God's. He shook his head. What was right, anyway? "This people can't win against iron chariots."

She nodded, resignedly, and lowered her head.

Heber wanted her support for his decision. He could not help these people. He rubbed her hand as he held it. "Besides, what would I do if something happened to you?" He lifted her chin so she looked at him. He was startled to see tears in her eyes.

He bent forward to hear her whisper, "But these people have God, Who can do anything."

Barak moved among the men scattered under the trees on Mount Tabor. Another group of men waited on Mount Ephraim. The rain had started at the beginning of the week. It hadn't stopped. Instead of moving farther north over the mountains, the clouds seemed to stay in this valley.

His men had no shelter, other than the leaf covering from the trees. They had built fires to keep from shivering, but no one was dry.

Barak looked at the sky. The black clouds held much more rain.

But You Have Not Obeyed Me

He shook his head. Drops of rain scattered from his hood. His skin was soaked. He shivered.

He had waited for Sisera seven days. He watched his men with concern. Would they leave? Not only had the rains come early for the winter season, but the men had herds of sheep and goats to move from the lowlands to the highlands before the rains prevented them from crossing streams that would become rivers. Their families depended upon their wool, meat, and milk to stay alive.

No man had left.

Yet.

But still there was no sign of Sisera.

Sisera knew of their presence. Barak didn't doubt that. Hadn't spies followed him throughout the land? Sisera would know their numbers, and they had nothing but slings, sticks, and stones to fight. Why did Sisera wait?

Barak drank from his vessel. The hot tea warmed his insides.

He looked down the southern road. His greater concern was Deborah. She hadn't come yet either. Had Sisera found her? Should Barak have sent more men to protect her on the way?

He shook his head as if that would remove the worry. After Sisera's threats, Barak didn't want her out of his sight. It had been months since Deborah had left him at his parent's home. Yet he still woke from nightmares of what Sisera had promised to do to her.

He didn't regret asking her to come, but wished she was already here. He'd feel reassured when she arrived. His thoughts wouldn't be divided between protecting her and battle.

A messenger came from Mount Ephraim, their other camp. "Shalom, Barak."

Barak turned from watching the road and tried to focus. "Be at peace."

The messenger coughed. "Sisera's men wait at the valley of Haroshet-hagoyim."

The valley of Haroshet-hagoyim was narrow, formed between the two mountains to the northeast from where they waited. Their camp would have trees for fires and grass for their horses. When they were ready for battle, they could ride into the Valley of Jezreel, where the valley widened into a plain.

Barak nodded. He took a swallow of his tea. It was already cold. He looked to the north to where Sisera's army gathered. Would God gather His people to be slain? "Any word from the south?"

The messenger shook his head and stepped back. "Nothing."

Resignation came over him. He couldn't wait much longer. He would obey and fight, but his reason for fighting—his glance met the messenger's. "The men are ready?"

The messenger nodded.

Barak nodded and looked back into his cup, as if that would give him the answer.

The day grew colder as more rain fell. And still they waited.

CHAPTER 16

Deborah looked again at the clouds to the north. How many more days of rain would they have before they reached Barak? She shook her head. If she had another delay, she didn't know what she'd do. When her escort, sent by Barak, had arrived two weeks ago, he had informed her that Barak had requested again that she come.

He was so stubborn.

He didn't need her there.

But she would go.

Maybe the strength of a man was measured by the woman who stood beside him. She hoped not. Her strength had been pretty small these last months as she waited for him to recruit troops while she ran their household and kept their village leaders looking to God.

The time had been long. She had grown weary, especially apart from Barak. She reminded herself this was what she must do, just like Barak must obey God in the north.

When the escort came, she had been separating the sheep who couldn't make the long journey to the high country. The mountain grass from the winter rains would make them fat. She lacked Barak's skill in evaluating the sheep. Even Lazor relied on Barak's knowledge. Without Barak, the process took longer.

She assigned servants to move the sheep. Those sheep who couldn't make the journey would be sold.

She took another day to pack for the trip north. She felt pressure to hurry.

She finished her hot tea the next morning before Lazor helped her mount her donkey.

Darkness still covered the ground when she rode out with the men Barak had sent for her. The group was somber, aware of the dangers of traveling, conscious of their purpose.

Lazor sent one man to scout the roads in front of them. They would be warned if Sisera's men came.

Barak hadn't elaborated on Sisera's threats, but Deborah could imagine what Sisera could do. Her own confrontation with him still brought fear. She shook her head to stop her thoughts from spiraling into panic.

The dark clouds, ominous when they had started out, now dumped their contents.

Deborah pulled her hood farther over her face to keep off the pelting rain, but it did nothing to prevent soaking her skin.

She gave her donkey its lead, as it followed behind the one in front of it. It plodded along, splashing through the puddles that were forming in the hard-packed earth. The farther north they got, the muddier it became. The road became one puddle after another. After trudging through a particularly deep puddle, the water up to its flank, the donkey became more obstinate about going through the puddles.

Cold water wicked up Deborah's tunic and drenched her legs. Her legs stayed numb. She shivered.

She felt isolated, seeing only what was in front of her own nose, feeling only the rhythmic gait of her donkey.

Traveling up the mountain, the cloud thickened. Sounds were muffled. The path narrowed so that she leaned toward the mountain to avoid hanging over the cliff on the other side. At least the rain kept her from seeing the cliff drop off into nothingness at her side.

The weariness of the day lulled her into complacency. She

must have dozed in the saddle, when she was jolted by movement under her. Her eyes flew open and she looked around in alarm.

The ground shook. Thunder rumbled beneath her.

A donkey brayed behind her.

Her donkey scrambled for its footing, pushing the donkey ahead of it up the path. They panicked and stampeded, causing all the donkey's ahead to run.

Deborah grabbed for the reins she had held only loosely. She lost them in his stumble and grabbed only its mane.

The men ahead of her circled the donkeys at a plateau.

Deborah clutched the reins finally and pulled her donkey to a halt. She breathed deeply.

When she had gained her breath, she looked back.

The path was gone.

So was the pack donkey that had been behind her.

She trembled. That had just missed her!

As the men settled the donkeys, Lazor found her. "Are you hurt?"

Deborah couldn't speak.

Lazor helped her off her donkey and stood beside her for a few moments before retracing their path. He stopped where the path had vanished.

Where was the group behind her?

Her legs shook. Glancing down the edge of the cliff, she swallowed. Rock piles, boulders and mud formed a clear path straight down the cliffside.

The donkey, immediately behind her, was gone.

Lazor cupped his hands over his mouth, "Is everyone all right over there?" His echo was muted by the rain. He called again.

This time, Deborah heard a faint answer. They couldn't tell what was said. "Did anyone go over?" Deborah's voice cracked as she realized how close she had been to the landslide.

Lazor and the scout exchanged silent looks.

The scout gestured. "I'll circle around from above and see who all is there. I'll bring them over a different way."

Lazor looked at the sky. "We'll need to camp soon. . . ."

The scout gestured to another man. "Go ahead and find a campsite."

In a moment, Deborah and Lazor stood by themselves. She continued to look down the cliff. "I was on that path when it started to slide." Her voice trailed off when she realized how close she had been to being buried alive.

Lazor nodded. They walked back to the donkeys. "Do you remember what was in the pack?"

She had thrown so many things together at the last moment, she couldn't remember what each pack contained. "My blanket, an extra tunic. I don't know what else."

Lazor took her by the shoulders. "You're shaking!" He wrapped a blanket from his pack around her and led her under a tree. "Stay here until we gather this group together. We'll camp soon. The others will join us after we have a fire and food ready for them."

She sighed, drawing the blanket tighter around her. It felt good not to be riding. And to feel warm.

When the donkeys were settled and the group adjusted, they continued on. Once they reached a flattened area, they made camp. All the men busied themselves with tasks.

Lazor broke branches and pulled out wool from his pocket.

"What do you have?" Deborah strained to see.

Lazor showed her. "I stuffed some wool in my pocket, probably not enough for the entire trip, but it'll make a good fire starter. I'll have this fire going for you soon."

She plopped beside him on a log and watched as he struck a rock against a piece of metal to spark a flame. After several attempts, he caught the wool with a spark. He blew gently, blocking any wind. He broke pine needles, adding them carefully. Finally he added larger pieces of wood. The damp wood sputtered and spit as the rain continued to fall.

Deborah stretched her numbed feet and hands toward the growing flames.

Warmth never felt so good!

Deborah couldn't keep her eyes open.

But You Have Not Obeyed Me

She must have dozed. Her head bobbed and her eyes popped open.

Lazor noticed and handed her a cup. "Here's hot stew."

She took the vessel, holding it with both hands. The steam drifted into her face. The meaty smells awakened her hunger. She sipped the broth. The warmth slipped down her throat and warmed her insides. She sighed.

As she ate, she became more aware of her surroundings.

The men squatted around the fire, all intent on eating. They were silent. Interrupted only by their slurping and chewing.

Deborah shivered again at how close death had been.

One or two men stood on guard at the camp's outskirts, tucked under overhanging branches. They stood alert, watching their donkeys' ears for any sign of an intruder.

She watched down the path. Would the rest of the group make it?

Lazor sensed her thoughts. "They'll make it."

She studied his face. He had always brought such peace to situations. He brought reassurance now.

"I'll wait for them. No sense you not getting your sleep while you can."

She didn't want to admit how tired she was, but riding that donkey all day was exhausting. "I should wait for the others."

Lazor shook his head. "So we can all be tired tomorrow? Why? Go to sleep."

She laughed. "Fine. It doesn't take much to convince me."

Lazor directed her to a tree whose limbs hung over a bed of needles.

She handed back his blanket he had given her after the landslide.

He shook his head. "Use it. I'll find another."

She fumbled for words. "Thanks, Lazor." She crawled under the lower pine limbs, and for the first time that day, didn't feel the rain. Even the sounds of the falling rain were muted. She sighed heavily and tried to unlace her sandals. The laces were coated with mud. She gave up and left them on. She wrapped the blanket tighter around her and lay down in the pine needles. She didn't' think she'd fall asleep for a long time. She'd listen for the rest of the group's return.

The pine's scent calmed her thoughts. She smelled deeply. The day had been long. They had so much farther to go.

The others settled for the night. They sounded far away.

And she slept.

When she woke, she tried to register where she was and what had woken her. The night seemed just to have started.

Lazor called to her.

She sat up, bumping her head on a low branch. She rubbed it as she crawled from under the tree.

Light barely broke through the clouds. Was it morning? She couldn't tell the time, only that it still rained. She pulled her hood farther over her face. And folded the blanket.

The cold rose from the ground. She stomped her feet to warm them, but only managed to feel how stiff her mud-caked sandals were.

Lazor held out a steaming vessel for her.

She took it and smelled. More stew. "Thank you." She sipped it, looking around.

Camp was packed.

The donkeys were saddled and loaded.

She looked at Lazor. "Did they make it?"

Lazor nodded.

"All of them?"

He smiled. "Yes."

She returned his smile. "Why didn't you waken me?"

He shook his head. "Finish your meal before it's cold."

She took another sip and chewed. She tried to hurry, but wanted to linger over its warmth. She sighed when it was gone. "That was good." She handed the vessel to Lazor to pack.

The cold already seeped back into her. She glanced at the donkey and cringed, dreading getting on it. Her legs felt stiff, her seat already sore.

Lazor helped her into her saddle.

Had she even rested? She swallowed a groan. She felt as if she'd already ridden for hours.

They started out. The donkey's gait only reminded her of all her aches. She tried not to think of Barak. Wasn't it his fault she was here in this rain? Her thoughts made her angry and hurt more.

At the midday stop, Lazor helped her from the saddle. He had just placed her on the ground, when he turned to grab the donkey's reins. It was uneasy and pulling away.

She lost her footgin at the sudden move and dropped to the ground. "Why did you let go of me?"

Lazor, now holding the reins, turned to see her on the ground.

She screamed at him. "Help me!"

He tugged the reins so he could step on them, and reached to help her up.

When she stood again, she sighed. Why had she yelled at Lazor? He wasn't the cause of her discomfort. He would have lost the donkey if he'd not grabbed the reins fast enough. "I'm sorry to yell, Lazor. I'm. . ." She couldn't complete her sentence. She was angry at Barak and was taking it out on Lazor. She shook her head. "I'm sorry."

Lazor held her until her wobbly legs could support her. "We're all tired."

Deborah studied him for the first time. Under his eyes were dark lines. He had waited for the rest of the group last night when she had gone to sleep. He probably hadn't slept at all. "I'm sorry." Was all she could think to say.

He offered her a drink from his waterskin.

She drank. The cold water made her shiver. But she shivered more by how she had treated Lazor. Even though she was tired, cold, wet, and hurt, she would try not to take it out on him. She would stop thinking about Barak's stubbornness and accept what she must do.

More than that, she would thank God for His deliverance. For He alone is worthy.

In the summer, it took four days to travel north. With the landslide, mud and rains, she couldn't even guess how much longer it would take.

Rains from the mountains filled seasonal dry stream beds. Waterfalls plunged over paths. Their donkeys stumbled and slipped. They circled around obstacles, veering back to the path, always heading north. They crossed streams only to cross back again later.

All this took more time.

Would they make it in time?

She plodded on.

The farther north they went, the path turned from puddles to mud, even out of the mountains on the main road. Rather than avoiding the puddles, she sloshed through them, no longer feeling her feet or legs. Mud caked on the donkey's hooves.

They stopped to scrape off the mud, only for them to replace it with the next step.

They toiled on.

Deborah couldn't remember so much rain.

When she looked north, all she saw was more rain clouds. She forgot why she even went. Was it so important that she be there?

She lost count of the days. And didn't care. No one talked or joked. All rode silently, doggedly, as if that was all they knew.

When they made camp that night, the scout approached her by the fire. "We'll make Mount Tabor tomorrow."

She stared at him, trying to focus on why that was significant.

Lazor sat beside her. He prompted her, "Should you send a messenger ahead to tell Barak?"

She nodded.

They would fight a battle after all this? She laid her head on her arm, exhausted.

CHAPTER 17

The next day was long, and they traveled late into the night the following day to arrive in Barak's camp. She paused before his tent and took a deep breath before pushing the tent flap open and entering. She flung off her dripping hood and shook off the drops that hadn't saturated her cloak. She removed her cloak and dropped it in a heap by the doorway.

Barak lay on his back, the goat skins only partially covering his chest. Even in the dim light, she saw his scars. She knelt beside him and touched one scar lightly. His wounds had healed well.

He was warm from sleep. He rolled over and opened his eyes.

She shivered. "Sorry, Barak. My fingers are cold."

He grabbed her hand and kissed it. "You're like ice." He wrapped his arm around her and brought her closer, covering her with a goat skin. "I'm glad you're here."

She lay beside him, listening to the rain fall on his tent. She closed her eyes, feeling the cold seep from her body. She wanted to rest for days before a roaring fire and be dry.

Barak's voice broke into her thoughts. "What has God told you?"

She looked into his expectant face. This was why she had come. He needed assurance. She put aside the trials of her journey and tried to smile. Even her lips trembled from the cold. "God gives victory."

He nodded, as if that was what he needed. "Tomorrow, we draw them into battle in the Valley of Jezreel. The main army will stand at the bottom of the hill. When Sisera approaches by chariot, our men will retreat across the Valley. We will draw Sisera to follow like flies to honey.

Then our men will shoot from the hillsides."

Deborah yawned. She tried to concentrate on what he was saying, but her eyes wouldn't stay open. She settled under the goatskin. The warmth felt so good.

Barak seemed wide awake now. His excitement bubbled over with his plans. "The men made bows from what they found in the forests. The wood isn't cured, but they're serviceable.

"The men have latched onto the passion of claiming their land for God. They want it back."

He looked over at her. "You're at peace?"

She was asleep.

Barak slept the remainder of the night better than he had for months. His mind was settled, no longer torn between the coming battle and Deborah's safety. She was here. And safe.

And the Lord promised deliverance.

Deborah was still sleeping, when he left the tent.

He tightened his cloak around him.

The grey mist hovered over the ground before dawn chased it away.

Rain still fell.

Barak approached the fire.

Lazor handed him a cup of tea.

"Don't you sleep?"

Lazor laughed. "When I must."

It was good the messenger had arrived yesterday to tell of their coming, for Barak had struggled to know if he should battle without Deborah. But he hadn't felt at peace. Now, with Deborah's presence, he could fight. "What took so long?"

Barak listened as Lazor reported of their journey. "God is moving the hearts of His people to remember Him."

They looked over the valley where they'd battle. The mist hindered much of the view.

Barak shook his head. "God keeps the men here in spite of this rain, fighting a battle so one-sided. How else can you explain why they haven't left?"

Lazor pushed his hands deeper into his cloak's pockets. "Our people are ready to listen to God."

Barak pointed to the far end of the valley. "We'll station men there in the valley as a decoy. The other men will wait on the hills. Thanks to the fog, they'll hear the chariots coming toward them, before the enemy will be able to see them."

Lazor looked where he pointed. "Will they stand still long enough?"

Barak pushed his hair from his face and shrugged. "Recruiting the men, having them stay here while their flocks needed tending and the rains fell, instilling hope . . . this whole thing is of God."

Barak wouldn't speak of his craving for justice against Sisera. He still relived the incident with Sisera. Was his quest for justice strong enough to carry him through battle?

Barak wasn't afraid. So why couldn't he shake this nagging worry? Did it have something to do with Deborah's prophecy: that victory would go to a woman?

Would Deborah have to fight? He'd die first. He hadn't considered himself dying, if they were promised victory. He shook his head. Victory assumed life. He sipped his tea. "Lazor, if I don't make it . . ."

Lazor leaned forward. "Victory is already promised."

Barak nodded, but not with enthusiasm. Had he missed anything? So much depended on what he didn't know. "What is the future but a guess and a hope?"

Lazor shook his head. "You know better. God gives more than a hope. He gives assurance. And God doesn't guess, He knows."

Barak smiled. "Our faith does rest in Him."

Lazor squeezed his shoulder. "I'll watch over Deborah."

Barak nodded. Nothing more needed said.

With that reassurance, Barak focused on the coming battle.

Several men had risen as leaders. Barak had assigned them over the archers and the rod and rock throwers who would surround the valley. Other leaders would stand with the soldiers at the far end of the valley as a decoy for Sisera's attack.

He couldn't test his battle plan, not without an iron chariot of his own, but the chariot's weight would be great. Would it be enough to do what he hoped?

He lifted his face to feel the rain falling. Here was the answer. He knew it.

God brought the rain to give His people victory.

Sisera rose that morning, not because the sun lightened the sky, but because one raindrop dripped through his tent and hit him on the cheek. He threw off his blankets and roared for his men to prepare for battle. He wanted this battle finished so he could return to the palace, eat a meal that wasn't soggy, drink wine that wasn't watered down by rain, and wear something that wasn't drenched.

He strapped on his armor over his damp tunic. The damp leather straps were stretched, chafing his skin. As he slid his sword in his scabbard to complete his dress, he demanded of his assistant, "Bring my chariot to my tent. Bring the men to the field."

A messenger arrived not long after. He bowed before Sisera, apologetically. "If you could come to the plains for your chariot—"

Sisera assessed him. His helmet did nothing to protect his face. Water dripped from his eyebrows and nose. His normally shiny armor seemed pitiful as mud ran down rivulets to drop at his mud coated boots.

Sisera shook his head and tried not to think of his entire army

But You Have Not Obeyed Me

looking this motley. He wasn't sure he wanted to know why the boy couldn't bring his chariot to him, but he asked anyway, "Because?"

The messenger raised his dripping face to meet his gaze. "The horses can't pull your chariot up the slope."

Sisera creased his forehead. Why was it so hard to obey a simple command? He had the best horses in the country. Why couldn't they manage to bring his chariot here? He shook his head in disgust.

He wanted this battle finished. He spoke in exasperation, "I'll meet you on the plains."

He stomped from his tent. Once he stepped beyond the layer of pine needles that cushioned his tent area, Sisera slid, nearly falling. He slowed his pace. He had to concede his horses couldn't have brought his chariot up that slope. But the admission did nothing to calm his aggravations.

When he reached his chariot, one glance at his horses, almost bowing to the rain's power, made him hesitate before stepping into his chariot. Their glory seemed muted by the dreary day. Their splendor thwarted by the rain-drenched harnesses.

He scraped off the mud from his boots against the chariot's side, before sliding across the iron floor. He grabbed the side to catch himself from falling.

His irritations was growing with every movement.

He snatched his reins from the footman in a gesture to gain control.

This was exactly why he didn't battle in the winter during the rains.

He cursed these people who had brought him discomfort.

Though he loved battle, he didn't enjoy battles in the rain. He determined to put an end to this battle soon.

He surveyed his men. Nothing filled him with pride and power as much as his army standing behind him ready for battle. Their numbers were staggering. Their skill comparable to no other nation.

Normally their armor gleamed in the sunshine, instilling fear in their enemy and respect for him. Today, no sun reflected off any armor; only the patter of rain against each piece of metal. The sound reminded him of how he had awakened. He gritted his teeth.

Nor could he see his entire army. The fog had settled over them. It was as if he was going to war with only a handful of men. He cursed the gods for the rain and shook his fist at the clouds. "For the sake of our gods, fight!" He snapped the reins and his horses charged.

The line of chariots leaped forward across the plains. Their horses' hooves splashed mire behind them like clabbered custard. Mud coated their helmets and shields. They advanced toward Barak's men waiting on the edge of the plains.

A stream gushed down the hillside and across their path.

Sisera swerved to avoid it, jerking hard on his reins, almost colliding with the chariot on his right.

The driver's eyes widened as he, in turn, veered not to be hit.

Once passed the stream, Sisera whipped his horses to action.

They wouldn't move.

He continued to whip them.

They strained against their harnesses, their muscles bulging in their attempts to obey, but they couldn't move the chariot.

Looking over the side of his chariot, Sisera saw his wheels sunk down to its axles in mud.

He looked across the front line of chariots. Several charioteers had collided when he had swerved. None were moving.

Chariots behind him had crashed into those on the front line. They couldn't advance or retreat. All stood unmoving, as if rooted by an unseen Hand.

Beside him, a man grunted, clutching his chest where an arrow stuck. Another fell from his chariot, splashing in the mud face down.

Men on the surrounding hillsides were shooting arrows, and throwing rods and rocks.

Sisera raised his shield over his head and glanced behind him to see how his footmen fared. The chariots had stirred the mud in front of them. The men who followed were miring down in it, trapped like animals stuck for slaughter.

Sisera pointed to the hillsides. "Find shelter."

When he stepped from his chariot, he sank to his calves in the bog. He lifted one booted foot, only to have his other sink deeper.

The valley was a trap.

Rain continued to fall.

But the fog had lifted. They were an open target.

And rocks flew as fast as the rain.

Keeping his shield over his head and back, he slogged to the hillside.

Rocks glazed off his shield and plopped in the mud.

One boot stuck fast in the mud. As he yanked, his foot sucked out of his boot. He toppled to gain his balance and fell. He lowered his shield to regain his balance.

A rock hit him on the shoulder.

He raised his shield in response, the effort requiring both hands to remove it out of the mud.

He wiped his mouth with his sleeve, leaving more mud on his lips and mouth. He spit.

Frustrated and needing to escape, he left his boot and stripped off his armor to lessen his weight.

With another step, he lost his other boot.

The sucking noise reminded him of a hog he'd given a wad of caramelized honey when he was a boy. He'd laughed until he couldn't breathe as the sticky, chewy stuff had mortared its mouth shut. Now the sucking noise brought the memory back. But this time he didn't laugh; he cursed.

His boots were lost. He didn't try to dig them out. He didn't look back. He fought through the mud to firmer, higher ground.

As men reached the hills, Barak's men waited with clubs and staffs. Skirmishes lined the bottom of the hill.

Sisera followed several of his men. As they engaged in battle, he darted through the gap, heading for the protection of some boulders.

Stones cut his feet. Cold numbed them. He slid to the ground behind the boulders to catch his breath.

He rubbed his shoulder where the rock had hit. His hand came away bloody.

With this break in action, Sisera gulped from his waterskin. With his first slurp, he swished the water around his mouth and spit out the mud he'd eaten when he fell. He wiped his mouth with his hand; then drank deeply. Its coldness went straight to his head. He shook it to clear the pain. He swallowed another mouthful, this time more slowly.

Sisera thought, for the first time, he might not win. His doubt brought panic. He'd always bullied his way to victory. This battle didn't allow that.

He fought against rain! How could he fight that?

He looked at the clouds.

The rain had stopped.

The fog had lifted.

He could see farther.

He couldn't hide.

He felt vulnerable and afraid.

Had the Hand of Barak's God brought his defeat?

To his left, a twig snapped.

A man rose from the ground and stabbed one of his men. The grunt was loud in the still forest. He crumbled to the ground. The victor searched the man, taking his dagger, but left his sword. The enemy searched for others.

Sisera hunched lower behind the boulders. He was glad he'd removed his armor to escape the mud, but now he felt naked without it. What protection did he have? He'd even dropped his sword.

In this battle of stealth, his sword would have been cumbersome. His wounded shoulder wouldn't have been able to hold it. He still wished for it. He felt defenseless without it.

Sisera tilted his head against the boulder and breathed deeply.

Sounds of fighting surrounded him. Not like two armies meeting with swords clashing and armor clanking. This fighting was silent—stalked like a lion. Its eerie quietness played on Sisera's mind.

His doubts increased. Would he survive?

Without turning his head, he looked around him. His skin crawled as if someone watched him.

Rage at his own helplessness burned within him. He bit his lip to keep silent. He was no animal to be hunted!

He rose and deserted the protection of the boulders. He would master this enemy. He left behind his shield; it's clumsiness made it hard to hide. It's absence made him feel exposed.

He slid from tree to tree, using them to hide. His movements sounded loud in the silence. He must escape.

Sunlight shone through the clouds, filtering through leaves and spaces between the trees.

He kept to the dark shadows. He'd compared this enemy running from his chariots, to mice scurrying away. Now who ran? He ground his teeth.

Rocks cut his feet.

Wet undergrowth whipped his legs.

He wished for his boots.

When he glided between low hanging tree limbs, water dumped on him.

Branches scraped his face.

Still he ran.

He reached a place where he could survey the valley. His entire fleet of chariots lay stuck in the slough. He spotted his own chariot, the god's emblem barely visible through the splattered mud. One horse lay at an awkward angle. The other fallen against it.

He had trusted in iron chariots and fine horses. He shook his head. How could they not have brought victory?

Where his footmen had once stood, masses of bloodied bodies made him swallow and turn away.

Buzzards already circled.

On the distant hillside, the underbrush moved where soldiers still struggled.

The battle was lost.

He felt empty. He had *never* lost. But in this one battle, he'd lost his chariot, his horses, his entire chariot force, his footmen. . . . He didn't even have his armor or sword. Everything he had trusted was gone.

He had only his life.

But even as he tried to gain confidence, he noticed movement on the hill.

One lone man followed him. He was a distance away, but he still followed.

Sisera licked his dry lips, wishing he could stop for a drink, but the man at that moment raised his head and saw him.

Sisera turned and fled.

Heber's tent lay in this direction. He would find protection and help. He left the forest and fled across the open grazing lands.

He felt the cuts on his feet.

With each step, his shoulder throbbed.

His chest hurt to breath.

He hadn't trained his troops to run. They stood and fought.

And won.

No man had ever pursued him like this.

The sunshine shone across a plateau. He could see Heber's tent in the distance.

He glanced behind him.

The man still pursued, but at a great distance behind him.

He would make it! He began to hope.

He approached Heber's tent warily, remembering how he had first came in full armor, fine horses and gleaming chariot. Now he arrived covered in mud, out of breath, barefoot, and limping.

He hesitated. Would Heber accept him after his last visit?

He was his only hope.

The tent flap was open.

Who waited there?

He reached for his sword out of habit and found his scabbard empty. He cursed its absence now.

Jael watched him come. "Turn aside, my master. Turn aside to me! Don't be afraid." Her voice sounded like music.

But You Have Not Obeyed Me

He breathed deeply, relieved. He was saved!

He limped into the tent.

She led him to a dark corner. She knelt beside him and wiped the mud from his face and body. Her touch warmed him.

She covered him with a goat-hair blanket. Its goat smell was strong, but warmed him.

"Please," he breathed deeply to catch his breath, "Give me water."

Smoothing his dripping hair from his forehead and holding his head up, she held a vessel for him to drink.

He touched her hands. His lips shivered as he sipped.

She had brought milk!

The warm milk coated his insides, soothing him. After it was empty, he sighed and dropped his head against the cushion. He was exhausted.

"Lay down. Sleep." She covered him with the rug and patted him. The rug was heavy, dry, and warm.

He was safe.

She rose from his side.

He grabbed her hand and gathered enough strength to say, "Stand in the tent's doorway. If anyone asks, tell him, 'No one is here.'"

Jael nodded and covered him again.

Sisera could hear nothing as the rug muffled all sound. The milk satisfied him. He felt drowsy and closed his eyes. When was the last time he'd slept warm, dry, safe, comfortable?

There was no rain here.

There was no danger.

No God pursued him here.

There was nothing to think about.

And so he slept.

But Jael remembered what Sisera would have done, if her husband hadn't arrived a few days before. This time, her husband wouldn't return to protect her, but he didn't need to. She held a tent peg, sharp enough to pierce the hardest ground and hold her house erect. She took a mallet and knelt beside Sisera.

His heavy breathing told her he slept.

She uncovered his head. She cautiously moved his hair, damp and curly from the rain, away from his face.

His breathing continued, slow and deep.

Moses's people had conquered city after city when their God had been with them. They had moved in the power of their God. Today, their God must have given them a taste of His power again, to make this arrogant, pompous general flee from battle and ask her, "Please."

Her fingers didn't waver as she positioned the tent peg over his temple and raised her mallet. She flexed her fingers, trying not to think what would happen if she didn't hit hard enough. She closed her eyes and struck the tent peg in one hard, strong blow.

Metal banged against metal.

She felt Sisera jerk beneath the peg.

She held onto the peg and pounded until it felt secure.

She opened one eye and looked.

The tent peg pierced through his temple and into the ground.

Sisera was dead.

Jael's arms shook. She dropped the mallet as if it were hot. She pushed the rug over his head and drug herself to her feet. She steadied herself against the table.

She had killed him.

Not just any man, but the second most powerful man in the country.

What if these people didn't win? What would happen to her?

She didn't feel sorry.

She felt relief.

She was safe.

Jael heard someone hail the house.

She closed her eyes and breathed deeply to calm herself. She pushed back her shoulders to appear strong as she answered.

A man stood, panting. "Shalom. I am Barak. I trailed a man whose bloody footprints led this way. Have you seen him?"

Jael studied the tent's entrance.

A few drops of blood lay smeared in the dirt.

She couldn't deny it, nor would she.

She motioned for him to follow her. She pulled back the rug.

Sisera lay as she had left him. A pool of blood seeping from the tent peg.

Barak looked a long time at the body. "You killed him?"

Jael could only nod. When he still didn't say anything, she added, as if in defense, "He came earlier to my house. My husband spared me his abuse."

"Where's your husband?"

Jael crossed her arms in front of her, trying not to shake. Had she saved herself from one man to be abused by another?

But when she met his gaze, his look showed amazement and disappointment.

She stepped back. Was he disappointed she had killed Sisera? Wasn't he an Israelite? Shouldn't he be relieved?

He had asked about her husband. He seemed concerned for her. "I'll be fine."

Barak looked back at Sisera, then at her. "Yes, you will." He walked from the tent, his shoulders hunched, his head bowed. He spoke to himself, but loud enough for her to hear, "A woman will receive the credit."

On that day, God subdued Jabin II, king of Canaan, before the sons of Israel. That was the first of many battles they fought to destroy Jabin.

But ever after, Barak led. He never asked Deborah to be by his side in battle again.

She wondered what made him change.

He had been so adamant about her presence, but when he returned and told of Sisera's death, Barak was different.

Now, beside the cook fire in the comfort of their own home, Deborah leaned against his feet and refilled his vessel with tea. She finally found courage to ask, "Barak, what changed you?"

Barak brushed her hair with his hand. He seemed deep in thought. "I've seen God deliver us with nothing but rain."

Deborah picked up her vessel and sipped. "That rain did a lot of damage. But that isn't what changed you. . . ."

Barak smiled, but it didn't cover the sadness in his eyes. "I watched Sisera from the moment his chariot entered the Valley. I saw him swerve his chariot and avoid collision. I watched him abandon his chariot and fall face down in the mud. I followed his every movement. When he reached the forest, I was there. I wanted him to feel hunted, to know fear. I lost him for a time in the forest, but then followed his trail to Heber's tent. I was *so* close. I wanted revenge—to cause him pain. I needed him dead." Barak drank his tea before continuing. He lowered his voice as he reflected. "But when Heber's wife led me through their tent, I saw blood pooled on the rug. My hope died.

"When she lifted the rug, I saw Sisera. Not as one I could execute justice upon, but as one dead.

"Jael had justice.

"I only received the achievement of a battle won.

"I didn't care about credit for victory. But I wanted to give Sisera justice." He lowered his head. He didn't want to say it; they were Deborah's words told before battle. "Justice was given by the hands of a woman. It wasn't what I thought."

Deborah leaned her head on his knee. "We can never understand consequences until we receive them."

Barak stared at his empty vessel, his frustration evident. "Instead of protecting you, I put you in more danger."

Deborah squeezed his leg. "God kept me safe."

Barak shook his head. "I feel something was left undone."

Deborah patted his knee. "The Lord gave victory."

Barak nodded, his gaze far away. "Nor will I forget."

PART V
GIDEON
JUDGES 6-8

CHAPTER 18

The noise sliced the quietness, rumbling like thunder through the valley, echoing over the hillsides. Gideon stood at the mouth of a cave, concealed but listening. He paused in chewing the flatbread he had carried in his cloak pocket for his meal. The sun still shone, hot and bright. This was no storm. It came from a different source.

When this noise had come before, entire villages trembled. Children huddled behind mothers. Fathers ran to protect their herds.

But this time, Gideon didn't run. He had learned he could do nothing.

How can one lone man protect his flocks and harvest against an army greater than a swarm of locusts?

And so the camels came.

And with them destruction.

The Midianites, who rode the camels, traveled through the Jordan plains and then through the Jezreel Valley. Once there, they spread out like spiders, snagging their prey. They seized the Israelite harvests and livestock. And when they returned home, they left nothing.

Gideon glared as the camels barreled through the valley below him. He had learned to hate these beasts of burden. They could travel four times what a loaded mule could travel in a day; and that through desert with little food and no water. But when they arrived at his village, they made up for it. A single camel could drink one-third its body weight in the time it took Gideon to put his cloak on and tie it around his waist. Not that he'd begrudge any animal water, especially after running through the desert. But their numbers were too great to count. And when all of them finished drinking, the stream was so muddied it was unusable for his own sheep, now hidden in the cave behind him.

Gideon's hatred increased as their flattened hoofprints, as big as a sheep's head is long, loped through his ripened wheat fields., stomping his year's food supply into the ground.

When they had first come, he had followed their destruction to his barn.

The door had been yanked open. Only one hinge still held.

Ten camels stooped in the darkened room, devouring his barley.

Gideon charged inside to chase them out.

They were bigger than he'd first thought! He came half-way up their back.

But in his anger to get them away from his grain, he didn't fear them. He grabbed the reins of one camel and yanked it toward the door.

The camel didn't budge. It paused in its chewing to regard him. It snorted, hot dust from its nostrils formed a cloud over him, like a desert whirlwind.

Gideon coughed but didn't relinquish his hold of the reins.

The camel paused in his chewing to swallow. Gideon watched his neck muscles bunch up and then expand.

Then that wretched animal spat on him!

The foul-smelling stuff covered his hair and face. He lost his meal, before wiping his face with his arm. He ran to the water trough outside the barn.

It was empty.

He never left it empty.

But You Have Not Obeyed Me

Those wretched beasts had drunk it all before entering his barn.

As he scrubbed his face and hair with his cloak's sleeve, unable to remove the stench, he heard laughter.

A soldier with drawn sword stood before him. It was the first Gideon had thought of the camels' riders.

"You've learned, it's not for you to tell my camel what it cannot eat? Eh?" He laughed again, pointing to the camel, still eating his barley.

Gideon swallowed the bile rising in his throat. He watched in helpless rage as the camels finished eating.

When they finished, the soldiers led them out of his barn, remounted their camels and moved on.

Gideon stared after them as they crossed his destroyed wheat fields, until he could see them no more.

He felt a hand hold his own. He looked down into the upturned face of his son. He squeezed the small hand and tried to smile.

Jether asked, "What will we eat this coming year, Abba?"

Gideon looked into his barn. His barley was gone. Only the dust from a few scattered kernels, and the dung from the camels remained. He swallowed, the smell still strong, but not as strong as the feeling of despair that settled over him. "I don't know, Son . . . I don't know."

And so began the Midianites' oppression of the Israelites.

In the first year of the Midianite oppression, the Abiezrite clan searched for anything to fill their hunger. Women combed the hillsides outside their village of Ophrah for herbs, as the men trapped and hunted wild game. They found hunting scant.

Nor could their flocks of goats and sheep, raised on the surrounding hillsides, supply their need. The Midianites stole the best of their breeding pairs for their feasts whenever they came.

The clan was left with only the weak and feeble to build their flocks.

Gideon returned from milking his goats. He placed the pail of milk inside the door for his wife to strain.

Rakaal looked up from the cook fire. When she saw the milk, she frowned. "You couldn't get more?"

Gideon hung his head, feeling rebuked. "The pastures were burnt when. . ." He stopped talking when he realized she wasn't listening. Why should he explain? She knew he hadn't caused the Midianite fires that swept through the hills burning anything green. Without pastures, the goats couldn't make milk. They had lost many young. But even as he didn't need to explain, he felt her blame.

Rakaal had turned from him. "The milk's not enough to make cheese." She seemed to find pleasure in telling him he couldn't provide.

Gideon knew that. What could he do?

As if by accusation, she added, "Your father has food."

Gideon's eyes had finally accustomed to the darkness of their room. The fire's smoke burnt his eyes. He wiped them with his arm. Wasn't it enough she belittled his ability to provide, without comparing him with his father? Gideon swallowed his angry response.

And how would she know his father had food? The thought gnawed at him.

Jether had listened during the exchange. But at the mention of food, he asked, "Abba, will we have something to eat?"

Gideon looked into the boy's upturned face. The months of want had hardened Gideon to the Midianite oppression, but they had exhausted his family. Jether's frail frame stood before him as a constant reminder of his failure to provide. He'd lost meat on his bones. Hunger and hope danced in his eyes as Jether waited for his answer.

Even if it was food from his father's hand, how could Gideon refuse? His shoulders slumped, and he stalked from the house.

But You Have Not Obeyed Me

He had reached the border of his empty barley field, when he heard, "Abba!" He turned with a sigh.

Jether ran to join him. "Abba, may I go with you?"

Jether's animated excitement melted Gideon's aggravations. He rubbed Jether's head. "Tell your mother."

As Jether ran to fulfill his responsibility, Gideon wondered if this was the best idea. Whenever he went to his father's house, they argued. He hated Jether having to witness the animosity.

But Jether's excitement over possible food was enough for Gideon to push those doubts aside.

They passed before the mountain where his father, Joash had erected an altar and Asherah pole for worship. It was situated in the center of the village, where all could partake.

When his father had introduced the altar, he told their clan this worship wasn't cumbersome, full of rules and restrictions, nor dependent upon a special tribe to sacrifice as theirs were. They wouldn't be expected to travel to a faraway city to offer a sin sacrifice each year. They would depend upon no one.

Gideon shook his head. That sounded like his father—independent and in charge. No wonder the clan followed him.

He had raised his five sons to follow in his footsteps. They controlled the clan, in more ways than worship.

Joash carved an Asherah pole depicting the fertility goddess with her adoring entourage of serpents wrapped around her seductive body.

Gideon everted his eyes from the pole. He noticed Jether studying it as they walked. Gideon turned Jether's head away. "Do not look."

"Doesn't Grandfather sacrifice to please the gods?"

Gideon swallowed. How could he explain to his son that the sacrifices were more for man's own pleasure? Jether was too young to understand what that meant. He nodded to the hillside. "The sacrifices are not for the young. When you become a man, you may look."

The answer was enough for Jether for the moment. Gideon

swallowed an inward sigh. How could he protect his son from what stood in the middle of the village for all to see?

He focused his own eyes on the path in front of him, rather than the pole up on high. How could he avoid looking, now that he was a man?

He wished his father had never built the altar. The sacrifices and worship consumed his thoughts. He shook his head. Even as a man, he shouldn't look.

The worship had replaced God. Now they thought only of their own pleasure. Instead of making them independent, as his father had proposed, it made them dependent on what never satisfied.

He strode faster. Trying to refocus, he thought about the Midianite invasions. He stopped abruptly. Was there a correlation between his father's sacrifices and their invasions? He had built the altar after the Midianites came to the land. He *did* always have food, even while his own clan suffered. The thought persisted.

Jether interrupted his thoughts. "Abba, please wait."

Gideon glanced at Jether. He was running to keep up. In Gideon's haste to run from his thoughts, he had almost run from his son. He stopped and waited.

Jether reached him. "Abba, hold my hand. Then I'll keep up."

Gideon took his little hand in his own. He smiled. Children reminded him of what was innocent. He could hold onto that.

After surveying Joash's yard, Gideon stepped inside the house. His father wasn't there. He let go of the breath he was holding. When his eyes adjusted to the darkened room, he saw his mother sweeping the floor with a wheat-stalk broom.

Jether ran to give her a hug. "Shalom, Grandmother."

Kachina hugged them both. "Be at peace. Hungry?"

Jether answered before Gideon could signal him not to answer. "Always."

Gideon looked at the vessels lining the wall. They were filled with grain. His own vessels at home held nothing. Why would his mother store what they had where anyone could see? His brows scrunched in question.

Kachina lowered her eyes and stirred the embers into flames, moving the vessel of water over the heat. "Your father kept his harvest. He wanted me to store it there. I don't ask."

Gideon nodded. How could his mother always tell what he was thinking? He shook his head and considered her words. When his father did things, it was better not to ask. Gideon must do business with other clan members, and he didn't want to be embarrassed by his father's treatment of them.

He remembered the frustrations that had brought him here. Gideon watched his mother grind the wheat. She was a strong woman, yet never allowed that strength to hinder her from serving his father. "How do you do it?"

Kachina paused and looked at him. "What?"

Why couldn't she read his thoughts now? Gideon struggled for the right words; then blurted out, "You control Abba, without letting him think so. You make him think he's in charge."

The water was hot. Kachina poured some into three vessels with mint leaves. She handed one to Gideon, another to Jether. "Be careful, Jether, it's hot." She hovered over him until he took a small sip.

"Thank you, Grandmother."

Kachina patted his hand; then looked at Gideon. "No one controls your abba, except your abba."

"But you tame him. You mellow the lion in him."

Kachina added water to the ground wheat and formed a ball, flattening it as she spoke, "You describe one of the mysteries of life. Man left to himself becomes wild. It takes a woman willing to be his helpmeet to bring his wildness under control. But how we do that . . ." She shook her head. "Perhaps because he must protect me and provide for me, that makes him consider carefully what he does—I don't know."

Gideon took a sip. He knew he wasn't providing much for his family. Did that make it acceptable for Rakaal not to follow? He had provided for her . . . before the Midianites. Or maybe he only thought he had. He was tired of trying to figure out what Rakaal was thinking. "How can I lead if no one follows?"

Kachina pushed her hair from her forehead. "It's hard for women to follow anyone. We think we know better."

Gideon held back a snort. Rakaal could tell him the same thing.

"But things go better when we submit." She laid the formed flatbread on the hot stones before the fire to cook. "Things with your father and I weren't always good." She looked off in the distance, as if remembering. "When we were first married, we had some big fights." She laughed, then shook her head. "But I finally learned to support him and respect him."

"Even when he made poor decisions?" Gideon could only think of his own failure to provide for his family. They had lost their third son when Rakaal couldn't make enough milk to feed him.

Kachina laughed. "Especially when he made poor decisions."

Gideon sighed. He received no support. "I wish it were as easy as caring for sheep. I understand that."

Kachina patted his arm. "You don't lead like your father."

Gideon sat back. He didn't lead at all, he thought. "So tell me, my wise Mother, how do I lead?"

Kachina looked into his eyes, her voice growing tender. "You lead with your heart. You feel for your followers, encouraging them to change *with* you. You inspire them to be great."

Gideon laughed. "When do I do that?"

Kachina nodded as if trying to convince him. "You lead by serving. Remember that avalanche a few years back? It was your leadership that brought all your father's servants home safe."

"That's not how it happened—"

Kachina put her hand up to stop him. "That's how Purah remembers it."

"Purah is faithful to a fault." Gideon shook his head. "And too loyal."

Kachina continued, "Your humility also makes you a good leader."

"I don't—"

Kachina smiled, "And I've missed your music. When are you going to play for us? Perhaps that will tame my wild savage."

Gideon shook his head. "When Abba and I get together, I just stir the waters."

"Your father doesn't understand you."

"Neither does Rakaal." Gideon wished he could call back the words. His wife didn't follow him. He couldn't even share his heart with her. She didn't even *want* to follow him. What could he do with that?

Kachina sighed. "Sometimes it takes some rough waters for someone to see the value of a person."

Gideon fingered his cup. He wondered how much more stirred the waters would have to get before his value was seen by anyone, especially his wife. Maybe he didn't have any value.

Kachina gave the finished flatbread to Jether.

Jether took a big bite. With his mouth stuffed, he said, "Guess what we're doing, Grandmother."

Gideon hadn't wanted his family to know what he was doing. He added evasively, "Jether's my helper."

Kachina looked over Jether's head to meet Gideon's gaze. "Not all secrets should be told, Jether."

Their quiet conversation was interrupted by a booming voice, "What secrets are we keeping from family?" Joash stepped into the house. His presence filled the room.

Gideon cringed and moved from the bench so his father could sit. Gideon shrugged, as if his project wasn't as important as it was. "What's a secret among family?"

Before he could motion to Jether, Jether blurted out, "Abba's making a secret hole to hide our harvest."

Joash looked at Gideon, his eyebrows raised in surprise.

Gideon braced himself for the berating he expected from his father. "Rakaal was tired of running to the caves for our food." He added, lamely, "When we have it."

Joash took the cup of tea Kachina offered. He swirled his cup as the tea steeped. When he looked up from his cup, his eyes penetrated Gideon's. "That's your problem, Gideon, you let your wife tell you what to do. Then you waste your time solving her problems."

Gideon gripped his vessel harder, the whites of his knuckles showed. "Feeding my family is my responsibility."

Joash laughed, nodding at Jether, who was stuffing his mouth with another flatbread. "You aren't feeding your family now."

His father's insinuation irritated Gideon. His condescending tone angered him more. He wished he hadn't brought Jether. But he couldn't feed him. Gideon looked again at the filled vessels. How did his father do it?

He swallowed any words of defense. By past experience, he knew they'd never change his father's mind. He backed farther into the shadows of the room.

Joash tipped his head as if considering the worth of Gideon's project. "It might work . . . if the Midianites don't find it."

Kachina added, "I wouldn't mind having a cellar to hide—"

Joash interrupted, "Don't, Kachina!"

Kachina shut her mouth. She pursed her lips into a thin line and blinked as if she was holding back tears.

Gideon studied his mother from the shadows. What had just happened between them? There was more than just the abundance of food here that was wrong. He couldn't ever remember his father barking at mother.

If his father was in a fighting mood, he wanted no part of it. Usually he was the recipient. He didn't know what to do with this attack on his mother. "Jether, it's time we went home." Gideon headed toward the door. He had found Rakaal's comment about his father having food true. But what he should do about it, he didn't know. He wouldn't ask for what they had.

Jether grabbed another flatbread and hugged his grandmother. "Thank you."

Kachina looked over his head while he finished his hug. "It's been a long time since we've heard your music, Gideon. When can you play for us?"

Before Gideon could say anything, Joash responded. "The entire village knows of Gideon's ability to make music." He emphasized ability, as if it didn't take much to play. His disdain was evident.

Gideon ignored the request and kissed and hugged her. "Thanks, Mother."

Joash added, "Dig your hole."

The sarcasm was lost on Jether. He enthusiastically responded, "Abba's making a big one!"

Joash answered, "Just so he doesn't die in it."

Gideon reached the door, when Joash stopped him. "Gideon."

Why must his father control everyone? He couldn't even leave when he wanted to. Gideon moaned inwardly, gathering strength for more insults. He turned back. "Yes, Abba?"

"Give up your hole. I have a job for you."

Gideon swallowed an angry response. First, he belittled what he did; then he expected him to drop everything to do his plans. Gideon never liked his father's projects.

"Take my flocks and your own, if you want, to the high country. Keep them there. They'll be protected from the Midianites when they come again."

The request surprised Gideon. It was a good one. His goats would give more milk and save their young. He could save his herd.

But normally his father used his servants for that job. Why send him? Who would care for his family while he was gone?

Before he could voice his concerns, his father continued, "Bring your family here to stay with us."

Why was his father being so generous? What did his father really want?

Kachina bounced on her toes. "We'd have the grandkids here."

Gideon looked at his mother. She seemed so excited.

He couldn't say no. But he didn't want to consent. Something held him back. He smiled sympathetically at his mom. "I'll think about it."

The moment they reached home, Jether shouted, "Guess what?"

Gideon sighed. He regretted bringing Jether with him. Did children keep any secrets?

Rakaal didn't want any guessing games. Instead she ridiculed, "What have you decided now? Another worthless hole?"

Gideon concealed his hurt. She had complained about going to the caves for their hidden storage of grain. He had dug the hole for her. What more did she want?

Jether couldn't wait for anyone to answer. "We're staying at Grandmother's."

Rakaal's eyebrows lifted. She looked over Jether's head at Gideon for conformation.

Was that hope he saw in her eyes? Why would she want to stay under his father's rule? He put his hand on Jether's shoulder. "I said I'd think about it."

"But if mother wants, you will." Jether was now jumping up and down. Latrell, his younger brother, followed, chanting, "We're going to Grandma's."

So much for making the decision. It sounded like it was already made for him. Gideon sighed. "Once I finish the storage cellar, we'll move."

The house ran him, instesad of him ruling his house.

In the following days, Gideon dug out the storage cellar. He lifted a bucket to the edge of the hole. "Here, Jether."

Jether grunted as he carried it to the pasture behind the barn.

Gideon called after him, "Spread it well, so it won't look like a mound anywhere."

Jether called back, "Latrell's dirt looks like glumps."

Gideon admonished, "Help him scatter it."

Rakaal came to the barn. She sat on the floor and dangled her legs down the hole. "How far have you gotten?"

But You Have Not Obeyed Me

Gideon set one of the support beams in place before glancing at her. He liked when she came to watch.

Her eyes sparkled, even in the dim light cast from the open barn door. She was beautiful.

"Would you like shelves?" He would have moved a mountain if it would please her.

She rolled her hair around her finger. "It doesn't matter." She looked at him then. Her sparkle died, as if he had doused the flame.

What had he said?

What was beauty, when her smile wasn't for him? He picked up his pick again, frustrated he couldn't even get his own wife to enjoy him.

She looked at the barn door.

The boys were still outside.

She lowered her voice, "I want you to finish so I can live at Joash's."

He leaned on his pick and stared. Hadn't she wished for her food to be stored closer than the caves? This hole was her idea.

She seemed happy he would be leaving soon.

Why had she called his father Joash? She hadn't referred to his father with respect, but endearment. The thought bothered him.

He didn't understand her. He was sorry he'd asked about the shelves. Sorry he'd dug this hole. Sorry . . . he wouldn't say it out loud, but sorry they'd married.

He started digging again. *That* he could understand. He'd finish this hole, hide what food they did have from the Midianites, and leave. If that would make her happy.

Jether brought back the empty bucket. "I caught up to you, Abba. You have no dirt."

Latrell pushed him aside. "It's my turn. Abba hasn't filled my bucket yet."

Gideon took both buckets and dropped them at his feet. If he was leaving Rakaal, he'd also be leaving his boys. He swallowed the lump the thought brought to his throat. He gathered Latrell and Jether into his arms. "I love you both." His voice broke, and he buried his beard in their shoulders to hide his emotions.

"I love you, too, Abba," they said as they squeezed him tightly.

He held them until Latrell squirmed to be let down. He boosted them to sit beside Rakaal.

He held Jether's gaze. "You're the oldest."

Jether sat up straighter. "I'm eight years old."

Gideon nodded. "When I'm gone, I expect you to protect your mother and brother."

Jether nodded. "I will."

Gideon nudged the buckets at his feet. "That means helping your brother do his work, instead of telling Mother how he didn't do his work. Understand?"

Jether glanced at the bucket and out into the pasture, then nodded.

Gideon noticed his look. "We'll finish the hole before I leave. The tasks Mother or Grandfather give you are important. Do them well. But the most important job is to protect your family. You'll be the leader until I return."

Jether took Latrell's hand in his own. "I'll protect them, as if I were you."

Gideon patted Jether on his knee. "Good. That's all I can expect."

Gideon turned to Latrell. "I expect you to help your brother."

Latrell held up his hand. "I'm four. I can tell Jether what to do."

Gideon shook his head. "You listen and obey. Jether shouldn't have to do your chores. He'll be busy with his own. Help him and your mother."

Latrell nodded. In earnestness, he squeezed Jether's hand.

Jether yelled. "Latrell, you're hurting me!"

Latrell let go. "I didn't mean to."

"You did that on purpose." Jether reached back to hit him.

Gideon grabbed his hand. "Jether." He waited until he had Jether's attention. "Help your brother and your mother when I'm gone."

Jether stood, tears forming in his eyes. "I don't want you to go. Couldn't we live with Grandfather and you?"

Gideon brought him to his chest again. "I don't want to go either. But we must protect our flocks from the Midianites or we won't have anything to eat." He stood him by the edge of the hole. "Right?"

Jether hung onto him as if he wouldn't let go of him. "I'd rather go without food than have you leave."

Gideon laughed, but there wasn't humor in it. "I must take care of you by protecting our sheep. And you must take care of your mother, so when I return, we'll be together again."

Gideon glanced at Rakaal. She had waited by the barn door during their exchange, as if the conversation bored her.

He frowned. Couldn't she even pretend she'd miss him?

CHAPTER 19

When the Midianites came, they didn't fight. They fed their beasts. They lived off other men's harvest and hard work. They feasted on meat slaughtered from the best herds. But they didn't select old ewes, unable to bear more lambs. They chose the young that would have brought a future herd. They washed the meat down with the best stolen wine. As they ate around their campfires, they hooted with laughter. Their fires burned late into the night, reflecting far into the darkness from where they enjoyed their meal.

No one opposed them.

They did whatever they wanted.

They were unstoppable.

And when they finished feasting and drinking, they hiked Joash's hill to give homage to their gods. They called for women to dance. They performed before the Asherah pole and sacrificed their spoils to Baal.

Every night, Jether listened on his pallet in the corner of his grandfather's house. The music and laughter called for him to see what he was missing. Maybe it would take away the hole in his heart from missing his father. Moving to his grandfather's house hadn't been what he'd expected. He wasn't hungry, that was true.

But nothing could replace his father. He missed him. Greatly.

He missed his father's squeeze before sending him to bed and listening as his father played his lyre. The music would drift over him as he went to sleep. He felt comforted. Complete.

It wasn't just that he missed his father, but he felt uneasy around his grandfather. He'd never felt that before. Was it because he'd always been with his father, who cushioned the harshness of his grandfather?

His grandfather didn't touch him. Most of the time, Jether wondered if he even noticed him. Other times, when he caught his grandfather's scrutiny, he felt like he'd done something wrong. He shuddered.

After cleaning out the ox stall in the barn, his grandfather had called him to stand before him. "Is this the best you could do?"

Jether had glanced at the floor where he'd shoveled the dung out. Because the Midianites had burned their fields, there was no straw for bedding. What more could he do? He hadn't known how to respond. He nodded.

His grandfather grabbed his shoulders and pushed them back. "Stand tall. Don't slouch like your father! And answer me!"

The words were thrown at him like a curse.

Jether trembled under his heavy hand, but pushed his shoulders back. He didn't mind being like his father, who always showed him how to do a job better without yelling at him. He swallowed, trying not to cry. He forced the word to come through his throat. "Yes."

A servant had come with more urgent news. Joash had left.

Jether trembled each time he completed a job. Was it enough? What more did he expect?

His grandmother smothered him with affection, as if to make up for his grandfather's gruffness. That was too much.

And his mother. He hardly saw her any more. She slept much of the day. How could she be that tired?

He had picked flowers in the pastures, hoping to cheer her. He ran into her room to give them to her.

Surely with the sun up for a long time, she'd be up too. But she wasn't. She was still lying in bed.

His grandfather sat on her bed, talking.

Jether had stopped short. He felt like he had intruded. But this was his mother.

His grandfather noticed him. "Leave! Don't bother your mother!"

How could he bother his mom with a gift? Jether had looked from the flowers to his mother.

His mom didn't defend him. Instead she nodded for him to leave.

He felt rebuked for doing something kind. It was a gift for her.

He stumbled from the room to the barn, where he threw the flowers at the oxen.

One ox nosed its head and ate them.

Jether watched until every last petal was chewed. He promised himself he'd never bother her again.

Now, he rolled over on his pallet and yanked the goatskin to cover his shoulders. He missed his father. He wished they'd never come to live with his grandfather. He nudged Latrell beside him. How could he sleep with all the noise?

It was late. He finally must have fallen asleep, when a light knock on the door woke him. He couldn't see who, but felt someone move through the room to answer.

Jether shifted so he could watch. When the door was opened, moonlight shone in his eyes. By the silhouette, he could tell his grandfather had answered the door.

It was one of the Midianite generals, Jether could tell by his cloak. What was he doing here?

"We need more!"

His grandfather answered, "I've given what I can."

"What about your wife?"

His grandfather's voice rose, "I told you, 'No!'"

"You promised to give us what we need. We need more."

Jether held his breath. What was his grandfather giving to the Midianites?

His grandfather sighed. "I'll bring another."

"Tonight?"

"Tonight."

The general seemed satisfied. He nodded. "Next time I come, we'll need more."

Grandfather took a long breath before he responded. "I'll find more in the village."

The general nodded. "See that you do."

When his grandfather shut the door, Jether didn't breath. Would his grandfather know he had heard?

His grandfather stood several minutes before walking to his mother's room. He entered without knocking.

Why would he go in there? Jether heard whispering, but couldn't tell what was said.

In a few minutes, both his mother and grandfather left.

Darkness returned.

Jether was left alone.

Where was his grandfather taking her?

He wouldn't sleep until he knew. He threw off his goat skin.

"Give me some blankets." Latrell's sleepy voice mumbled.

Jether shook him. His father's admonition to protect his mother came back to him. "Come with me. Grandfather has taken Mother somewhere."

Latrell sat and rubbed his eyes. "Where'd they go?"

Jether whispered, "Shhh. Don't waken Grandmother. I don't know. Hurry!"

He grabbed Latrell's hand and they tiptoed out the door and into the darkness. Jether led them to a hillside overlooking the Midianite camp. He focused on the campfires below.

Men lounged by fires, asleep. This wasn't where his mother had gone. Jether pulled Latrell behind him.

"Where're we going?"

Jether silenced him with a finger over his lips. He whispered in his ear, "Follow me."

They strode around the hillside to the army's camels.

His father hated camels, especially after being spat on. But they intrigued Jether.

They were corralled by ropes behind their camp and separated

But You Have Not Obeyed Me

into groups. Mares with young nursed in one roped off region. Did they bring the mothers to feast from his people's harvests? The thought made Jether angry and he shook his head to study another area. This area held mares without calves. They seemed agitated, straining against the ropes to join another roped section of camels. Here, bulls bellowed. Their mouths were flecked with white foam as they pushed toward the mares.

Those bulls would do anything to join the mares during the rutting season. How could a flimsy rope hold them back?

Jether whispered to Latrell, "What would happen if the rope fell?"

Latrell's eyes widened, then he smiled and nodded.

Latrell's response encouraged Jether. After glancing at the campsite, he knew no one would notice.

In circling the camels, trying to get closer to the bulls, Jether noticed lights on his grandfather's hill where the altar and pole stood. That was where the noise came from, their drums which had kept him awake.

He pulled Latrell closer to see. His abba's words came back. He mustn't look until he was a man. But wasn't he being a man by protecting his mother?

He whispered, although by their music, no one else would hear him, "Look for Mother."

He couldn't make out any faces, even though the torches and the fire on the altar were bright. All he could see were silhouettes and shadows dancing before the altar.

The Midianites didn't bring women with them.

Where had the women come from? Did his grandfather provide them?

They danced. Before the pole, men cut themselves, calling to their god to make them acceptable.

Jether covered his ears to their screams of pleasure and pain.

He was afraid, but continued looking for his mother. What would he do if he found her?

Latrell whispered in his ear, "What are they doing?"

Jether, wanting to seem older, said, "Worshiping." But this

wasn't for the pleasure of any god. His abba's words to turn his head from the hill echoed in his mind. He felt uneasy. He shouldn't be there. He shouldn't have brought Latrell with him. What should he do? How could he protect his mother?

He glanced back at the camels. Maybe if he cut the camels' corral rope, he'd distract the people on the hill, so he could find his mother. "Let's go back to the camels."

Latrell nodded.

He picked his way through the dark to the ropes that held the bull camels. Keeping hidden by the trees, he approached the rope corral. He swung the rope, feeling its tension.

Latrell bumped into him.

"Watch where you're going!"

Latrell moved back a step. "Why'd you stop?"

"Shhh." Jether slipped his knife from his cloak's pocket. The knife had been a gift from his abba before he left. He had felt grown up when he'd received it. Now he unsheathed it carefully and turned it in the moonlight's shine. It would cut easily through the rope.

Even though the night's coolness required a cloak, he was sweating. He wiped his hand down his cloak before sawing the rope.

It's fibers cut his hand as he held it still.

The rope became harder to hold, as the bulls strained against it. The final fibers holding the rope together tightened.

Jether sawed again.

The rope snapped and lashed his face.

The rope fell.

The bulls surged forward. Their bellowing increased. Bulls paired off, attacking each other, kicking and biting to claim their mate.

Jether closed his eyes. He had expected something else. Not this horrible battle.

Latrell grabbed his hand. "Let's leave. I'm scared."

Before Jether could answer, someone grabbed him.

"What are you doing here?"

But You Have Not Obeyed Me

Jether could only whimper, "Take me to my grandfather, Joash."

R ough hands grabbed his feet.

Jether kicked out. "Quit it, Latrell. Let go!"

A slap to his head made him stop. "Enough!" A gruff voice barked.

Jether's eyes flew open. The morning's light streamed through the open tent flap blinding him. When his eyes could focus, it wasn't his brother who held his feet.

His eyes widened as the soldier took his own knife and raised it.

Jether shut his eyes tightly, willing himself not to flinch. He tensed for the stab of pain.

When nothing happened, he opened his eyes, one at a time.

The rope that bound his ankles was cut.

His feet tingled.

He wiggled his toes to regain his circulation.

He dared to lick his dry lips and tried to swallow.

Jether watched as the soldier resheathed the knife. That was his! He felt down his cloak's side, with his tied hands to make sure. He could feel nothing. What would he tell his father?

Tears stung his eyes. He blinked to keep them from falling.

He looked for his brother. Where was he? He remembered being caught, tied, and thrown into this tent the night before. But what had happened to Latrell?

His father told him to protect his family. He had not only lost his knife, but his brother and mother. He swallowed, unable to stop his tears. He brushed his arm over his face. How could he have failed so much? What could he do now?

The soldier pulled him to his feet and shoved his shoulder. "Walk."

His feet still tingled. He stumbled from the tent. He wiped his face again so he could see where he walked. Where were they going?

When his grandfather's house came into sight, Jether breathed a sigh of relief. He was safe. But the closer he came to the house, the more his relief changed to a different fear. What would his grandfather do?

When Joash answered the door, he looked from the man to Jether.

Jether cringed by his look.

"What's the meaning of this?"

The general pushed Jether forward.

Jether stumbled and fell at his grandfather's feet.

"Because he's yours, he's alive."

Joash motioned for the man to follow him some distance from the house. They talked in low tones.

Jether strained to hear, but couldn't.

When they finished, the general left.

Jether watched his grandfather's straight back and strong shoulders as he returned.

Jether lowered his gaze and chewed his lips. What would he do to him?

"Hold out your hands."

Jether couldn't stop his hands from shaking as he held them out to his grandfather.

Joash cut the cord. He wasn't rough, but he wasn't kind.

Jether rubbed his hands together. With his head down, he watched what his grandfather would do.

His braced himself for rebuke and punishment.

When his grandfather spoke, Jether was surprised at his calmness. "What did you do?"

"I wanted to make the camels quiet."

He seemed incredulous. His voice rose. "You what?"

Jether quivered, but told his story. "Abba told me to protect Mother. I didn't know where she was. When I looked, I lost Latrell." He breathed a big sigh. He felt relief. His grandfather would find Latrell and make everything fine.

When Jether finished his story, Joash looked toward the hill where the altar stood. "You saw them worship?"

Jether nodded, hesitantly. Remembering his father's warning not to watch. "But I was trying to find Mother."

Joash leaned into Jether's face.

His gaze seemed to penetrate into Jether's thoughts.

He willed himself to stand tall. Nothing infuriated his grandfather more than to see him cower; he'd learned *that* from doing his chores. He almost didn't hear the question.

"What did you see?"

Joash squirmed under his scrutiny. Was he disappointed? He had disobeyed his abba. What could he have called it? "Dancing." He grimaced, remembering the screams and drums. He added quickly, "But the camels were more interesting."

Joash leaned toward Jether. "You saw no faces?"

Jether swallowed, wanting to bow his head, but struggling to resist. He shivered under his grandfather's stern expression. He couldn't find his voice. He shook his head in answer.

Joash shoved him into the house. "To bed with you."

Jether hesitated. He was confused. He had hoped his grandfather would tell about his mother and brother's return.

He expected to be disciplined.

His grandfather didn't say anything more. He seemed more interested in what he had seen on the mountain than his own mother and brother. He wished he'd paid more attention to the worship. Maybe that had been important.

But as he entered the house, Latrell wasn't lying on their pallet. He didn't dare ask his grandfather. After all, he hadn't punished him yet.

Jether couldn't dispel the feeling his grandfather knew where Latrell was, but all wasn't fine.

CHAPTER 20

Gideon put more sheep dung on his fire. His breath formed a cloud before combining with the fog rising from the frost-covered grass. His flocks grazed close to the fire, as if their own wool coats didn't keep them warm enough. The sun rose over the mountain and distant hills. When he poured the hot water into his vessel, he smelled the fragrant mint leaves. They would settle his empty stomach.

Gideon tucked his head farther into his cloak's hood. He liked this time of day. The sheep would get their water needs from the grass, before the sun melted the dew. Darkness stayed long in the morning hours until the sun broke through the clouds.

Normally this was a peaceful time, but his father had sent word by a messenger. Their clan had lost their entire flocks to the Midianite invasion. His and his father's alone were safe. But Jethro assured Gideon, "All is well with our family and land."

Gideon would have felt better to see his wife and children for himself. He missed them. Missed Jether. He still turned to watch for him, following him around like his own shadow.

He tried to receive comfort from his father's messenger, but they seemed false. Why did he feel uneasy about staying? But what could he do in the valley when the Midianites were raiding again?

He slurped his tea. It wouldn't satisfy his emptiness, but he hoped it would help him forget it for a time. Did his family have enough?

Again that uneasiness about his father's plan.

"A peaceful time, is it not?"

Gideon turned quickly to see who spoke. He was angry for allowing someone sneak behind him. He studied the stranger.

The man smiled. His cloak was coated with frost. His beard was ragged, his head uncovered, his hair windswept. He'd traveled far by the looks of his worn sandals. He held no sword or visible weapon. He seemed safe enough.

But why would anyone come here?

Gideon adjusted his hold on his vessel and nodded.

The stranger stepped closer, eyeing his flock. "You have a good-size flock."

Was he a spy from the Midianites? Gideon answered warily. "It's fair."

The stranger squatted before the fire and stretched his hands to its warmth. "The Lord wants our people to remember Him."

Gideon heard but didn't understand. Had he ever heard about their own God?

The man continued, "The Lord, the God of Israel says, 'I brought you from Egypt, out from slavery. I delivered you from the hands of the Egyptians."

Gideon had heard of Egypt's powers a long, time ago. No threat came from them now. They were gone. Like a puff of smoke.

His mother had told him stories of God causing Egypt's ruin. But weren't they childhood stories, told to give pleasant dreams?

This man spoke like the stories were true.

Gideon wanted them to be true, but it seemed too much to hope. If their God had saved them from Egypt's bondage, couldn't He save them from Midian's?

The man continued, "The God of Israel is the One Who said, 'I am the Lord, your God. Don't worship the Amorite gods in whose

But You Have Not Obeyed Me

land you live, but worship Me.' But you and your people have not obeyed Him."

This rebuke jarred Gideon. What was he to obey?

The stranger stood with a quiet, calmness.

Gideon directed a wayward yearling back to his flock with his staff. "You remind me of childhood stories about a God Who could do anything. But weren't they stories for children?"

The man smiled and looked at the sky, as if he spoke to God, saying "Your people have forgotten Who You are." He shook his head, the smile leaving his face. When he looked at Gideon, his eyes pierced Gideon.

Gideon stepped back in alarm.

"Have your people forgotten how God showed Pharaoh His strength by changing the river to blood? Or how He killed the Egyptian herds, yet not one of their own were touched? Those are not stories for children. But warrior stories of greatness. They instill courage in our people about Who our God is."

Gideon listened. For the first time seeing these stories as true. "And the stories of food and water in the desert—?"

The man nodded. "True."

Gideon looked over the hills. His flocks were nothing compared to what they had once been. His insides rumbled, reminding him of his own family's needs. He swallowed, trying to understand. "If this God could do so much, where is He now?"

The man looked at the sky once more. He lowered his voice, almost reverentially, "God is waiting for us to remember Him."

Gideon shook his head. It was too much to imagine—that a God could deliver them from the hand of the Midianites. They were so many. And it had been so long.

Yet stories of Egypt and even of the perils of the desert seemed real now. Hadn't his people survived much worse?

Gideon began to hope.

It was time for the wheat harvest. Gideon returned home to harvest his fields. He expected the Midianites' return, yet wanted to be near his family. He stayed with the flocks until he reached the foothills, sending Purah ahead to move his family back to his own house. He was excited to tell Rakaal of the prophet's visit. He burst into his house. "Rakaal!"

Jether ran and hugged Gideon. "Abba! You're back!"

Gideon grabbed Jether and twirled him. He nestled his beard into his chin to hear his giggle. "You've grown to be a man while I was gone. I've missed you." After he put Jether down, Gideon looked around the room. "Where's Latrell?"

The words caught in the air and hung.

He glanced at Jether.

His head was down. He swallowed but wouldn't look at him.

Gideon felt dread creep from his toes to grab his heart. He walked to Rakaal and touched her shoulder.

Rakaal knelt by the fire, not even acknowledging his presence.

He dropped his hand from her shoulder, the joy over seeing his family replaced with concern. "Where's Latrell?"

She stirred the embers into flames, adding kindling to build the fire, as if that was more important than his long-awaited presence.

Gideon's enthusiasm over sharing the prophets' words were forgotten. Even his words of deliverance seemed impossible in this dark, silent room.

Rakaal finally stood. She assessed him.

Under her scrutiny, he pushed back his unkept hair, smoothed his soiled cloak, straightened his wayward beard.

She sniffed, her nose high as if his sheep smell were offensive. Her contempt was clear.

Gideon looked away, unable to meet her scrutiny. Maybe he should have bathed in the stream before bringing the sheep down the mountain, but he couldn't wait to see her. Would it have made any difference to her?

He clenched his hands into fists. He wanted to shake her. "What's wrong?"

But You Have Not Obeyed Me

She announced, almost with pleasure, "Your barn is gone."

He looked through the open door across his fields. He hadn't come home by way of the orchard where the barn had been. But now across the fields, he saw the charred remains of his barn. He walked to the doorway, leaned against the frame, and allowed a groan to escape his lips.

He had tried to prepare himself for anything the Midianites might do. He should have expected this.

The building could be rebuilt; but his barn had been a reminder to him of strength, protection, refuge.

He swallowed any comment.

There was more.

Rakaal followed him to the door. "Your secret cellar—the one you'd hidden so well?"

Her accusing tone struck fear in him.

Gideon waited. Why couldn't she continue? She hadn't cared whether the hole was dug. Why did she care if they found the food? He'd hide the food in the caves again if he had to. What could be so wrong?

He looked again for Latrell. It seemed empty without him. He put his hand on Jether's head, a silent gesture of blessing and peace.

His father had assured him all was well—his family was fine. He hadn't told him of his barn, but that could be rebuilt. He watched Rakaal's face.

Her face twisted in pain. She formed the words, throwing them like a knife. "Latrell." She licked her lips as if to gain strength.

Gideon looked again around the room for him. He felt panic, dread—the knife twisting his heart.

"Latrell hid there when they came. But they found him. They used him before their gods."

Gideon swallowed. He couldn't grasp what she said. He looked at Jether, then at Rakaal. "They didn't hurt you?"

Rakaal shook her head. "I was at your father's."

Gideon was confused. Why was Latrell here while Rakaal

stayed at his father's house? She wasn't making sense. "Rakaal," He touched her shoulder.

She winced, as if she couldn't stand his touch. She glared at him.

In that look, Gideon felt undone, as if he'd caused their son's death, as if he should have stopped the Midianites. He whispered, "I'm sorry."

She shouted. The volume, so different from the words before, "I'm sorry? You allow foreigners to steal my children for their pleasure and all you can say is 'I'm sorry'?"

Gideon lowered his head. He couldn't even mourn his son's loss before she berated his failure. He braced himself for hearing more, but this time, she stopped.

He hung his head to conceal his own tears.

He was sorry he'd come home. He braced himself against the doorway, and looked over his ruined fields to the charred remains of his barn. His eyes strayed to the hills he had come from. It'd be so easy to run away and not return. Hadn't he found peace and hope in the hills?

A movement caught his eye.

A buzzard circled high over his once secret hole. He'd been so sure it would be safe from detection. It should have protected Latrell if he had hidden there, too. He didn't understand it. Maybe it was too much to process in his grief.

He followed the buzzard's movement, drifting in smaller circles higher in the sky.

Rakaal wasn't finished. She followed him and touched his arm. Before her touch would have brought healing, now, he cringed, wondering what else she must say.

"His body still lies there."

Gideon sucked in his breath. He would bury his son—he squared his shoulders—and mourn his loss.

The prophet's words seemed forgotten in some pleasant past. Only the despair of living remained.

But You Have Not Obeyed Me

Gideon walked through his wheat field to the ashes that had once been his barn. He stood over the secret door and grunted. So much for secret. It was like they had known about it. The thought stuck. Had his father told them about it? He shook his head. This was his own grandson's life!

The trapdoor he had concealed stood open. This hole had been nothing but trouble since he'd started it. Why had he ever thought it such a good idea?

Before seeing the body, he'd dig the hole. Maybe by then, he'd be prepared to see his body.

He had hidden his tools in the hole. He wouldn't retrieve them now. Instead, he broke a burnt beam from the barn and strode to the edge of his pasture. He stood under a sycamore tree whose limbs stretched over the pasture.

He took off his cloak and stabbed at the ground with the broken beam. With his hands, he scooped out the loose dirt.

He felt he wasn't alone. He wiped his face with his tunic sleeve and looked up.

Jether stood behind him. His lower lip trembled.

Gideon had forgotten the boy in his grief. Now he opened his arms.

Jether ran to him.

Gideon hugged him tight, crying with him. Had he been wrong in leaving? Would he have been able to stop this murder?

He didn't like his questions.

He didn't have any answers.

Jether stepped back and wiped his nose with his fist.

Gideon handed him his cloak.

Jether wiped his tears on its sleeve. When he raised his face, he had fresh tears. "It smells of sheep and goat. I missed that smell."

Gideon ruffled his hair. "I would, too, if I didn't have my flocks."

Jether gulped for air, but couldn't force any words out.

Gideon waited. He didn't rush him. He felt his own need to grieve.

When Jether could speak, he mumbled, "It's my fault."

Gideon patted his knee and allowed Jether to sit on his lap. "What's your fault?"

Jether told his story of how he and Latrell had searched for their mother, to protect her. When he finished his story, he said, "They brought me back to Grandfather's. Latrell wasn't there. I never saw him again."

Gideon was silent for a long time. He was beginning to see why his father had sent him away. Had Rakaal gone to the temple willingly? Had his father consented to Latrell's sacrifice or just accepted and covered it afterward?

How could his father tell him "all was well" with his family? There were too many questions and too many unknowns.

A stifled sob stopped his ponderings.

Gideon squeezed Jether. "This wasn't your fault."

Jether buried his head in Gideon's chest. Through muffled sobs, Jether spoke, "I took him with me. He'd never have been caught . . ."

Gideon shook his head. "Your grandfather knew both of you were missing?"

"I told him he was with me. He seemed more concerned about what I saw."

Gideon considered the Midianite worship. Human sacrifices and women prostitutes were expected.

His father always had plenty to eat. His father's scheme made sense now. Gideon's absence made his family available for his father's use.

He rubbed Jether's back; then pulled Jether from him so he could watch his expression. "Do you feel safe with your grandfather?"

Jether hesitated, "We've never gone without food."

That didn't answer his question. Gideon studied Jether. He wasn't saying something. Was he afraid? "What is it, Son?"

Jether swallowed. "Grandfather talks with a Midianite general at night."

"He talks with the Midianites? You are sure?"

Jether nodded.

But You Have Not Obeyed Me

"What did they say?"

"They wanted more of something. They threatened to take Grandma, but Grandfather said, 'No.'

"When they returned me to Grandfather, they said it was only because I was his that I'd been returned. I should've told them Latrell was, too. Maybe he'd be alive, like me." His voice trailed off.

Gideon held him, trying to reconcile this story with Rakaal's. What had really happened to his son?

Did he want to know?

Life settled into a routine. Rather than the calmness he had known watching his flocks, Gideon felt the displeasure of Rakaal. He tried to ask about Latrell's death, but he couldn't say anything without her spitting at him in anger. He could do nothing to please her.

He found reasons to stay away. In the foothills outside their village, he found a cave for their food. Staying busy helped him grieve his son's death.

Jether worked beside him, like a shadow, He seemed almost afraid not to be in his presence. His clinging actions made Gideon wonder what had happened that night.

His thoughts turned to the prophet. He had told him to obey the Lord.

But what did God want him to do?

Not knowing left a hole, like the loss of his son, only deeper. He was missing something, but he didn't know what it was.

He hadn't told Rakaal about the prophet's visit. The time never seemed right, as if she might listen.

Nor had he returned to his father's altar since he'd come from watching the flocks. He felt cleaner, like his mind could focus, rather than be consumed with the next sacrifice.

But the loss made him restless.

If God had saved their people long ago, why did He allow them to suffer now? How could he bring his people to remember God?

The wheat was ripe. Most of his clan had already harvested. Gideon had taken longer. He had prepared a hiding place, where no one would find it.

Rakaal challenged him one night, "Why haven't you finished the harvest?"

Gideon wasn't sure he preferred her questions to the silence he had become used to. "I protect our harvest."

She spit out, "We have no harvest."

Gideon shrugged. Why did he bother telling her? Nothing he did was enough for her. "If I hide it, we'll eat through winter."

"Bah. You dig like some mouse scrounging for a grain of wheat."

Rakaal made him feel worthless. While he had tried proving his worth by providing for her, her disdain for him had only grown.

What could he do?

He didn't have the servants his father had, nor would he ask for their use. He worked alone and felt alone. And worked harder to finish the harvest.

Many days, after rising before the light of the sun, he'd work until the moon had risen. Rather than return home to sleep, he'd fall asleep exhausted in the cave where he stored the wheat.

He set up his wine press under a tree in a field of his father's, close to his shocked wheat. He wouldn't return to his non-existent barn to thresh it. He wouldn't build another barn. Not for a long time. The memory only brought pain.

He dragged one shock close to the wine press to separate the chaff from the kernels. He put the freed kernels in a jar to take to the cave. Like Rakaal's description, he felt like some rodent hoarding his winter's stores.

He winnowed several shocks of wheat.

He didn't pile all the shocks at one time. They'd be too conspicuous and attract attention. Instead, if he were caught by the Midianites, only some his wheat would be stolen. He would still have what he'd hidden.

He had just returned from the cave and started threshing another shock. The earlier morning breeze had stopped and the still air made separating the chaff harder. He wiped his head; his tunic dripped with sweat. The chaff stuck to his sweat, making him itch. He glanced up from his work, frustrated it took so long to do so little.

A stranger stood before him.

He stopped and stepped back. He had heard nothing. How could anyone have approached him without his knowing? He looked for others, but saw no one else.

The man spoke, "The Lord is with you, O valiant warrior."

Gideon swallowed a laugh. Valiant warrior? He was hiding his wheat from his neighbors and the Midianites. Was this man flattering him to get his wheat?

He wiped his brow. Shifting his threshing tool, he tried to think. He couldn't be some unknown neighbor. A nieghbor wouldn't have referred to God, but to Baal-peor.

He had to be God's prophet!

Gideon thought of his questions since the other prophet had visited. "O my lord, if the Lord is with us, why has all this happened to us? Where are the miracles told to us by our fathers? Didn't the Lord save us from Egypt? But God has forgotten us and given us into the Midianites' hand."

The man studied him for a long time.

Gideon dropped his bold look. His tongue burned from his accusing questions. Who was he to question God?

The man answered, "Go, deliver Israel from the hand of the Midianites. I have sent you."

Gideon wiped his dusty hand down his sweaty tunic. "How should I deliver Israel? I'm the youngest son of my father."

The man's gaze didn't waver from Gideon's face, almost like his father addressing him as a child. "I am with you. You shall defeat Midian as one man."

One man? Gideon stepped back, as if he already felt the point of a Midianite's sword. How could he defeat them alone?

When Gideon met his gaze, he saw confidence, not the scorn

he would have seen on his father's face. This man expected him to do what he said.

Gideon sensed his own worthlessness. He must give this man from God something—a sacrifice. "If I've found favor in Your sight, show me a sign. Prove to me who you are." This man wasn't just a prophet sent from God. This was an angel.

Would he still be here when he returned? "Please don't leave until I return. I'll bring you an offering."

The man smiled. Humoring Gideon with his response, "I'll stay."

Gideon was relieved. He could do something for this God he wanted to know. A burden lifted.

Then doubts. What if he didn't stay for the sacrifice? He wanted reassurance. Gideon turned back. "Until I return?"

The man nodded. "I'll be here when you return."

Gideon smiled for the first time. "I'll be back." He ran to for one of his goat kids. They grazed in the foot hills, where a whistle, warning of Midianites coming, would signal the keeper to push them into caves in the hills. He hurried to his flock, greeting his herdsman with a nod. With no time to explain, he pointed to the best kid.

His servant helped separate it from the herd.

Gideon slit its throat.

They skinned and prepared the meat.

As they worked, Gideon told of the angel's visit.

The servant listened. His eyes growing big.

Gideon sliced the choice cuts of meat into chunks. He used the herdsman's meal basket to carry the meat to the cave where he'd hidden his wheat in jars. There he sorted the wheat kernels, making sure no weed seeds or rocks were mixed with them. He ground the wheat, using the rock and pestle he kept hidden there.

When he gathered the food, he hesitated before going to his house.

Rakaal would ask too many questions and scorn his visitor.

He didn't want to have to try to convince her.

But You Have Not Obeyed Me

But with the fine ground flour and the meat, he hurried home to retrieve embers to cook the meal for his guest.

When he reached his house, Gideon glanced around for Rakaal.

She wasn't there.

Though relieved, he was concerned. Where would she be?

He felt the urgency not to keep the man from God waiting. He knelt beside the cooking embers from breakfast. Using a piece of kindling, he scooped embers into a vessel to keep them glowing until he reached the man of God.

White broom plant lay beside the fire for coaxing the embers to flames. He grabbed a handful and stuffed them in his tunic's pocket.

With all the necessary items gathered, he hurried back to the tree.

As he came closer, he looked for the man. Where was he? Panic made him run. He stumbled, almost spilling the meat and the flour, but caught himself from falling.

Then he saw the man.

He was resting against the tree.

Gideon sighed in relief. He brushed off his knees and tunic and readjusted the meat, flour, and embers.

Slowing his pace, Gideon, this time, watched his steps.

When he reached the tree, he was out of breath. He knelt, and made a depression in the dirt. He didn't want smoke to carry the smell that might bring others. He combined some chaff from winnowing with the white broom plant to place in the depression he had made.

He poured the embers from the vessel into the kindling, blowing softly as he did. Flames sparked to life. He consciously slowed down his movements, so he wouldn't blow out the embers.

Gideon snapped off twigs from branches, broken from some past storm. He fed them to the growing flames. Soon he added bigger pieces. He concentrated on his work, keeping it hidden from the village and neighbors.

Once the fire was burning well, he poured water from his waterskin into the jar, along with the meat pieces. He placed it over the fire to heat. While waiting for the meat to cook, he added water to the wheat flour and formed a ball, flattening it on a rock for bread. He shoved a flat rock closer to the fire so he could cook the flatbread when the meat was cooked.

All this was done in silence. Gideon concentrated on his tasks. They reminded him of his life with the sheep and the peace he had felt.

When he had done all he could, he leaned back and spoke, "Our people have forgotten our God. A prophet told us to remember Him. How can we, without someone who knows Him?"

The angel smiled and nodded. "I'll tell you of Him." And as they waited for the meal to cook, he did.

Gideon heard of his people's history. How Abraham was promised a son and received him, though he was old. How God was faithful to bring His people back to the land He promised to Abraham. He heard about this God Who cared for His people.

When the meat was cooked, and the bread had baked, the angel pointed to the flat stone where Gideon had formed the bread. "Lay the meat and bread here."

Gideon obeyed. When he had done as the angel asked, he sat back to allow him to eat.

Instead, the angel touched the food with the end of his staff.

A puff of flame ignited the sacrifice and burned it, leaving only ashes.

Gideon blinded by the flame's light, blinked to clear his eyes. When he looked for the angel, he had vanished!

Gideon fell on his knees before the smoldering ashes. He trembled, feeling his unworthiness after seeing the power of God's messenger. "Truly, I have seen the angel of the Lord face to face!" Would he die?

As he bowed before the accepted sacrifice, Gideon heard the voice of God, "I give you peace. Don't be afraid. You won't die."

At God's words, Gideon felt a peace he had never felt before. It seeped over him like oil spilling over a wound, healing, protecting, giving assurance. This peace wasn't dependent upon his performance, as faulty as it would be. It was dependent upon God's Word. Like a rock he could stand on. He stayed on his face, praising God for sparing his life. And for giving him peace.

When he finally rose to his feet, he was surprised the sun was low in the horizon. The day was almost past.

Gideon felt a freedom he had never felt before. Like dipping in the stream, only it cleaned his insides. He touched the rock where the ashes had left a black mark on the stone. He had been made acceptable in God's sight, not by his own merit, but by God accepting the sacrifice. A weight lifted that he hadn't even known he had been carrying.

He had to do something—to remember this spot where he had talked with God—to honor God for accepting him. He scrambled around the field, piling stones to make an altar.

He had new life, new purpose. He didn't move as one surviving, but as one who was alive, set free, complete, and whole. He could move mountains, *if* God told him!

He spoke out loud, "I'll name it, 'The Lord is Peace.'" He continued his prayer, "You have told me to defeat Midian as one man. I don't know how, but I'll be Your man."

Gideon had loitered as long as he could over the altar. The stars had come out, and still he hesitated to go home. Would this peace last? Would this confidence give strength to stand before his wife? He drew a deep breath and resolved to return home.

How could one lone woman decimate his confidence? Surely, God was stronger than Rakaal's words.

With this new resolution, Gideon quickened his pace home. But even as he came within a few paces, he slowed. He breathed heavily to steady himself before entering his house.

It was dark. Not even a candle was lit.

Rakaal must be asleep.

Gideon breathed more freely.

Smoke from the cookfire still lingered.

He could smell bread. His insides grumbled. He stilled its rumblings with his hand.

He crept to their pallet in the corner of the room, his eyes growing accustomed to the darkness. He sat and removed his sandals and placed them ready for morning. He lay beside Rakaal, carefully covering her with the goat skin.

Her voice startled him out of his quietness. "Where were you?"

Gideon's heart beat faster. He rubbed his hands down his tunic. They scratched against some of the white broom plant he still had in his pocket. The feeling of wellbeing was gone. In its place he felt chastened, like some schoolboy caught without his lessons finished. He swallowed; then plunged to answer her. "I've met with God." He wasn't sure what else to say. Now he felt guilty for talking with God instead of finishing the harvest. He couldn't please her. He added, to justify taking the time to talk to God. "And He is worthy."

Rakaal lay on her back. Gideon could hear her intake of breath.

He wanted to share with her what he felt—the freedom and peace. Yet he was afraid if he did, the feeling would leave.

She would explain it away.

It would vanish.

He was torn. If he didn't speak, he felt he would burst. Wasn't that why he had stayed to praise Him?

Yet in Rakaal's presence, he felt restricted, afraid to share his thoughts, lest they be condemned as trivial or wrong. He had said enough. He closed his lips and tried to calm the rushing of his heart.

But Rakaal wouldn't leave it alone. "You're a fool. Anyone who believes that has my sympathy. God has forgotten us."

Gideon licked his lips and found his tongue. He didn't want to argue with her, but he must defend God. "He hasn't forgotten. He merely waits for our return."

But You Have Not Obeyed Me

She humphed. "Our return? Where have we gone? We've gone nowhere. *He* has vanished."

Gideon thought of their history. He normally wouldn't have continued correcting her. He would have remained silent. But tonight, confidence pushed him to say more. "We've forgotten His Words and must return to His way."

Rakaal laughed. "As if by some magic, we obey, and He brings food? Gideon, do not deceive yourself."

A knife couldn't have pierced his heart more. He wanted Rakaal to support him. He wanted to share his purpose—his mission. But any time he tried, she exposed his insides to the buzzards for their fill. He couldn't share his feelings, when he couldn't even tell her his purpose. He closed his lips and refused to respond.

Rakaal turned over and pulled the goatskin with her.

Gideon was no longer covered. He felt the cool breeze of the night's air settle over him, just as her words of condemnation and worthlessness seeped back through him.

He put his arms under his head and looked up at the darkness. What would God have him do?

Although the night had been late when Gideon had finally fallen asleep, he awoke early, before the sun had risen. He put on his sandals and stretched by the door of his house. He pushed back his hair, scratching his head as he did.

He still felt peace. But more than that. He felt driven to do something. He splashed water on his face from the basin by the door. The cold water roused him. He shook off the droplets before wiping his face on a cloth by the basin. He walked toward the village.

On the hillside overlooking the village, the altar of Baal-peor stood silhouetted against the rising sun. The pole of Asherah reached toward the sky as if mocking his people.

God spoke, "Pull down your father's altar of Baal. Cut down

the Asherah pole beside it. And build an altar to Me where they stand."

Gideon took several steps toward the hill. The Asherah's pole was strong. How could he do it?

God answered, "Take your father's bull and a second bull, seven years old. Pull it down."

Gideon considered. Two strong bulls pulling downhill would do it. He nodded.

"Offer the second bull on the altar. Use the wood from the Asherah pole."

Gideon heard no more instructions.

God's voice was gone.

Gideon scratched his head, considering the task. It was one thing to tell Rakaal that God was worthy. But another to prove it to his father.

That could bring a war.

The altar of Baal-peor honored lasciviousness. Baal-peor literally meant god of the opening. During worship, Baal required women to offer themselves.

The Asherah pole represented Baal's female counterpart. Men emasculated themselves before her to achieve greater sexual fulfillment. When the night's sacrifice was over, they left, weakened, and unfulfilled. Yet they lived for the next time they would worship, their thoughts consumed by the next sacrifice. This addicting power of Baal-peor drove men to more worship.

They never thought their weakness would last. They gave their strength to strange women.

The Midianites, by introducing God's people to this worship, needed nothing more to destroy the fight of God's people.

This worship consumed their lives.

Their strength was gone.

And they didn't know it.

Their God was forgotten.

And they didn't even miss Him.

CHAPTER 21

God was worthy. Gideon wanted his own people to know their unworthiness could be washed clean. They could have purpose, greater than pleasing themselves, greater than life itself. Gideon looked at the altar on the hill. The sun peeked over the mountain and shone on the altar giving it a glow that seemed to cover the destruction caused during the night.

It was one thing for Gideon to tell God He was worthy. It was another to show his father. His father was a leader in his house, in his community.

Gideon wondered about Jether's comment about the Midianites coming at night to talk with his father. Could he be leading the Midianites too? He shook his head. He couldn't think about it.

He must plan. How would he remove his father's altar? And use his father's bulls to do it.

He'd have to take his bull by the horns and just do it!

He laughed at his boldness, then sobered at the reality.

God help him.

He would have to.

He was feeling weak just thinking about approaching his father to ask. Ask? How could he even ask?

He'd test his courage with Rakaal, while he ate that morning.

It was nice to have the recent harvest.

He expected the Midianites to come any day now.

Everyone did. They lived looking over their shoulders, waiting for their return. And when they did, everyone knew they would go back to hunger. But until then, all lived hoarding their harvest, and eating as if they might not eat for a long time.

So when Gideon bit into the flatbread, he savored the fresh taste. Rakaal always could season it just right, with salt evaporated from the Dead Sea water. She nurtured several plants outside their house, which she added to flavor the bread. She didn't grind the wheat too fine, giving it the crunchy, chewy flavor he liked.

Gideon savored it. "This is good."

Rakaal shrugged. "What are you doing today?"

Gideon stopped chewing. How did she always know when he was going to do something? Could she read his mind? He paused, trying to think how to tell her. Why did he need to tell her? "I'm going to see my father."

"What for?" She pressed.

Even when he tried to keep things from her, she pressed until he would blurt it out, then instantly regret it when she told what she thought of his idea. Couldn't she encourage him, even if it wasn't a good idea? When she had finished telling him how the idea was completely senseless, he would agree and then do what he'd always done—what she wanted done.

Today, he wouldn't concede. Today's task wasn't his own. It was God's. And he would obey it, with or without Rakaal's approval. He pursed his lips. "This is good flatbread."

"You will be finishing the harvest today, won't you?" Rakaal pressed him farther, "You aren't pursuing something for that God, are you?"

Gideon kept his eyes down. How could she make him feel like such a little boy? He wouldn't look her in the eye.

What had happened to the peace of the day before? Had it taken wings and flown away with Rakaal's words? Gideon tried to call it back. With renewed confidence, he raised his eyes to look directly into hers. "God is worthy. I must do what He wants me to do."

Rakaal's eyes widened at his boldness. Her lips opened to speak, then shut again. It was she who looked down this time.

But it didn't take her long to recover. When she looked at him again, she said, "You better hope your God doesn't make a fool out of you."

Gideon laughed, growing bold by his declaration. "If what He calls me to do is seen as foolish in the eyes of His people, it's not God that's a fool."

What had gotten into him? Gideon never stood against Rakaal. Why did he feel like he should now? Maybe he hadn't lost all his manhood before the altar of Asherah. Or maybe his God had given him another chance to gain it back. Not that he wanted to fight with Rakaal. He only wanted to have her support him in his dreams.

Years ago, after each harvest they had sung and spent time as a family. He smiled remembering the evenings. He'd play his lyre and Jether and Latrell would dance to it.

Gideon thought about his lyre. He hadn't played it since . . . since the Midianites had come. There was still a reason to play. God was still worthy. He would not forget what God had done. He would play again.

He stepped more resolutely to his father's house. He'd need plans. He stopped at his father's barn to see the two bulls. One was already harnessed to the grind mill, treading in circles to make flour.

Everyone expected the Midianites any day. They wanted the harvest hidden when they did. Urgency could be felt.

Gideon looked to the hillside where a lookout notified them of any dust approaching.

Gideon nodded to his father's foreman. He had already assigned the tasks for the day. Still Gideon dallied. How could he take the bulls when they needed them? Would he be able to ask his father to use them?

Someone spoke right behind him. "Shalom, Son."

Gideon hadn't heard his father approach. It irritated him he could do that to him. Gideon turned his head. "Be at peace, Father." He nodded to the man at the top of the hill. "They should be coming any day now."

His father smiled. "My wheat will be hidden by the end of the week. Then we'll enjoy the sacrifices all the more." His father looked at Gideon, his gaze seeming to pierce into his thoughts. "You finished your harvest?"

Gideon felt reprimanded, as if he must be reminded of what was important. He licked his lips, trying to tell his father what God had told him to do. He'd been a fool to think he could ask his father for help. Gideon turned from studying the mountain where the altar and the pole stood. He hadn't answered his father, and that would irritate him. But he had other things to do.

His father looked at him accusingly. "Did you come here for something?"

Gideon hesitated, then shook his head. "I should get back home."

His father nodded toward some of his servants. "Take Purah and Cael with you. Rakaal tells me you're behind in your threshing."

How did Rakaal know he hadn't threshed all day yesterday? Why would she tell his father? Gideon remembered her absence yesterday. Although unusual, he'd thought she was gathering herbs or something. Why had she come here to report his doings? It seemed bad enough she found fault with his decisions, but to tell his father? Gideon didn't understand. He knew better than to ask his father why she was here. He'd just give Gideon that knowing smile and laugh. Instead he nodded. "Thank you, I could use them."

He started to leave, then turned back, trying to tell him his mission one more time.

His father had already turned his attention back to his own winnowing.

Gideon headed for home.

Throughout the day, Gideon looked to the mountain top where the altar stood and wondered how he should do it. It seemed so easy when God explained what he should do, but now as he planned how he was to get the two bulls, harness them, lead them . . . the job seemed almost impossible.

He went back to the oak tree to thresh his wheat.

Purah and Cael proved invaluable, bringing the shocks from the field, threshing, and gathering the wheat into jars.

He alone took it to the caves where he hid them. The less people who knew of his hidden storage, the safer it would be when starvation hit the village.

But as he worked, a plan grew for obeying God.

The sun was growing warm, almost overhead, when Gideon glanced toward the house.

Rakaal was coming to him.

His heart raced. Was something wrong? Had the Midianites gone around his land to hit his father's first?

But she wasn't hurrying.

He watched her come.

When she was close enough for him to see, it was clear she carried a basket. Had she brought the noon meal? Why?

As she reached the tree, Gideon reached out to take her basket. One smell told him he was right. "You brought the noon meal?"

She shrugged. "Thought you might be hungry."

She hadn't brought his noon meal for a long time.

He looked at her awkwardly, like he was just a boy wondering if he should ask to hold her hand.

She seemed not to know what to say. She picked at her sleeve, then looked into his face.

He had forgotten how beautiful she was. And how mesmerized he had been through their courtship.

"How's your father?"

His father? She had just talked with him yesterday. Why would she be concerned? Gideon studied her carefully. Why would she ask? Was that the reason she had brought his meal? He coughed before answering, "He's fine."

Rakaal seemed to catch herself, as if she had revealed too much. She tried to explain, "I mean, with the pressure of the harvest before the Midianites coming . . ."

Gideon studied her more intently. She seemed to care more for his father than—he shook his head. He couldn't consider that. "Thank you for the meal." Why did he give a formal response, as if they weren't husband and wife? Yet the thought struck him, how much were they?

She didn't stay, but gave the meal and left.

Her actions made Gideon wonder. He asked Purah and Cael, "Do you see Rakaal at my father's house often?"

Purah choked, then caught himself before he turned away.

Cael kept his head down. "I'm too busy caring for the bulls to notice."

Gideon could tell by Cael's nervousness, he lied. But his response led him to ask another question. "Cael, I have need of my father's bulls tonight. Would you harness them for me?"

Cael's eyes widened. He was a faithful servant to his father. He would do anything asked of him. He nodded slowly. "I could."

Gideon felt his plan developing. He felt a bond with these men, more so than with his own family. Maybe because he worked with them. They spent hours caring for the herds. He had shared what the man of God had told him. They seemed receptive to knowing God.

He would need help to carry out God's plan. "Purah, would you bring my father's straps, the ones he uses when he hauls stones in his wagon?"

Purah looked unsure. "Tonight?"

With his hesitation, Gideon nodded toward the mountain. "To give God His rightful place."

Purah followed his glance to the top of the hill where the altar stood. His eyes widened. He looked at Gideon with new respect. "You'll remove your father's altars?"

Gideon smiled at his response. "I'll obey God."

Purah considered Gideon, "You heard from God again?"

At Gideon's nod, Purah answered without hesitation, "I'll help."

"Good." Gideon stood to return to work. "Who else would you trust?"

Cael considered, "My three brothers."

Purah nodded, his face showed excitement and hope, "And my two; also Nadir, another of your father's servants."

Cael added, "If we're involving your father's servants, maybe even Dand and Ferdi."

Would they be loyal to him or his father? He'd find out tonight.

Thinking of loyalty, Gideon wondered about Rakaal's strange behavior. She held no devotion to him. He'd been given too many hints not to conclude what he didn't want to know—Rakaal was visiting his father. As he picked up his threshing tool, he asked, "Whom does my father sleep with?"

Purah, caught off-guard by the change of subject, responded, "Anyone he wants." He realized what he said, "I only meant . . ." and shook his head to soften his words.

Gideon saw his expression. He didn't want to ask, but he needed to know. "Including my wife?" Gideon looked at Cael.

Cael looked down, but not before Gideon saw his pity.

Gideon looked at his threshing tool. "Why don't you both refill our waterskins. I need to be alone."

Purah squeezed his shoulder. "She isn't worthy of you."

When they were out of sight, Gideon took out his pain by threshing wheat.

CHAPTER 22

Gideon returned late that night. He entered his dark house quietly. He could see the forms where Jether and Rakaal lay. He felt by the embers for any flatbread left, but found none. He grabbed a handful of wheat kernels, and popped them in his mouth, not feeling hungry. As he chewed, he looked at the bed he had shared with his wife for thirteen years.

He wouldn't sleep before he met with the others to destroy the altar, even though he was tired from the day. He hadn't resolved anything by threshing. He was still angry. If anything, he was more determined to destroy the altar. Not only for God's sake, but for the destruction of his father's ways on his own life.

The moon wouldn't give its light on this night. They would work in darkness, even on the hill where the pole usually stood silhouetted against the moon.

Now, in the dark, he felt his way to the wall and grabbed his lyre and went outside. He leaned against the wall of his house.

Music had calmed him when he was growing up. Would it soothe him now? The strings had grown loose through disuse. He plucked one as he tightened it to bring it back to pitch. He repeated it until all the strings were tuned. He strummed, thinking back over his marriage. What could he have done differently? Should he have moved away from his father? Would that have made a difference?

He strummed absently. His fingers were stiff and not calloused enough to play a clear note.

Growing up, he had watched his father get whatever he wanted.

His brothers had married and moved away, taking control of their own homes.

But when he married, his father said he must stay nearby to help. Shouldn't he have stayed to help? Or would things be different if he'd put distance between his father and his family?

At first, it had been hard to leave Rakaal and his boys, but as the distance between Rakaal and him grew, it became easier to find a reason not to come home.

Rakaal didn't respect him. She disdained his presence.

He found it harder to come home. If it hadn't been for Jether, he wouldn't have.

He always thought it was his fault. He wasn't the strong leader like his father.

But when he was with his servants, they expected him to lead. They shared that camaraderie that comes by working together. He was confident. They trusted his judgment. He felt their respect.

When he stood before Rakaal or his father, he only remembered his failures. And so did they.

He hadn't doubted Rakaal's word about Latrell's death until today; he just couldn't understand it. He had no cause to question her truthfulness. Jether's story was skewed by his own blame and youth. Yet it had bothered Gideon.

But now . . . as he doubted Rakaal's words, Jether's story made more sense. Was Latrell's death caused by his father's worship? Had he allowed his own grandson to be sacrificed?

But more than his son's death was the death of his marriage. What could he do now? He felt nothing for Rakaal. Yes, she was beautiful, but beauty without respect becomes an empty vessel—hollow, pretty, but useless.

He wouldn't fight, demanding her respect. Where's respect in that? It would be duty without heart. He would demand from no one.

He understood obedience when his heart wasn't in it. Hadn't he done that for his father many times? He wanted service without coercion, but out of love.

By allowing his father to control his family, had Gideon created Rakaal's disrespect? And led her to desire his father? Was he to blame?

He was no closer to any answers, but he must meet the other men at his father's.

Yet he lingered.

He didn't want to see his father. He wasn't sure he could control what he said.

He felt, rather than saw, Rakaal beside him.

He stopped playing. He couldn't look at her.

She touched him lightly on the forearm. "You're going to your father's tonight?"

He looked at her hand, but didn't feel its warmth. How did she know? Gideon couldn't find his voice to answer. He nodded.

"Take me with you." Her voice pled.

Gideon swallowed. Her request was like pouring salt on an open wound. He bit back an angry response. "What about Jether?"

She shrugged. "He knows where to find me."

Gideon nodded, processing her comment. Had everyone known, but him? He was thankful for the darkness that hid his shame. He asked, although not sure he wanted to know, "Is he mine?"

He almost sensed tenderness in her hesitation. But her answer eliminated that.

"He's your father's."

The night sounds shouted at him. Crickets' chirping scolded. An owl's call echoed over the still, night air, as if its talons had already grabbed his heart from his body.

Gideon pushed on with his questions, since she was talking. "Was Latrell's mine?"

Rakaal hesitated. "Yes."

He swallowed. Was that why Latrell was used for their worship and Jether saved?

He found his voice, "Why, Rakaal?"

Her hand still lay on his arm. It trembled. "Your father leads with authority. His household doesn't go without."

No one doubted his father's authority. And he definitely manipulated circumstances, even stealing from his own family to make sure he didn't go without. Gideon leaned his lyre against the house and stepped away. "I'll take you."

She squeezed his arm. The first gesture of support and kindness Gideon could remember from her in a long time. He almost changed his mind, wanting to fight for her. But her support was only because she would leave.

Together they walked across his pasture, through his orchard, and around the mountain to his father's house. When he reached it, he walked Rakaal to the door.

She slipped in, as if she was expected and welcome.

Gideon turned back to the barn.

The men, recruited by Purah and Cael, stood in the darkness against the barn.

He must focus on the task before him. He strode to the barn. This task he would do. And willingly.

He spoke with authority and confidence that he didn't feel. "Ready, men?"

Cael held the lead rope harnessed to the bulls.

The others answered by stepping forward out of the shadow.

Gideon smiled for the first time in a long time. "Then let's move out."

The path wasn't clear. Darkness hindered finding the trail.

The bulls had been pushed hard through the day to finish the wheat, now Cael snapped the air with his whip, struggling to keep them moving.

When they reached the top, Gideon directed the men to tie the straps around the altar and direct the bulls down the hill. Dirt had sifted between the boulders. Rain cemented the dirt to form secure bonds.

The oxen strained against their harnesses.

The men wielded their axes at the crevices, jarring the stones loose, weakening the bonds.

The altar finally budged. As the bulls moved, the altar slid across the ground, leaving a flattened trail.

When the bulls reached the edge of the hill, Purah unfastened the straps.

Cael pulled the bulls away from the edge.

The men shoved the altar over.

Gideon stood at the edge of the hill, listening. The rocks fell, bouncing and crashing to the bottom of the hill. He could smell the dust as it rose from the valley. Then all was quiet.

The silence instilled a rightness in his action. It gave an inward strength.

Gideon bounced on his toes as he turned to survey the pole. He couldn't wait to finish the task God had given. "Let's take it down, men. Let's get our strength back."

He attacked the pole, wood chips flying. He felt power rise in his blood over the rightness of his action.

The men swung their axes, catching Gideon's passion. They chopped the pole into pieces, as if their manhood had been restored and they would again live as God intended.

When the pole cracked and fell, the men cheered.

Gideon led the men in praise, "God is worthy."

They built another altar. This one to God.

When the altar was complete, Purah put on the altar a splintered piece of the pole.

Other men followed, until all the pieces were heaped on the stones. They would sacrifice their futile attempts to *be* right on the altar where God would *do* right.

Gideon killed the seven-year-old bull on the altar before God.

The men circled the altar as the flames consumed the sacrifice.

Gideon watched the fire burn the wood and lick the meat.

The flames lifted toward heaven in a sacrifice of obedience.

The day had been torn by pain, anger, and failures. They seemed little, compared to what God would do.

Gideon looked around the altar at the ten other men. He felt a kinship with these men, who had bonded under darkness to do what was right. The flames lit each face, reflecting a yearning to serve God.

Gideon raised his arms to the sky. "God is worthy."

CHAPTER 23

When morning came, the villagers rose, and as was their habit, looked to the hilltop for reassurance of their coming pleasure. What they saw caused an uproar. "Where's the Asherah pole? Whose altar takes the place of Baal-peor?"

The shouting was heard. News spread. Crowds formed. When they tried to find blame, someone recalled hearing Gideon, son of Joash, shout from the hilltop during the night, "God is worthy." Wasn't that proof enough of who was responsible?

They moved as a mob to Joash's, irate over their pleasure being thwarted. They pounded on his door.

Their noise woke Gideon, who had slept in his father's barn for the night. He wiped the sleep from his eyes and ran his hand through his hair. He watched from the barn door to see what the commotion was about.

Before his father's house, twenty-five men stood.

His father stood by his open door. "What's the meaning of this?"

A self-imposed leader demanded, "Bring your son that he may die."

Gideon stepped back into the shadow of the barn's door, but strained to listen.

Joash raised his voice to calm them. "What has he done?"

"He deserves death. He's torn down Baal's altar and the pole of Asherah."

Joash looked at the hillside. His face showed surprise, but he quickly masked it. He raised his arms for quietness. "I put up the altar, didn't I?"

The nods from the crowd showed they were listening, but someone from the back of the crowd demanded, "But it's our place to worship."

Joash nodded. "But will you fight for Baal? Must you protect your own god? Shouldn't Baal protect you? If he can't even protect himself, what kind of a god is he?" He paused to allow the people to consider his words. "Let Baal contend against Gideon if he needs it."

Gideon swallowed. His father had protected him. Maybe to save his own reputation in front of the men, but it encouraged Gideon. For now his life was spared.

Gideon studied his father from different eyes. He got what he wanted, but protected his own, in a warped sort of way. His father attracted men and women alike to follow him.

Gideon knew he wasn't a strong leader like his father. Should he fault Rakaal for wanting better? His inadequacy as a leader could almost excuse her behavior. But not remove the hurt.

Gideon watched the crowd leave in twos and threes, drifting back to their own homes. When they had all left, Gideon had a clear view of his father. He caught his father's eyes.

His father nodded to him, any emotion masked by his stern features.

Rakaal stood behind Joash. She had stood with him while he confronted a mob, but she couldn't stand by Gideon when he did what he was supposed to do. Her fickleness and lack of loyalty pierced his heart anew.

Joash turned and placed his arm around Rakaal's waist and led her inside the house.

Gideon watched from the barn's doorway, swallowing the anger that wanted to control him.

But You Have Not Obeyed Me

Gideon returned home to thresh wheat. Why? He didn't want to eat, let alone live. When he approached the oak tree where he had met the angel, he remembered the peace, but this time he had none. He lashed at the wheat, as if he could beat his thoughts into submission by separating the wheat from its chaff.

He was startled when someone spoke behind him, "If you're grinding the wheat into flour, you're doing a good job."

Gideon stopped threshing and turned.

Purah stood behind him. "Shalom."

Gideon shrugged. "It's safer than returning to my father's house."

Purah nodded.

"Everyone knew but me, didn't they?"

Purah shrugged. "Most don't want to know what Joash does, except when it pertains to their work."

Gideon threw the threshing tool to the ground and stretched his arms above his head. "Urgg. This wheat is worthless."

Purah shook his head. "I think it served its purpose."

"Maybe it did." Gideon looked toward his father's pasture. "What brings you here?"

Purah seemed apologetic, "Your father."

Gideon snorted. "Should have known. And what does my father want from me now?"

"A messenger arrived. The Midianites have crossed the Jordan River and are heading this way."

The cloud of self-pity fled. His people finally had enough warning to prepare for their coming. He remembered the angel's words, "Go in your strength and deliver Israel." Gideon grabbed his cloak from the ground and tied his waterskin to his belt. "How many?"

"They've recruited the Amalekites and others from the east."

"I'll meet you at my father's, I must grab my trumpet."

Purah nodded and turned to go. But he turned back, his voice was grave, "Gideon."

When he had Gideon's attention again, he continued, "Joash's men are for you."

Gideon blinked. Not only had his father's servants helped destroy the altar and pole, but they would support him now with the Midianites. Gideon stretched out his hand. "That means a lot."

Purah grabbed it and they embraced. "Now hurry."

Gideon ran to his house. As he ran, he planned. If they could attack the Midianites unexpectedly, they may have a chance, but what about the additional Amalekites and others?

After grabbing his trumpet, he ran to his father's house. He didn't stop at his barn or house, but ran to the top of the hill where he had sacrificed to God. He grabbed a breath before blowing his trumpet. The trumpet alerted their clan of danger.

Men hurried to the base of the hill by Joash's barnyard.

Gideon returned to the bottom of the hill and waited for his father to organize the men as he always had done in a meeting. When Gideon caught his eye, his father gestured for him to speak. Gideon swallowed. Why had he deferred to him?

Gideon raised his arms.

The men quieted.

"The Midianites have crossed the Jordan and are on their way here. They bring the Amalekites and others."

A man from the back called, "They'll be angry when they see their altar destroyed and the pole gone. How will you protect us from their anger?"

Gideon looked at his father.

Joash smiled, his arms crossed.

Had he known they would respond like this? Had his father protected him from the mob, only to feed him to a bigger enemy?

Gideon swallowed. He'd never led men into battle. What did he know?

He looked over the gathered crowd.

But You Have Not Obeyed Me

Purah and Cael stood in the back with his father's other servants. Purah nodded, confidently.

Gideon looked toward the hill where he had sacrificed and proclaimed, "God is worthy." He was still worthy. Gideon felt strength come upon him. It wasn't his own. "Abiezrites, sons of Gilead, men of our family, the Lord's angel has promised deliverance."

Murmuring swept through the crowd. "Is this the youngest son of Joash? We've watched him grow up, herd sheep, and play instruments. *He* will lead us?"

But Purah answered their murmurings. "What courage would it take to remove the pole and altar from our midst? Gideon did it. And God is with him."

The men listened. They looked to the hill. The pole was gone. In its place was an altar. They turned to Joash, who had always led them before.

Joash leaned against his doorpost, his arms crossed. He gave no consent, merely shrugged.

It was enough to turn the crowd to Gideon. "What shall we do?"

Gideon silently thanked God and nodded to Purah. "Prepare for battle. Meet me at Midian's spring on the north side of Moreh's hill in three days."

As the men left, Gideon joined the servants at the back. "Cael, send men to Manasseh, Asher, Zebulun and Naphtali. Tell them to meet at the spring of Midian."

Cael turned to go.

Gideon stopped him with these words, "The Lord go with you."

Cael smiled. "I haven't heard those words in a long time."

Gideon nodded to the altar. "It's time you did."

Gideon watched the men leave. He saw Cael speak to others who would carry the message to the northern tribes. He knew the Spirit had directed him as he spoke of battle; but now as he thought of how they would fight this battle, he doubted. The comments about him were true. He was the youngest of his father's sons. Why didn't God use one of his brothers? They were more qualified.

These men had watched him grow up. They saw how his father had delegated him to pastures, while he took his wife. And now they were supposed to follow him?

Where was the peace he felt when the angel had sent flames to consume his sacrifice? Where was the confidence he had when he pushed the altar over the hillside?

This was battle.

What had he been thinking?

All around him the servants prepared.

How should he prepare?

The day was far gone. It had been an exhausting several days and nights. Gideon would sleep in his father's barn rather than return home. He stretched on the hay and pulled a sheepskin over his legs. He propped his head on his arms. Although tired, sleep wouldn't come. Gideon listened as the barn sounds grew quiet and the men went to bed.

He had sent for Jether to come during the day.

Jether hadn't wanted to sleep inside the house. Now he lay beside him. His breathing took a steady rhythm as he slept.

Gideon adjusted another skin over Jether. He was a good child.

He thought of his father. The image of Rakaal standing by his father burned in his memory. The pain wasn't so great. Had he accepted what he was? The least of his father's sons? Not worthy of anything good?

But even as the self-pity crept into his thoughts, he thought of the angel of the Lord. He had chosen to visit him. And told that deliverance would come by him.

God was worthy. But was Gideon a worthy leader for his God?

What if the other northern tribes refused to come? Would they be massacred? The angel had said, "delivered," not "hope to be delivered." He turned over on the sheepskin, shifting the lumps of hay. How long would he toss before he could sleep? The sheepskin was wet from his sweat. He rubbed the wetness, thinking. It was unusual for the skin to make him sweat.

He spoke to God, "I'll put a fleece of wool on the threshing floor. If there's dew on the fleece only, and it's dry on the ground, I will know You will deliver Israel through me, as You have spoken." He took the sheepskin to the middle of the threshing floor. He flattened out the curled edges.

The moon shone on the skin's whiteness. It stood out against the dark ground.

He felt silly for asking God to show Himself. Didn't he already know God was worthy? But this wasn't about whether God was worthy. This was about whether he was worthy to help God.

He went back inside the barn and lay down again. The question would be answered in the morning. He stretched out again, feeling more than tired. Even his mind was tired of going over what had happened over the past several days, and over what could happen at the spring of Midian.

This time he fell asleep.

CHAPTER 24

Before the sun rose over the mountain, Gideon was awake. He stretched, feeling the hay scratch him where normally the soft skin of a goat would caress him. He rose quickly, anxious to see if God had done what he asked. He didn't bother to put on his sandals. He looked around for anyone watching. He didn't want anyone to witness his test. He felt embarrassed by his insecurities. He hurried to his father's threshing floor. The ground was dry on his feet. He stooped. He took a big breath as he reached toward the skin. When he touched it, he gasped. The skin was soaking wet. He lifted and squeezed it. Water dripped from the skin. He tapped his toes to the ground again, reassuring himself it was dry. He studied the puddle formed by the dripping skin.

Gideon nodded, breathing deeply. "God is worthy and has told me He would deliver Israel through me. I must believe that."

That day as Gideon prepared for the journey north, rolling cloth for a tent, walking among the servants at his father's house who would be going with him, he felt the weight of leadership.

His father had been absent. Gideon had watched the house many times, waiting for him to come and speak to him.

He didn't.

Gideon wondered if he should tell Rakaal good-bye before he

left for battle. The few times he had caught sight of her, she had hurried from the house, only to carry or dump wash water. She hadn't looked his way.

Would he miss her? Had she given him anything but disrespect and disdain? He shook his head; she had given him children. Then he corrected himself, not Jether. He had treated him as his own, had thought him his.

He felt his cheeks flush as he thought of how everyone had known, but himself.

He had been too busy watching his father's sheep to know what his own family was doing. He lowered his face in shame. How could he not have known?

He spent the day in misery. Trying to avert his thoughts and his eyes from what happened at the house and to prepare himself for battle.

He had draped the sheepskin over the fence to dry in the sun. Every time he glanced at it, he felt a renewed confidence in what God was going to do through him. He almost wanted to salute it. To tell God, "You don't know who you're working with."

But God did know him. Better than he knew himself.

When the day was over, and he was again lying on the hay with the sheepskin over him, he felt little and unsure. What if he had heard wrong? He was leading men into battle. Some would die. What if he hadn't heard right?

He spoke to God again, "Please let me speak once more. Let me make another test. Let the fleece be dry and the ground around it covered with dew."

He rose in the darkness to lay out the skin, patting the skin for reassurance. And returned to his hay to sleep till morning.

Gideon had slept so little over the past several nights that when morning came, he woke with a start. The sun streamed into the barn door. He heard the servants cleaning out the stalls. Had he missed the test?

He ran to the threshing floor. When he reached the sheepskin, his feet were covered with dew. He paused before touching the fleece, hesitant to confirm God had chosen him. Could he bear it if God showed him "No"?

His father's voice stopped him before he touched the fleece. His scorn evident in his voice. "Running around without your sandals like a little boy?"

Ignoring his father and unable to wait for God's confirmation, Gideon grabbed the fleece.

It was dry and soft!

He hugged the fleece to his chest. God had chosen him to deliver His people. He did have worth, at least in God's sight.

His father crossed his arms and loomed over him. His lips twisted in scorn. "Not only are you running around barefoot, but you're hugging your blanket like you can't part with it. How do you expect to lead an army?"

Gideon heard the disdain, felt the rebuke, but this time didn't cower under it. Instead, he stepped toward his father. "My God has chosen me. He is worthy."

Joash's scorn faded as confusion clouded his face.

Gideon softened his voice at the change of his father's expression. He wanted to convince his father. "God has given us victory."

Joash's jaw tightened. "You speak of victory when you know nothing of fighting. How will you lead men when you can't even lead your family?"

Gideon stood taller. "I don't have to win the battle. It's already promised."

His father taunted, "You know the future?"

Gideon smiled. "I know the God of the future. He has promised victory."

"You boldly take men into battle, but will you faint when their spears brings blood?"

"God has promised deliverance from the Midianites as one man."

His father's snorted. "You think that one man is *you*?"

"God has shown me with this dry fleece and wet ground. He is with me as I go to battle."

His father's eyebrows lifted and he studied the fleece. "It was left overnight here?"

Gideon handed it to his father. "Feel for yourself."

His father touched it, tentatively at first, then squeezed it. He studied the ground around it, lifting his feet in the dampness. He looked again at Gideon. "You asked for this sign from God?"

Gideon nodded. He could barely voice what he felt. God had accepted and affirmed him for delivering his people. And his father witnessed it!

His father dropped his hand from the sheepskin, as if he didn't want to acknowledge God's sign or Gideon's worth. "Did He tell you to take down my high places?"

Gideon looked to the mountain, then met his father's gaze. "Yes."

"You weren't afraid of me?"

Gideon laughed. "I was more afraid of God's displeasure. Isn't that why the Midianites overrun us, because we've forgotten God?"

Joash lowered his voice, "I thought you responded because of Rakaal."

Gideon swallowed. He didn't want to talk about her with his father. He shrugged, "My anger helped."

The change of subject away from God seemed to renew Joash's confidence. He demanded, "You owe me for my ox."

Gideon spoke with confidence, "I'll repay you."

Joash humphed. "How?"

Gideon smiled. "When I return with victory." He raised his eyebrows and looked toward the house. "There will be payment for all things taken."

Joash laughed. "If you return. If you win. You boldly promise what you do not have."

Gideon gained confidence. "I've learned well from my father. You promised my family would be cared for. Your word may mean nothing, but I speak truth."

Joash stepped forward and slapped him.

Gideon licked his bleeding lip but didn't retreat. "What did you tell mother when you brought Rakaal here, that she'd have grandchildren to keep her busy, so she wouldn't notice what you did with my wife?"

Joash raised his hand to strike again, but dropped it. "Your mother knows why I brought them here."

Gideon didn't know why he said it, but he continued, "To protect my family or sacrifice them?"

Joash paled. "I couldn't help Latrell—"

Gideon swallowed. Rakaal had been so adamant about what had happened to their son. He knew now she hadn't lied. She had retold the story given by his father.

His father had found the hole, hidden his own deeds, then later convinced her of Gideon's folly. Realization of his father's deeds made Gideon spew out the words, "You disposed of his body so Rakaal would blame me."

Joash looked keenly at Gideon. His eyebrows raised in surprise, then he quickly masked it. "The Midianites needed payment." He shut his mouth, and swallowed.

Gideon shook his head in unbelief. His father had consented to abusing and sacrificing Latrell. His hole hadn't trapped him and brought his death. He hadn't been the cause of his son's death. Relief filled him. The guilt he had carried had been a burden. He no longer carried it.

The blame lay on his father. His father had used the hole as a convenient place to dispose of the body. And to give a reason for Rakaal to hate Gideon more.

Gideon swallowed his anger. He wanted to strangle his father. "You promised me you would protect my family. You told me they were safe."

"How did you . . ." Joash looked toward the house, as if unsure of what Gideon knew. Joash shrugged, not finishing his thought.

Gideon didn't want to know what else his father had done with his family. He shifted the sheepskin in his hands. "I have things I must do. Was there something else you needed?"

Joash searched Gideon, like he was evaluating him for the first time. He shook his head.

Gideon nodded. "Then I must prepare for victory."

CHAPTER 25

The Midianites and their allies marched through the Harod Valley after traveling up the Jordan Valley. They camped in the valley before the hill of Moreh. Their numbers were great. Their discipline strong.

Gideon watched them pass as he drank from the spring of Harod. He had cut arm holes in the sheepskin and worn it inside his cloak, to remind him of God's promise. Now he reached inside his cloak to pat the skin. God would remain true.

As he watched under the shadows of the trees, surrounding the spring, he heard God's voice.

"The people are too many for Me."

Gideon gulped. He could tell that too. "Yes, Lord, there are many comgin against us. I have asked the northern tribes to come and my own people. What more should I do?"

"Tell your people, 'Whoever is afraid, leave.'"

Gideon squeaked, "You mean, I have too many men? But what is that against them?"

God was clear. "Israel has too many men. They will think they won."

Gideon didn't understand. "Don't we want to win?"

God explained, "Israel will boast that their own power saved them."

Gideon nodded. He remembered his position as the weakest son. It did keep him humble. "I'll tell those who are afraid to go home."

So Gideon stood before the men.

Purah stood at his side. "Cael has done well. There are 22,000 men who have come."

Gideon nodded. He felt proud so many had come to fight. He looked to the clouds, as the man of God had done. He understood God's request, but he didn't like it. He raised his arms for them to listen.

When they were quiet, Gideon spoke, "My brothers, my fellow tribesmen, my neighboring tribes, thank you for sacrificing to come for battle."

He pointed to the other hillside, where they could see the tents of the Midianites. "Look at our enemy. They're like grasshoppers covering the grass. They are seasoned fighters, taking our food for seven years. They have camels and horses.

"You are brave to come this far to help your brothers. But—" and he paused a long time. He remembered his father's scorn. "But I don't know how to fight. I've never led men into battle.

"We have no horses. We're not armed with weapons.

"If you don't want to fight, but do it only out of duty—if you are afraid; it's no shame. I'm afraid, even though God has talked with me.

"But if you are afraid, go home. No one will shame you. None will think less of you. Leave before the new day begins." Gideon turned from the group and went to his tent.

Purah followed him. "What were you thinking? What a way to instill courage and strength in your men! We needed all those men. Don't you see, even with all those men, we are still outnumbered?"

Gideon reached his hand inside his cloak and stroked the sheepskin. "Men who fear spread fear."

"But they are a body that might tire the Midianite's hand from swinging another time at a fearless man."

Gideon shook his head. "Remember when we destroyed the pole and the altar?"

Purah nodded, "There wasn't an army fighting against us."

"I obeyed the Lord then, and He protected me."

Purah's eyes blazed. "You didn't see the wrath of your father afterward."

"God protected me." Gideon looked at him with an intensity that caused him to drop his eyes. "God told me to tell the men who are afraid to go home." He paused for his words to sink in. "This is God's victory, not mine or yours." He waited until Purah looked him in the eye. "For Him to have the victory, we must do it His way. You do want to win, don't you?"

Purah sighed. "Yes. But—"

"There can't be 'but's' when we obey God. It's His way, or we don't win."

That night as darkness crept over the camp, Gideon stayed by his cook fire. He didn't want to watch as the men left. Darkness allowed them to leave without feeling shamed. No one could see who left. Didn't he have fear?

Purah sat beside him.

Gideon leaned toward him. "You're unusually quiet tonight. What's on your mind?"

Purah tried to smile. "Don't you think about the battle?"

Gideon laughed. "The thought doesn't leave my mind."

"Then how are you not afraid? I feel like I should go home, only you have told me to stay."

Gideon ran his fingers through his hair, then stretched his legs toward the fire and wiggled his toes. "I don't know enough about battle to tell you this fear doesn't go away.

"But you know the fear of sleeping with a lion's roar. You've been there with me, when we've heard one. There's a fear that paralyzes you and shame you. And there's a fear that pushes you to do what's right, in spite of the fear."

Purah leaned forward. "How do you know which fear you have?"

"You won't until the final moment when you must kill or be killed."

Purah looked at his hands, "Some men know now. They don't wait for battle."

Gideon took off his cloak then his sheep skin. "Some men think only of the cause of their fear. The enemy is too many, too big, too much."

Purah interrupted, "But they are."

Gideon nodded. "They are. But there is more to a battle than what you can see. When you dwell only on what you see, you will fear. You'll be defeated before you start."

Purah nodded.

Gideon gave the sheep skin to Purah. He had told Purah about the test he'd given to God. "This skin reminds me God is the unseen factor in this battle."

"I don't understand."

"Neither do I. I don't understand how God will win this battle with less men. God has told me He will win with only one man. I don't know how. But I don't look at the many men on the other side. That gives me fear. Nor do I want to see how many of our men are leaving. That too will give me fear. I look at the one God on my side. That gives me peace."

Gideon swallowed as he strode to the hillside to speak again to the men the next morning. He hadn't watched them leave, but he heard them and could feel their absence. They had left quietly. It was good to tell Purah that God would win, but when he looked over the campsite, he almost cried. The camp had shrunk by half!

Purah approached him on the hillside. "By my count, we have 10,000. Not nearly enough."

Gideon nodded. He lifted his waterskin to drink. The water

was muddied from all who had drunk, and had been stirred by the Midianites with their horses and men above them. He spit out the first swallow before taking another.

He had followed God's words and didn't know what else to do. So he waited.

As he waited, he heard God again. "The people are still too many. I will test them. Bring them to the spring to drink. There I will tell you who stays and who must go."

So Gideon told the men to drink at the spring. They came in clans and tribes.

God told Gideon, "Have them drink. Separate those who lap with their tongue like a dog from those who kneel to drink."

Gideon told Purah and Cael to separate them as God said.

Those who lapped weren't many. Would God send those away?

Purah hesitated, "They are separated, Gideon. Now what?"

Gideon waited for the Lord's instructions. But his heart sank when he looked at those who lapped like a dog. He sensed what the Lord wanted. He didn't want to hear. He wanted to resist. He fought with his thoughts. Surely, the Lord wouldn't send all those away except that handful! But he determined in his mind to obey whatever the Lord said.

Then the Lord spoke, "Tell those who kneeled at the water to go home."

Gideon choked.

Cael patted him on the back. "What is it?"

Gideon raised his arms and signaled the men to listen. He faced those who knelt before the water. "You have done well. May the Lord reward your willingness to fight. The Lord has said to go home, but leave your trumpets and your provisions."

There was a collected gasp as the men looked at the group who had been selected to fight.

Purah could see better on the hillside. He had already counted them. "Gideon, there are but 300 men. Are you sure you heard right?"

Gideon raised his arms again. "Those who haven't been

selected, please stay in your tents at the time of battle." He didn't want the Midianites to know how few were left to fight.

The men shook their heads as they walked away.

Purah grabbed his arm. "That's the whole army. How can we fight with those?" He pointed to the meager sum.

"I am the least of my family. The least of my clan. The least of my tribe. Yet God has chosen me. He will win the battle for us."

Purah looked at Cael. His expression showed he wasn't believing the victory.

Gideon grabbed his arm. "How did you drink?"

Purah's eyes widened; he stuttered. "I can't remember. Don't send me away. I've been through too many storms watching sheep with you for you to do this alone."

Gideon raised his eyebrows. "You don't remember?"

Purah stuttered, "I can't say."

Gideon sighed. "Help organize the provisions that remain." Gideon turned to hide his smile. He needed Purah, but also needed to remember God was in charge.

CHAPTER 26

Gideon swallowed as he watched the men eat around their campfires that night. They had separated from those chosen to fight. Gideon stretched. He drank deeply from his waterskin. He knew he wouldn't sleep, not for a long time.

Purah nodded to his flatbread, uneaten by his side. "Nervous?"

Gideon shrugged. "I've never led men into battle. I don't want to fail."

Purah looked for Gideon's cloak.

Gideon was sitting on it.

"You take off your cloak with its sheepskin lining, then forget what God has told you?"

Gideon nibbled a bite of flatbread, only to reassure Purah. "Waiting is hard."

"You're a shepherd and a farmer. You know waiting is necessary." Purah encouraged.

"Since when are you my advisor?"

"Since I stood beside you during those shepherd and farming times. I was there when you hacked down the pole of your father's. Remember?"

Gideon nodded. "You've earned that advisor status. You're right. I'm nervous."

Gideon motioned for Purah to follow him.

Purah put down his flatbread and brushed dirt from his tunic.

They moved away from the tent. When they reached a place where the valley stretched before them, Gideon sighed.

They studied the valley in silence. The smoke from the Midianite campfires below smelled of roasted meat and bread, mingled with camels and horses. The twinkling lights of their scattered campfires and torches seemed like looking at the heavens with all its stars.

Their noise carried up the hillside as if Gideon was right there with them.

Gideon bit his lip and a groan escaped his lips. What if he had heard wrong?

Even as he second-guessed himself, he heard the Lord speak, "Go to the Midianite camp. I will show you."

Gideon hesitated. How quickly his talk with Purah was needed for himself.

The Lord knew. "Take Purah with you. What you hear will encourage you that I am with you."

Gideon wiped his hands down his tunic. He looked at the sky, already showing stars. He turned to Purah. "Come with me."

"What do you have in mind?"

Gideon nodded to the Midianite camp. "We'll spy them out."

Purah stretched. "Sure, let's see, not only how we're outnumbered, but that heir swords and spears are sharper than anything we've ever seen. That'll help you sleep."

Gideon didn't respond. He was already walking toward their camp.

They circled around to the back side of the camp. They could smell the camels and horses before they reached them.

"Wow! Would you look at that!" Purah whispered. Their camels couldn't be numbered, like sand on the seashore.

"Shhh." Gideon swallowed. The memory of the camel spit brought bile to his throat. He couldn't fight against one lone camel, let alone these numbers.

They reached where the tents were pitched, like a city scattered before them.

But You Have Not Obeyed Me

Gideon and Purah dropped to the ground and crept on their bellies. The sand under them covered their noise, but left a trail. They had almost reached one of the tents in the outer perimeter when they heard talking.

A troubled voice said, "Listen, I had this dream. A loaf of barley bread fell into our camp and knocked my tent flat."

Another voice interrupted, "This's nothing but the sword of Gideon, son of Joash. God has given Midian and all the camp into his hand."

Gideon swallowed a gasp. He bowed his head in the sand, and praised God for reassuring him of victory.

Purah grabbed his arm and squeezed. His eyes sparkled with a new confidence. He moved to whisper in Gideon's ear, "Heard enough?"

Gideon nodded.

They crept back to the shelter of trees. When they could stand, they rested a few moments before returning to their tent.

The victory was already his.

Gideon motioned for Purah. "Call the 300 men. Divide them into three groups."

"Now? No more waiting?" Purah smiled.

Gideon nodded.

When the men were divided, Gideon told the plan. "We'll surround their camp. Make sure you can see the next man in the circle. Everyone take a pitcher with a torch inside and a trumpet. Look at me and do what I do. When I blow my trumpet, blow yours. Then we'll shout, 'A sword for the Lord and for Gideon.' Any questions?"

The men shook their heads. The three groups separated and circled the Midianite campsite.

They strode out with only the moon's light and the glow from their torches in their pitchers. By the time Gideon with his hundred men circled the camp, it was the middle of the watch.

Campfires had burned down to embers.

Most men slept.

Those on watch couldn't be seen at this distance.

Gideon saw the two men on either side of him only by the shadows cast by the glow from their lanterns. Around the hillside, the mellow, softened glow of all their lights shown like specks through their vessels.

He nodded and lifted his trumpet to his lips.

Those on either side of him followed him.

Gideon paused for all to follow their neighbor. Then he sucked in a breath and blew the trumpet. In unison the trumpets around the circle sounded.

The charge echoed off the hillside, repeating the blast long after he had stopped blowing.

Gideon lifted his pitcher above his head. He waited for the others to see. Then threw it to the ground. All the pitchers hit boulders and dirt beneath them, echoing around the valley like thunder crashing.

Three hundred men in deep, strong voices shouted, "A sword for the Lord and for Gideon!"

Then they waited.

The Midianite camp sprang to life. Men stumbled from their tents. They ran confused, unorganized. In their panic and fear, they pulled their swords and killed one another. As the one-sided battle grew more intense, men ran for their camels and horses. They fled, heading out of the Harod Valley.

Gideon heard the cry, "Their escaping!"

He called to Purah, "Purah, get the men who wait in the tents. We will pursue the enemy as it flees. Tell them to take care of those who remain."

He saw movement across the circle as Purah moved to obey.

Gideon considered his next move. The enemy had too much of a lead for his whole group to be able to outrun them and block them from crossing the Jordan River.

The tribe of Ephraim lived close to the Jordan River where they would have to cross. He wanted no one to escape and later return to terrorize the Lord's people again. He shouted again. "Cael, can you hear me?"

Cael shouted from the right of him, "Yes, Gideon."

"Go to Ephraim. Tell them to stop the Midianites before they cross the Jordan."

"I'm on my way."

Gideon called to the remaining 300 men, "Follow me. We'll block the Harod Pass."

The pass acted as a bottleneck, minimizing the soldiers who could go through. When Gideon reached the Pass, many of the Midianites had already passed. Gideon circled his men to the front to stop others. As the Midianites poured through, Gideon and his men confronted them.

Those soldiers who were called from their tents routed the remainder of the army from behind, pushing them through the Pass.

The Midianites would be surrounded and conquered.

As the number of the retreating soldiers petered out, Gideon called his men to pursue those who had already escaped down the Jordan Valley basin. As he ran, he heard his name called.

He looked back, Purah was running to catch him.

Gideon stopped to wait.

When Purah reached him, he stood breathing deeply.

"You routed the army from their campsite?"

Purah nodded between gasps for air.

"The remainder will be destroyed at the Pass. I'll pursue those who cross the River."

Purah again nodded. He pulled his waterskin from his belt and slowed his breathing so he could take a gulp. He almost choked.

Gideon began running to the Jordan pass.

When he reached the Jordan, Gideon saw a line of men guarding the Jordan River. He slowed to a walk as he approached them. "Did you catch the leaders?"

Rather than answering, one of the Ephraimites confronted him, "Are you Gideon?"

Gideon nodded. The man reminded him of his father when he was angry. Behind the man, the group scowled, holding their hands to their swords' hilts. Why were they angry?

Cael stepped forward.

Gideon asked again, this time to Cael. "Did you catch the leaders?"

Cael nodded, and started to speak, "Only two—"

The other man stepped before him. "Why didn't you call us to fight?"

Gideon looked from Cael to the leader. He drank from his waterskin and wiped his mouth with the back of his hand. He ran his fingers through his hair. "And you are?"

"Whitcome, from the Ephraimite tribe." The man stepped toward Gideon with his hand on his sword's hilt and repeated his question. "Why didn't you call us to fight?"

Gideon was confused. If they had captured two of their leaders, why was this man angry? He looked at Cael for an answer.

Cael shrugged.

Gideon lowered his voice. "Whitcome, you captured two of the Midianite leaders?"

The man nodded. He seemed to restrain himself from saying more.

This man was angry at him! Gideon smiled. He couldn't take time to fight his own people. He must pursue the real enemy. He couldn't be distracted discussing what he should have done.

He'd learned from his father to give him credit for good, and take the blame for wrong. He tried that approach with Whitcome, "What have I done in comparison with you? Haven't you gleaned the grapes of Ephraim better than our spoils of Abiezer? You have captured and destroyed two great leaders of Midian. What have I done in comparison?"

Whitcome swallowed.

Gideon gave him time. "I merely ran them into your hands. Who am I, among such great warriors?" He gestured to those who stood with Whitcome.

Whitcome adjusted his sword and dropped his hand. "We did catch two of the leaders: Oreb and Zeeb."

Gideon extended his arm to shake and embrace him. "God is worthy."

Whitcome took his arm and they embraced.

But You Have Not Obeyed Me

Gideon couldn't waste time talking, but knew it was important for Whitcome to tell his story. "How'd you do it?"

Whitcome smiled, "We overtook Oreb at the boulder just before crossing the Jordan. He was killed there by my son's arrow."

Gideon looked at the lad to whom he gestured and nodded.

"While our archers were shooting at their camels, they reached the trees." He pointed. "There by the River. They were sheltered. Radford's winepress lay hidden under its limbs. And so did Radford. He threw his knife and struck Zeeb in the chest. He fell from his camel and died. We surrounded his soldiers easily after that."

Gideon laughed. "What victory you have brought!"

Whitcome nodded.

Cael gestured to leave.

Gideon embraced Whitcome again. "I must cross the River to finish off any stragglers returning to their land. Will you continue to block the River from any others who come?"

Whitcome nodded. He drew his sword and pointed to the camels and horses they had seized. "We are delivered from the Midianites."

Gideon smiled. "We are indeed."

Gideon, with his 300 men, crossed the Jordan River. The place was narrow and the water was low, but the men were tired. Half-way across, Gideon watched his men struggle. He hadn't eaten much the night before. They had fought through the night and day. His stomach rumbled. He reached the other side, stumbling out of the river. He caught Cael by the shoulder, "How are you doing?"

Cael wrung out his cloak and tightened his sandals. "Not used to running so much."

Gideon smiled. Cael wouldn't tell him how weak he really was. He didn't want to be left behind.

Gideon looked into the canopy of fig trees, growing along the river bank. They weren't in season, nor did any fruit still cling to the branches.

They must have food soon.

He touched Cael's back. "I'll run ahead and ask for food. Catch up when you can."

"Wait!"

Gideon looked across the River. Purah was stumbling into the water, almost drowning himself to catch up with him. Gideon laughed. "Don't you know the meaning of rest?"

Purah gasped unable to answer for some time. "When you rest, I'll rest."

Gideon laughed. "I'll rest as you cross the River."

Purah half-walked, half-swam the river to reach the other side. He was still winded and stumbled out of the water as Gideon grabbed him. "Must you always try to be by my side?"

Purah stood. "I can't advise you from the other side of the mountain, can I?"

Gideon laughed. "Come on then, but don't slow me down."

When they came to Succoth, the men of the town stood across the road that entered their town.

Gideon approached the man who appeared to be their leader. "Please give bread to my men. They are weak from battle. We pursue the kings of Midian."

The man was slow in answering. "Do you have the kings already, that we should give you bread?"

Gideon pointed across the River. "Ephraim has killed two. We only chase two more."

The man shook his head. "Without victory, we can't help."

Gideon pointed to the stragglers of the Midianite army running through their village street. "We have the victory. We just have to claim it."

The man spat at Gideon. "You have no victory without those kings."

Gideon wiped the spit off his face, took a drink of his water-skin slowly, then stepped forward and grabbed the man by his tunic and held him to his face, "When we have the last king, I will return. And when I do, I will thrash your bodies with thorns and briers." He threw the man away from him.

The man landed hard on the ground. He jumped up and brushed himself off, looking at the group of men that stood behind him.

Gideon looked at his men who had joined him. "Let's go." He didn't look back.

The man called after Gideon, "You come back and try."

From there Gideon and his men traveled to Penuel. Again men from the town met him before their village. He almost begged for bread. Some of his men could barely walk. His own body felt hollow and weak.

The men shook their heads.

Gideon pointed to their high place of worship, "When I return safely, I'll tear down this tower."

He turned to go.

The leader of Penuel yelled to his retreating back. "Those are bold words for a man who has been controlled by the Midianites for seven years!"

Gideon didn't respond but kept pursuing the Midianite army.

After passing Succoth and Penuel without receiving food, Gideon and his men were discouraged and faint. They passed through the fields of another small village. They gleaned from the wheat, chewing on the fresh kernels. They drank from their waterskins and felt refreshed enough to continue.

Gideon placed his hand on Purah's shoulder. "And you, my advisor. I'm thankful you finally caught up to me and stayed with us."

Purah nodded. "All I could think of was to catch up with you. Now I can only think of how great food would taste."

CHAPTER 27

The Midianites with their allies of the east and the Amalekites had marched into Israel. Their swordsmen had numbered 135,000. They had camels and horses. They had skilled soldiers and kings; 120,000 men had fallen from Mount Gilboa through the Haron Pass to the wilderness. Two kings were reported as killed on the other side of Jordan. Only Kings Zebah and Zalmunna remained. When they arrived at Karkor, they set up camp with their remaining 15,000 men. They did not guess that the Israelite army still pursued them.

Gideon had his 300 men and what they held in their hand and their God. They reached Karkor as the sun was setting.

They came over the rise of the hill. Before them spread the remaining Midianite army of 15,000, making camp.

Gideon had mentally anticipated meeting them and finishing the battle. Now as the sun was setting, he felt he should be finished. He wanted rest, but rest for him now meant rest for the enemy. They were close to their enemy's territory, where recruits could be summoned.

His men were exhausted. They had gleaned from wheat fields they'd walked through, but they'd had nothing substantial for the entire day. Gideon didn't know how long he could even stay on his feet.

He watched his men. They'd been dragging since the last wheat field they had gleaned from. When he lifted his head and saw the campsite before him, his eyes lightened.

Purah seemed to read his thoughts. "They make their camp as if they don't expect pursuit. They're closer to their home; they're confident we didn't follow."

Gideon looked at Purah. "Hurrying in battle can mean lives."

Purah smiled. "Aren't we on God's time?"

Gideon looked again at his men. Three hundred against 15,000 still seemed like a feat. He sighed.

Purah added, "Didn't God promise victory?"

Gideon nodded. "But, we have the victory."

"With two kings still alive?"

Gideon's shoulders drooped. "We'll attack once the sun is down. That will allow us some rest."

When the sun went down and the camp was quiet, they circled the Midianite camp from the east, blocking any escape to the cities of Nobah and Jogbehah.

They approached the campsite, seeking out any guards. No alarm was given as Gideon's men entered one tent after another and left none alive.

Purah called him over to their camel corral. "Look at this, Gideon."

The moon had risen, shedding light over a roped area where two camels wore blankets. Golden ornaments in the shape of crescent moons and stars dangled from their harnesses and reins.

Gideon whispered, "Not only are their kings decorated for easy identification, but their camels."

"Without camels, they must run, just like us." Gideon looked for Cael. He motioned for him to take the camels. A running king would be easier to catch than a riding king. Cael strung together the camels and led them from camp.

By the time someone alerted the camp, it was too late.

Two kings fled with their army.

Gideon pursued them, overtaking them easily on foot.

But You Have Not Obeyed Me

When the kings, Zalmunna and Zebah, were tied and bound, the army of Gideon rested.

Cael brought the camels to Gideon while they rested. Gideon approached them warily, remembering his first encounter with them.

Purah slid the blanket from the camel and handed it to Gideon.

Gideon fingered the golden ornaments. Crescent moons symbolized the god of fertility. Life and death depended upon the light from both the moon and the sun.

Purah started ripping them from the blanket. "We won't need charms to remember God. He has given us the victory."

"Wait! Wait!"

Purah stopped, looking questioningly at Gideon. "We aren't going to worship their gods anymore. Are we?"

Gideon ran his hands down his tunic. "Of course not, but the ornaments are gold."

Purah raised his eyebrows. "But God has given us the victory."

Gideon took the gold. He held it like it was his right to have.

Purah looked at him strangely, but handed him the others ripped from the blanket. "Do you want the purple robes and blankets from the camel, too."

Gideon held the blanket to his chest. It was soft. No wind would blow through this material. He looked into Purah's face, measuring his words. "We're permitted battle spoils, aren't we? Didn't Joshua allow his men their due? We'll take it back with us. Haven't they stolen from us these seven years?"

Purah nodded. He gave Gideon the blanket he had pulled from the other camel.

Gideon motioned to the kings. "Bind their hands."

Cael interrupted, "Wouldn't it be easier to kill them now?"

Gideon nodded. "The other two kings were killed at Ephraim, without witnesses. Our clan needs to see victory and know deliverance."

Purah laughed, "Rub it in your father's face, a little, eh?"

Gideon shrugged and smiled. "Perhaps."

Purah gestured to their robes. "You'll allow them to wear their robes?"

Gideon shrugged. "Why not. We will have them soon enough. Does the king make the robe, or does the robe make the king?"

Cael pointed toward the camel herd. "What do you want with these?"

Gideon had learned to hate them for what they meant to his people. They brought destruction to his village They starved his family. He had no use for them. "Kill them."

Purah nodded. "You could sell them to neighboring countries."

Gideon spat. "So they could return when we aren't ready? No, kill them and we will eat."

Purah pulled his knife.

Cael stepped forward to stop him. "I'll rope his front leg and bend it back first, so it doesn't kick you."

Purah stepped back quickly. "Good idea."

After Cael roped its front leg, he nodded to Purah.

Purah again stepped forward.

Cael stopped him again. "Aim between his front legs on his chest. Stab deep."

Purah looked at him. "How did you become so skilled at killing camels?"

Cael shrugged. "All animals' hearts lie deep within their chests. But I've seen too many incautious servants of Joash's get picked up and thrown by the teeth of the camel they were trying to kill."

Purah winced. He extended his sword to Gideon, "Do you want the honors?"

Gideon looked at Cael then back at the camel. "What do you think we could get for them in Nobah?"

Purah stepped back more. "A lot more than a meal."

"This *is* a king's camel," Cael added.

Gideon gestured to the camel struggling with his front leg tied back. "Do you know enough to take care of them until we sell them?"

But You Have Not Obeyed Me

Cael shrugged. "All animals need food, water, and shelter. These things need less."

Gideon shook his head. "I've seen them empty my barn of its grain in a matter of moments and slurp my spring dry just as fast."

Cael's eyebrows lifted. "After going without for days. It seems merited."

Purah looked at Gideon. "If I didn't know better, I'd think you were reconsidering. Why do you hate them so?"

Gideon grunted and turned away. "It's just a beast. Why should I hate it?"

Purah pressed, "You do. Cael, look how he purses his lips together, almost like when he approaches Joash."

Gideon walked away without saying anything more.

They ate and warmed themselves over a fire fed by camel dung. They felt good.

Gideon posted a guard over the kings and their camels.

As they started back to their own land, they didn't run as they had when they left. But they hurried. They had news of deliverance. Of victory. Of success.

Gideon and his men attacked Penuel, killing its men. After taking the city, Gideon led his men to the hill outside the city. They destroyed the pillar and altar.

From the hill, Gideon looked at the city. "Joshua warned us we'd become like the people we conquered, if we forgot God." It was too easy to forget.

They traveled through the wilderness, where many of their people sought refuge from the Midianite oppression. Nothing grew without great effort. No streams fed the cities.

As they approached Succoth, Cael captured a youth outside its walls and brought him to Gideon.

Gideon fingered the hilt of his sword. "Who are your leaders?"

The youth noticed Gideon's hand and swallowed, shifting back and forth on his feet.

After a silent pause, Gideon smacked his sword in his open palm. "Give me the names of all the rulers of your city."

The lad backed into Purah who stood behind him. He jumped as if he'd been stabbed. He regained his footing, and stammered, "I'm not sure, I can remember all of them."

Gideon smiled and stepped toward him, holding the young man close to him. He lowered his voice to almost a whisper, "Start with whom you know."

The youth barely mumbled.

"Speak louder."

He gave more names.

When he had finished, Gideon had seventy-seven names.

Gideon turned to his men. "Find and bring them here."

When they were brought, Gideon stood before them.

Some lifted their chins in scorn. One, who had been the spokesman for the group before, glared at them. "We told you, don't bother us without the kings."

Gideon shrugged and waited.

Gideon motioned Purah to bring the kings from his tent.

As they were paraded before the seventy-seven men, Gideon noticed, with a concealed smiled, that their eyes widened. Their mouths opened in surprise.

Gideon's smile widened as they gawked at the king's purple robes and their amulets that jangled from their sleeves and hems.

It had been good to allow them to keep their robes for now.

"You taunted me, saying 'Are the kings already in your hand, that we should give you bread? Behold your requested kings.'" Gideon motioned to his men. "You made my men go hungry, weary from battle." He paused while he studied each man. "What did I promise when we returned with victory?"

The princes and leaders remained silent, not meeting Gideon's gaze.

Gideon paced in front of the men. "I told you I'd return. Here I am. What else did I tell you?" He paused as he looked over them.

But You Have Not Obeyed Me

"No one remembers? Let me tell you. That I would thrash you with thorns." He walked away from the group and motioned to his men.

They grabbed them and forced them through the hills covered in thorn bushes.

The sun grew hot.

Sweat dripped from their bodies.

Many had been seized from their homes without a cloak. Now the sun beat upon their uncovered faces.

Thorns gouged their legs and arms, shredding their tunics as they were marched through the bushes.

The city leaders stumbled, fell, and refused to rise. They pled for mercy.

Purah turned to Gideon. "Are they as tired as we were after fighting through the night and pursuing the army all day without food?"

Gideon shrugged and turned away.

The other warriors shook their heads and pushed them harder.

When the sun set and the cold began to creep into their uncovered arms, Gideon called a halt.

They would not soon forget Gideon's victory, and their refusal to help.

Gideon nodded to his men. "Let's go home."

They had become a tight group of men. Men who faced their fear because the cause was more worthy than the reason for their fear. Men who followed a leader who knew truth and obeyed. As his men walked ahead and behind him, Gideon held his head up, proud to be a part of them.

As they drew closer to home, Gideon's steps seemed less enthusiastic. The last few days of battle and travel had changed him. But would the people at home have changed? Probably not. Why would they, without conflict? Didn't conflict sharpened a man? But shouldn't oppression have taught their people about

God? It seemed oppression only reinforced self-reliance, selfishness and self-destruction. Gideon shook his head. It required constant focus to remember God.

They reached the River. After the harsh sun of the wilderness, the green foliage from the trees around the water gave rest to his sun-scorched eyes and parched skin. He kneeled to refill his waterskin and smelled the freshness of green plants around him.

With his men rested from battle and satisfied with food, crossing the River waseasy. Victory gave a lightness to their step. Gideon sensed it in his spirit; he saw it with his men. They joked with each other. They even sang. It was like they could now live. He found himself smiling.

Even as he saw what freedom was doing for his men, he noticed the two kings trudging to keep up. Bondage sapped their energy. When freedom lies within a man, no obstacle can bind him on the outside. But without it, a man is broken and incomplete.

He dropped back to walk beside the kings. "What did you think when you heard us on the hill of Moreh?"

Zebah pulled his robe closer around him, as if the memory made him insecure. "My messenger had informed me of your God's power the night you attacked. He told of your God's power. I went to sleep thinking, 'What a mistake we had made to come.'"

Zalmunna nodded. "When I heard your trumpets and the crashing, I rushed from my tent in time to see all your lights surrounding us. My heart melted for fear."

Gideon smiled. "What made you start killing your own soldiers?"

Zebah's brow wrinkled. "We didn't kill our own."

It was Gideon's turn to be confused. "Who killed them then?"

"Your men."

Gideon gestured to the 300 men around him. "None of my men are missing."

Zebah studied Gideon more closely. "These men resembled you, sons of a king."

Gideon scratched the back of his neck, trying to think who

they could mean. Could they mean his brothers? They had lapped like a dog and been told to stay in their tents. Had they entered the Midianite camp against his orders? Or was this afterward, when Gideon had pursued the fleeing army? He wasn't sure he'd ever know. But realization came that his brothers were gone. "They were my brothers. Sons of my mother."

They walked in silence.

Gideon lowered his head and considered. He found his voice. "If only you had let them live, I would not kill you. But now . . ." He shook his head. He couldn't finish his thought.

As they approached their village, Gideon watched his men strut and shout with victory. It was easy to walk with their shoulders back and head high when they were conquerors! Before he'd had to force his feet to move; now he wanted to dance!

News of victory spread.

People joined their procession.

Gideon had been right. His village needed to see the victory.

He led them to his father's house. Even from afar, he could see his father watching them from the doorway.

As they neared, Gideon caught his father's eye. He couldn't remember his father looking with such pride at him.

Jether ran to greet him, "Abba! You brought victory!"

Gideon hugged him.

He commanded his men to bring the kings before him.

He handed Jether his sword. "Victory is complete when these kings are dead."

He held the sword suspended between them.

Jether's eyes widened as he looked from Gideon to the kings. He backed away, shaking his head. He couldn't return Gideon's gaze.

Gideon encouraged him, "They've killed your uncles. Rise. Kill them."

But Jether continued to refuse.

Gideon glanced at his father. He read his disdain for Jether. Gideon swallowed and lowered his sword. He would have felt proud to have Jether complete their victory. But he could see his fear and knew he couldn't push him past it.

Zebah taunted, "Rise up yourself and fall on us."

Zalmunna spurred him, "For as the man, so is his strength."

Gideon raised his sword and stabbed both kings. He wiped his blade on the grass at his father's feet.

Gideon yanked the crescent ornaments from their robes and threw them at his father's feet. "Payment for the ox I sacrificed to the Lord."

His clansmen fell on their knees before him. "Rule over us, Gideon, both you and your son, for you've delivered us from the Midianite's hands."

Gideon looked at his father. He saw the pride in his eyes. He had finally pleased his father. But this was not his doing. It was God's.

He turned to the men before him. He felt disgusted. These men would follow him, now that victory had come. Weren't they the same men who had days before came as a mob to kill him? They were no different than the men of Succoth, who wouldn't feed them when they were hungry until they proved their worth in battle.

Nor had these men stayed in battle. They had been sent home, to fearful to fight.

Gideon had told them there was nothing to be ashamed of, if they were afraid.

But now at their request, he saw them differently. They couldn't stand beside him in battle, and now they wanted him to rule over them in peace? Could he trust them? Would they change with another wind?

Before he could answer, Rakaal stepped from behind his father and approached him.

Gideon watched her come. What did she want? Would she now embarrass him publicly before the entire village? He had to calm the whirlwind of emotions that she stirred inside him.

She stopped before him and looked him in the eye. Without saying a word, she stepped behind him and grabbed his arm.

Gideon had to remind himself to close his mouth.

Now she would in support him publicly? After everyone but he had known of her previous deception?

He would have to sift through his emotions for her in private. He patted her hand and left it over hers.

The men still waited for his answer. They seemed to assume he would accept.

Maybe that was why Rakaal was by his side.

He cleared his throat; then drank from his waterskin. He coughed and looked at his son. His head was bowed as if he knew he'd disappointed him. Gideon took Jether's chin and lifted it to see into his eyes.

Jether's chin trembled and his eyes brimmed with tears.

He answered the men, without his eyes leaving his son's face, "I won't rule over you, nor shall my son rule over you."

Rakaal's hand trembled on his arm.

Would she leave again? Or would she stay by his side?

There was light in Jether's eyes. He hadn't been crushed by his refusal.

Gideon paused, looking upward. Finally he studied the men around him. "The Lord shall rule over you."

He pointed to those who had fought with him, "But I would ask each of you to give me an earring from his spoil."

The Ishmaelites had fought with the Midianites. They were known for their gold earrings.

Purah laughed. "Should be an easy request."

Purah yanked off the robes from the dead kings and spread them at Gideon's feet.

The men who'd fought with Gideon reached into their belonging and stepped forward as each fulfilled his request, throwing an earring on the robe.

When all the men had given, Gideon looked at the gold collected there. He then looked at the hillside where the altar of the Lord now stood. He licked his lips, his voice had grown hoarse with emotion. "The Lord is worthy."

The clansmen left first. Then, standing before his 300 men, Gideon swallowed the lump in his throat. In the short days of battle, these men had become closer than brothers. How could he express his gratitude, respect, and pride for their service? "We fought, in spite of our fears, for the victory promised by God." He grabbed each man's hand and embraced them.

Their families finally tore them away to return to their own homes.

His father remained standing by his door. He had watched the entire procedure. Now he offered his hand. "Welcome home with victory."

Gideon couldn't remember the last time his father had touched him, other than to administer correction or control. The effort it took for him to extend his hand and embrace his father showed how far Gideon's courage had brought him.

No other words were shared.

Gideon gathered the corners of the robe to carry the gold home.

Jether walked beside him.

Gideon was encouraged by him at his side. He placed his hand on Jether's shoulder as they walked. "You were afraid to kill the kings?"

Jether nodded, keeping his head bowed.

Gideon squeezed his shoulder. He remembered his fears. His own father belittling him hadn't helped him conquer his fear.

God also knew his fears. But He didn't belittle or scorn them; He gave assurance. Gideon hoped he could do the same as God had done for him. "Son, look at me."

Jether raised his head, his eyes brimmed with tears.

"Do you think I wasn't afraid?"

Jether nodded. His hand twisting his tunic.

Gideon shook his head. "I did what was right, even though I was afraid."

Jether's eyes widened. "You, Abba? Afraid?"

Gideon patted his shoulder. "I was afraid. I told God my fears. But do you know what He told me?"

Jether shook his head. His eyes not leaving his father's face.

"He was with me." Gideon looked toward his house.

He heard Rakaal walking behind them. His own heart seemed torn by her presence. What would happen when she grew tired of him again? Did he want to trust her?

He turned his thoughts back to what God had promised. He spoke more to himself than to Jether, "I had to believe God when He promised victory. I had to trust God when I was afraid. And He proved faithful."

Gideon glanced back at Rakaal as he finished. He wasn't sure how he felt about her.

Did she return only for the victory and gold? Or would she support him when he made a mistake and needed reassurance?

The knot in his gut returned. He had lived without it for days.

Battles helped him forget.

Now the battle was over, he must return to normal life.

Would that be enough for Rakaal to stay with him? Or would something else draw her away?

Would something else draw him away from God? So easy for him to hold a grudge, yet expect God to forget his own faithlessness.

When they arrived home, Rakaal sat at his feet. Her eyes sparkled in the candlelight's flame. "What are you going to do with all this gold?"

She sat like a queen. Her question reminded him of her fickleness. She hadn't come for him, but for the gold.

He brushed her question aside. "I'm hungry."

Rakaal built a fire and made flatbread.

Gideon watched her, mesmerized by how she moved, how beautiful she still was. It reminded him of why he had married her.

When Gideon had eaten, he pointed to the mound of gold before him. "Now about that gold . . ."

She leaned against him, actually listening to what he had to say.

He liked the feeling. He paused, relishing her respect. He fingered a gold piece. The shine seemed deceiving, like her beauty. But he still wanted it. Did he want to be deceived by her support? He drew a breath. There was much to consider. "There's about 1,700 shekels here, not counting the crescent ornaments and pendants."

Rakaal gasped.

Her response encouraged Gideon, "I'll make an ephod, a gold breastplate for worship, and put it in Shechem where our victory will be remembered."

Rakaal squeezed his arm, interrupting his thoughts. Her voice was almost a whine, "You won't give away all your gold, will you?"

Gideon felt elated by her touch. Almost like when they had courted. "What would you want me to do with it?"

"Couldn't I have a few of the crescent ornaments?"

Gideon squeezed her. "But they're from the camels."

"It would be enough for me." She let go of his arm and snatched the ornaments.

In that revelation, Gideon knew what he must do.

Gideon permitted Rakaal to come home, but didn't allow her back into his heart.

Gideon followed his father's example, by taking other wives and concubines. He would never allow his heart to be broken by trusting too much in another.

He had seventy sons.

In Shechem where he worshipped and wore the ephod of gold, he had a concubine.

She gave him a son.

He named him Abimelech.

By placing the gold ephod in Shechem as a reminder of their victory, his people remembered—not that God was worthy, but that they were capable of fighting and winning. Thus the gold became a snare to Gideon and the people.

God's people lived undisturbed forty years, the remainder of Gideon's days.

His village deferred to his leadership.

Gideon died and was buried in the tomb of his father Joash, in Ophrah of the clan of Abiezrites.

When he died, the sons of Israel returned to Baal-berith.

The people did not show kindness to Gideon's descendants, in spite of the good he had done to Israel.

Nor did they remember God was worthy and had delivered them from their enemies.

PART VI
ABIMELECH
JUDGES 8:33-9:57

CHAPTER 28

Now Gideon had not been dead long before Abimelech, Gideon's son by the concubine living in Shechem, attended a wedding for one of his relations. During the wedding, after much wine was served, Abimelech boasted, "I could lead the city to greatness."

Another protested, "You have the help of your seventy brothers."

Abimelech stood and raised his wine vessel. "Which is better for you, to obey the whims of seventy men or just one man?" He paused for them to consider. "I am your bone and flesh."

Others picked up his cause. "He *is* our relative."

Abimelech looked around his relatives. He had only meant it as a jest, but they were considering it. The more he thought about it, the more he knew he could rule better than his brothers. He had never been allowed to rule; his brothers squelched any of his attempts with criticism about his mother, making him feel inferior and stupid. His brothers would never step aside and give him the city. He must ensure they wouldn't interfere. "What will you give to help me rule?"

One man lifted his vessel and promised, "Ten pieces of silver."

Abimelech nodded. "Your help is but a start." He looked around at his other uncles and cousins. "Who else?"

When the men had finished their vows, Abimelech had seventy pieces of silver. He bowed to them. "You honor me with your confidence and means."

Abimelech went to the temple of Baal-berith. He found men who neither worked nor showed wisdom, but loitered at the temple for the next sacrifices.

Baal-berith was an addicting cult. Its worshippers carried small idols in their pockets or tied around their necks. When the urge for pleasure pressed upon them, they would kiss the idol. It sufficed until they could return to the temple where they could find fulfilment for their sensual needs.

These men never left the "service" of the temple.

They couldn't be trusted. They were temple grazers. All temples needed them. Not all were willing to sacrifice their children to the gods. These men coerced "willing" participants.

Abimelech could use them, because they were void of any conscience. Right was determined by what they must do to be pleased. He called for their attention, jingling the silver in the bag tied at his belt. "Looking for more than sacrifices that will be over after the night?"

The men moved closer to Abimelech. But because they were thieves, they didn't crowd too close. They kept their hands on their knife handles, and listened with skeptic ears.

Abimelech lowered his voice to a whisper. "The city has made me leader."

One man challenged, "What's that to us?"

"Because, if I lead this city, I determine when we sacrifice." Abimelech stared at him until he dropped his gaze. He knew what would motivate these men. He nodded toward the temple stairs. "I also provide the women for the sacrifices."

One man, leaning on one of the temple pillars, asked, "What must we do?"

Abimelech smiled. "Remove the other leaders."

The man straightened. "Aren't you're one of Gideon's sons?"

Abimelech had never felt proud of his heritage. His brothers reminded him of his inferior status and his lack of an inheritance.

He ignored the man as he surveyed the circle of men. "You'll be well paid."

One man, shorter than Abimelech by a palm's length, shifted. "I want payment before we began."

Abimelech fingered the silver through the bag. "I said you'd be paid well."

The man's laugh scorned Abimelech. "And we trust you, because?"

Abimelech held his eyes without wavering. "You speak of trust when no man trusts you?"

The man didn't lower his eyes, nor did he waver. He shoved both hands deeper into his pockets. He took his time in returning Abimelech's gaze. "I trust no man."

Abimelech steeled his expression to hide his surprise. This man's indifference might be just what he'd needed. "What's your name?"

"What's a name but a requirement to fulfill or a dream to be sought or a hope to be found. No man needs to know my name." The words were spoken, not with spite or resentment, but merely to give boundaries, a warning not to cross his line.

Normal business was conducted on knowing their name and heritage. Wasn't that why Abimelech was willing to destroy his father's name? He was tired of being called the son of his father's concubine. By eliminating his half-brothers, wouldn't he become the son and rightful heir of who Gideon was? He'd be the son of Israel's judge.

This man questioned him, while he did nothing but loiter at the temple? Abimelech swallowed his rising anger. How could he rule a city when he couldn't even pay men to follow him? He didn't know how to respond. He waited.

The other men seemed to wait for this man's response. He led these men with some invisible cord. If Abimelech could win him, he would have them all.

The silence seemed awkward. Like he was being evaluated. Abimelech shifted under the scrutiny.

The man shrugged, finally deeming him worthy. "When I choose to respond, they call me, 'Zebul.'"

Abimelech breathed a sigh, relieved by his response. What would he have done to force an answer from him? "You do well to respond, Zebul."

Before the man could say anything more, Abimelech addressed the others, "We'll leave at the break of dawn. Meet on the north road to the city." Without another look, he strode away. His silver jingled against his leg with each step.

The hair on the back of his neck rose. Was he safe to turn his back on this group of men? He jingled his silver louder as if that would hide his pounding heart and still his troubled doubts.

That night as Abimelech rehearsed his plan to his wife, she listened without comment. He stuffed his mouth with a piece of flatbread filled with lamb. With his mouth full, he asked, "What do you think?"

Sable swallowed her mouthful. She didn't look at him when she spoke, but stared behind his head. "Your brothers haven't treated you well, but—"

"I'm nothing more than dung on their sandals. Always giving me the crust of bread when they took our best wine and sweet rolls."

Sable licked her lips. "I like the crusts of bread."

Abimelech ripped another piece of flatbread from the circle in front of him. "This flatbread is hard." He scooped from the pot between them. "The meat is tough." His tone harsher than before, he listed what his brothers had done to him.

Sable had stopped eating and rubbed her chin. "But do these things warrant death?"

Abimelech spewed his uneaten food. "If I'm to lead this city, they must be gone!"

Sable was silent for a moment. "But do you *want* to lead?"

He shouted at her. "Of course I want to lead! I'm tired of my brothers telling me what to do."

Sable placed another warmed flatbread in front of Abimelech, bending it to make sure it wasn't hard, then sat back. "Doing what you want and leading are two different things. Are you sure you want to solve the problems of a city? You don't like dealing with difficulties of our harvest . . ."

Abimelech bellowed, as if by being louder he could prove his point better. "What has that got to do with ruling a city?"

Sable drank from her vessel. She leaned forward. "Maybe nothing, maybe everything. If the people don't have food, they'll blame you."

"Don't be stupid. How could our people ever go without food? Our valley is the most fertile land in the entire country."

Sable refilled her vessel from the pitcher in front of them. "This is good wine."

He hated when she tried to redirect him. As if he was some child to be distracted.

She laughed lightly. "Remember the wine came at great cost—and you didn't like all the problems you had with the workers." She spoke in a soothing voice. "I don't know; you don't like making decisions—"

"This is entirely different."

Sable sighed and conceded. "Maybe, but you—"

"I want to do this. I must do it."

Sable finished the wine in her vessel. "If that's what makes you happy, then do it. But is it worth murdering all your brothers?"

"That's what makes it worthwhile. How could it not?"

Shechem's grape harvests were always plenteous. Streams flowed from springs through the summer, giving their area more water than most of the country. Their wines were known throughout the country for their sweet, rich, mellow flavor. Isn't that what had brought his father to his city?

The group that met with Abimelech outside the city left Shechem's harvest behind them as the sun peaked over the mountain.

The distance to Ophrah took a day's journey. Abimelech liked the idea of ruling Shechem. Normally his half-brothers would dictate what new regulations he must follow, while they took payment from Shechem's harvest. They controlled the temple sacrifices, often giving cast-offs from their own temple.

Abimelech shook his head. Much of his plan had sprouted under the wine's influence and his arrogance of the moment. Now with time to consider, twenty worthless men from the temple, and men from Shechem who wanted to watch how their silver was used, he began to doubt. Did he want to lead? Or as his wife suggested, did he merely want to do what he wanted?

He looked at the group of men who traveled with him. They followed him. He had enough men with him to move the entire town of Ophrah. He could boss people around like his brothers did. Didn't that make him a leader?

He loosened his cloak as the sun warmed him. He kissed the idol strung on his neck and looked back at the men following. Perhaps he shouldn't judge them so harshly. He drank from his waterskin, brushing against his hidden knife as he returned his waterskin to his belt. The bulge in his sleeve cuff where he'd sewn the silver so it wouldn't jingle reminded him to be alert to these men.

A voice spoke by his side. He jumped.

"What's your plan?"

Abimelech swallowed. He'd allowed someone to creep up beside him. He couldn't do that and live long with these men. When he glanced sideways, it was Zebul. He should have known. He swallowed his anger. If Abimelech didn't win him, he would have a dangerous enemy. And who would follow him then?

Abimelech swallowed his condescending response, "We eliminate other leaders."

Zebul nodded. "How?"

Zebul hadn't questioned why he was killing his own family.

Abimelech spoke with greater confidence. "My plan is simple: to kill them in bed."

Zebul rubbed his beard. "And their families?"

He hadn't considered the family members. He pushed off his hood, so he could glance sideways at the man beside him. If killing his brothers wasn't repulsive to this man, he could show his power publicly. "I make my brothers pay for their father's destruction of the altar and the tower—"

Zebul tilted his head. "Making a new altar would show your power."

Zebul accepted his plan without hesitation. There was something that prompted Abimelech to ask, "What would you do with the families?"

"The women—" Then he shrugged.

Abimelech understood. The temple was hard on the prostitutes. Often they took too much wine and drugs. When they were no longer useful, they were thrown in the streets to die. Regular replacements were needed. Abimelech nodded. "We'll take what women would serve our temple's needs."

"And the others?" Zebul continued to look ahead, giving Abimelech no indication how he should respond.

Abimelech stumbled over a tree root. Recovering his steps, he massaged his cloak where a knife lay hidden. Abimelech needed more time to think. This man had challenged him before he had come, and now acted as if he was helping plan. Why had he decided to help? "You don't trust many people, do you?"

The man laughed. "Neither do you, or you wouldn't hang onto that knife you think you've hidden in your cloak."

Abimelech dropped his hand from his side. Had he been that obvious? He continued walking, but didn't respond to the man's comment. Zebul made him feel uneasy. He couldn't hide anything from him. Yet he wanted his approval.

During their noon break, Abimelech refilled his waterskin and stretched his legs as he sat against a tree. He grabbed a dried fig from his sack.

Zebul sat in front of him and gestured to his sack, "I'd like one."

Abimelech stared at him. He didn't like anyone demanding from him. It reminded him of his half-brothers. But he couldn't make Zebul an enemy. He needed him. Abimelech tightened his lips, forcing himself not to say anything and pushed the sack toward him.

Zebul seemed not to notice his hesitation. He grabbed a handful and bit a fig tentatively. "Mmm. Sweet. Ever notice without the skin of the fig, the fruit is just seeds and sweetness? The skin gives the fruit its texture." He chewed, savoring it.

Wasn't Zebul just a worthless, homeless tramp? Abimelech considered the fig in his own hand. He took a bite. The skin *did* give it texture.

Zebul dug into the sack for an almond. In one smooth, quick chop, he unsheathed his knife and cracked the shell while he held the nut between two fingers.

Abimelech reminded himself to shut his mouth. He hadn't even seen him unsheathe his knife, let alone strike. And he hadn't even nicked his fingers. Yet there was the unshelled nut.

Abimelech stopped chewing to watch Zebul pick the meat from the shell with the tip of his knife. He shoved the meat into his mouth with his knife and slid it off with his tongue.

"Take an almond," Zebul crunched and talked at the same time, "Its fiber adds to the sweetness of the fig to give a sweet-salty taste. Perfect for sustaining us on our journey."

Abimelech found himself reaching into his sack for an almond to test what Zebul had said. He didn't want to show his ineptitude with his knife, so he dug until he found a broken almond piece, already shelled. He chewed with part of a fig still in his mouth. The mixed flavors did give a feeling of fullness. He watched Zebul with new respect. Maybe he wasn't so worthless.

Zebul finished his handful, shelling the almonds as before. He drank from his waterskin and sighed. "Makes water more precious."

But You Have Not Obeyed Me

Abimelech felt for his water; he needed a drink, too. He drank. It *did* taste good.

Zebul leaned closer to Abimelech and lowered his voice. "It *is* necessary to remove your brothers."

Abimelech's plan had been approved. He pushed his shoulders back.

Zebul's scraggly beard didn't seem so threatening, instead it enhanced his sincerity. There was more to Zebul than being a worthless tramp.

Zebul wasn't finished. "But you aren't a leader."

Abimelech choked on his water. What was he saying? That he wouldn't help him?

Zebul lowered his voice and Abimelech leaned closer. "You kill your brothers, not to rule, but to make yourself feel worthy." Zebul took another drink and wiped his mouth with the back of his hand. He leaned against the boulder behind him. He stroked his beard and shook his head as if considering. "It won't be enough."

Abimelech pulled away from Zebul. How did he know how his brothers made him feel? He could lead. He'd do a better job than his brothers!

Zebul lowered his voice, making Abimelech lean forward to hear. "When you compare yourself with someone else, you'll never be good enough." Zebul pulled his knife from his sheath and stroked it with the tip of his finger. His touch was so light, it didn't bring blood, in spite of how sharp it had been with the shells. Zebul raised his head slowly and stared Abimelech in the eye. "You must become the standard; then you will succeed."

He dropped his knife in its sheath and grabbed an apple from Abimelech's sack. He rubbed it on his dirty sleeve and took a bite. "Sweet. Just like your promises of better sacrifices." He raised his eyebrows and stood, showing he was finished with this conversation. "Better keep your promises." He melted into the crowd.

Abimelech felt like a reprimanded child. But what could he accuse Zebul of saying? He hadn't shown disrespect or insubordination. Had he threatened him? He couldn't tell. Abimelech rehearsed their conversation.

Zebul observed everything.

Abimelech took an apple from the sack and bit into it, chewing slowly. When was the last time he'd noticed what he ate, except to complain about it?

How did Zebul know he couldn't lead? Maybe it was like Sable had said; did he want to lead? He shook his head to dispel his doubts. He *had* to lead. That was why he must kill his brothers.

Zebul made him uncomfortable, and at the same time he wouldn't feel secure without him. By talking with him, he figured out what he should do. Was it his plan or Zebul's? He couldn't tell that either. The thought made him uncomfortable. He stood and called the men together. "Men, here's the plan. Each group will capture several of my brothers. Meet at the base of the hill where we'll sacrifice them. If any opposes you, kill them. By our sacrifices, the gods will confirm before their village that I am leader. Any questions?" He looked around the group. He met Zebul's eyes and glanced away quickly.

Another man stood beside Zebul. He covered his mouth and whispered.

Zebul shook his head slightly, his arms across his chest.

Abimelech stared. He couldn't remember where, but he knew that man. He cleared his throat to hide his momentary pause. "Any questions?"

There were none.

"Let's attack at the same time to avoid anyone escaping." He looked at Zebul for confirmation.

Zebul gave a slight nod.

Abimelech led off down the road again. He wished his pace could outrun his thoughts. But it didn't. Why couldn't he lead? Why did he look to Zebul to help him?

And who was that man beside Zebul?

Instead of answers, Abimelech found he had more questions.

But You Have Not Obeyed Me

The men had refilled their waterskins and taken a break to eat again before completing their journey as the sun was setting. It had been some time since Abimelech had come to his father's village. He never came as a child. Abimelech remembered pestering his mother about seeing his father. When he got older, he felt the tension between her and his father's wives. He also felt the half-brothers' rejection. It was better to stay away. But even the distance couldn't keep him from feeling inferior. When they came to his city, people respected and deferred to his brothers, even when Abimelech stood with them.

Now, Abimelech could hardly wait to prove his worth. His excitement of leading, rather than being forgotten or looked over, consumed him. His steps grew lighter the closer he came to their village.

The road wound through the mountains and brought the group to Gideon's house first. Gideon's name had been changed to Jerubbaal, after he had destroyed the altar of his father. Now Gideon's oldest son, Jether, lived there.

The moon was starting to rise when they approached Jether's house. Abimelech motioned for some of the group to circle the house to prevent escape. He pounded on the door, bouncing on his toes, as he anticipated bringing Jether to his knees.

When the door opened, Abimelech couldn't see who answered, but recognized Jether's voice. "Abimelech! What's wrong?"

Abimelech felt a catch in his throat. He could almost feel Jether's concern. He steeled his resolve with thoughts of ruling without interference. "I must speak with you."

Jether opened the door wider and stepped out, not even putting sandals on his feet.

Abimelech spoke to Zebul at his right. "Seize him."

Zebul grabbed Jether's wrist and wrenched it behind his back, before he had time to respond.

"What is it, Jether?" a voice came from inside his house.

Jether looked first at Abimelech; then to the darkened opening. "It's Abimelech. I'll work it out."

Abimelech laughed and hissed, "This time, big brother, you

will not work it out." He motioned for Zebul to tie him. Abimelech ripped a strip of Jether's tunic and tied it around his mouth. "It's with pleasure I stop your words."

Before he pulled the cloth tight, Jether murmured, "Abimelech, you will always be the cur of the family. My father wouldn't even acknowledge your existence."

Abimelech yanked the cloth tighter and tied it. "Silence! You were always the spoiled, favored one. I will enjoy seeing you die."

Jether's struggles stilled at the words, and his face visibly paled in the moonlight.

Abimelech pushed him toward the mountain. "We waste time. We have others to get."

Before leaving Jether's house, Abimelech pointed to the cellar. "Men, take his wine. We'll need it to sacrifice."

Several men yanked open the door. They returned with full hands.

"Bring it to the mountain." Abimelech pointed to the base of the mountain where his father had once sacrificed to God. He pointed out a group of men. "Take him to the top. Prepare the sacrifice. I'll return with the others."

The process continued.

At last Abimelech hiked the hill. A pile of wood had already been prepared. His brothers were surrounded by guards. He smiled and called for the drums to play. The beat would motivate his men and drown out his brothers' screams. "We'll begin with Jether, the firstborn."

Zebul shoved Jether to the altar.

Several men threw him on the altar.

Zebul raised his sword and with one swift motion, swept down. As his knife hit Jether's neck, he grunted from the exertion.

Jether sucked a final wheeze before his head fell to the ground and rolled to Abimelech's feet.

Abimelech blinked. He hadn't seen Zebul's arm move. He looked at the torches lit around the circle. He kicked the head away from him and turned to his other brothers. "You thought you could lord it over me. Didn't you? This is what happens to

But You Have Not Obeyed Me

those who treat me with disdain." He pointed to another brother. "He's next."

And so the night continued.

As the mound of bodies grew, he instructed the fire to be made hotter to burn their bodies. The wood was heaped high. Their bodies thrown on top.

The smell of burnt flesh and hair filled the air.

Abimelech wrinkled his nose and called for wine.

They drank to their success.

They drank to worship Baal.

They drank for their own pleasure.

Wine masked many things.

More brothers were brought. Some wives were included.

Abimelech smiled. "Baal will indeed be worshipped."

And so his revenge was satisfied as the night progressed.

Zebul pointed to a crowd coming. "The village men come."

Abimelech called, "Baal calls us to sacrifice. He demands we give up the old and prepare for the new. These men have lorded it over you. They have taken the credit for Baal's success. Baal alone should be worshipped."

The drums beat.

The sacrifices continued.

The village men cared not who was sacrificed, as long as they were pleased.

They were not disappointed.

CHAPTER 29

But not all weren't disloyal to Gideon's sons. One man remembered Gideon's victory over the Midianites. He knew his obligation to Gideon's sons. This man left the mob arriving in Ophrah and hurried to find Jotham, Gideon's youngest son. When he arrived, he didn't knock on the door, but called through the window where Jotham slept. "Jotham!"

Jotham stirred, "Hod! What is it?"

"Danger. Abimelech's killing your brothers. Hurry!"

Hod waited outside while Jotham opened the door. "Run to the hills."

Jotham stooped to tighten his sandals. "I must get Hepsiba."

The man pushed him. "I'll bring her. Go!"

Jotham looked back into his house before stepping into the moonlight.

The man pushed him again. "They'll be here soon."

They both looked toward the torches lighting up his lane. The mob was coming.

Jotham embraced the man. "Take care of her. Keep her safe." He let go and ran.

The man entered the house and woke Jotham's family. He carried two of the children and led the others into the orchard. He motioned for them to lie down in the ridge between grape vines.

When he looked back, he saw the glow from the torches had reached the house.

They'd be safe for only a short time. He'd take them to a cave in the mountains. His sister's family would be safe.

The night was spent. Sacrificing was over. The men lay exposed on the mountain, waiting for the sun to warm what their drinks had not. But their hearts remained cold and hardened.

Abimelech lay where he had stumbled and fallen. He reached for his cloak, which he had tossed aside while dancing, to cover his nakedness from the night's worship.

The drums had long since stopped, but the pounding in his head had only begun. He held his head as he struggled to sit up. He alone remained of all his family. He would rule over this people. He'd receive the respect he craved. He would be worthy. He bent over and vomited.

Abimelech kicked a vessel. He chased clumsily after it, as it rolled out of his reach. He licked his lips in anticipation when he finally held it between both hands. Raising it shakily to his lips, he swallowed. Much of it spilled over his chest and dripped down his bare legs. What he managed to pour down his throat burned as he swallowed. He fell, rolled over and closed his eyes. The pounding in his head continued.

The men of Shechem had returned to their city. Not as they had left, as a mob controlled by their desire to destroy and conquer, but as stragglers wasted from sacrificing. Days later when all had returned, they assembled by the pillar of their city under the oak tree, known as the diviner's oak.

Abimelech stood before them. "Men of Shechem, we have achieved complete victory. No longer will you be subject to the

But You Have Not Obeyed Me

rule of many, but only to me, one who knows your needs, lives by your side, and wants your best."

The men raised their voices in assent.

A voice Abimelech recognized as Zebul's rose from the back of the crowd, "Long live King Abimelech!"

Their words grew into a chant that resounded around the hills.

Abimelech stood taller. He raised his arms for silence, bowing his head to acknowledge their praise. "We have done well. Our city will be blessed."

When the men started to leave, Abimelech watched for Zebul in the back of the crowd, "Zebul!"

Zebul turned back.

Abimelech walked the remaining distance between them. "You're swift with your knife. And skillful with people. I remember those who help me. I'll need a lieutenant."

Zebul's eyes flickered to the men who were leaving; then looked down, but said nothing.

Abimelech followed his glance and saw the man who had spoken to Zebul earlier. He was looking back. Abimelech watched him leave before turning back to Zebul. "I'd like you to be my lieutenant." He extended his hand.

Zebul shook Abimelech's hand without looking at him. They embraced.

Abimelech wondered how a king should act around his subordinates. He couldn't seal every oath with a hug. He released his hand as if it were burnt and stepped back, straightening his tunic, nervously looking around to see if any watched. He coughed. "I give you authority to make my reign secure."

Zebul slid his hand down his tunic where his hand rested on his knife handle. "You're in good hands."

After Abimelech had been declared king, Hod returned to his house. He prepared meat, cheese, fruit, and wine and left the city by the southern road. He circled around the city and headed north toward the hills of Gerizim. When he left the road surrounded by hills, he glanced at the many caves in despair. "He could be anywhere." He studied the way he'd come. No one followed him. He called out, "It's Hod. Where are you?"

His voice echoed over the hills as he waited an answer.

Movement high on the hillside caught his eye.

Jotham waved from a cave.

Hod hurried to him. "Shalom." He dropped his bag of food and embraced him. "All is safe?"

Jotham nodded. "By God's great mercy and your provision."

Hod handed the food to Jotham. Only then did he take his waterskin from his belt and drink. He wiped his mouth with the back of his hand. "They've made Abimelech king."

Jotham stopped untying the bundle and looked at him unbelievingly. "They what?"

"Abimelech's been anointed king."

"What about my brothers?"

Hod hesitated, looking at the ground. He fumbled with his waterskin, tying it back on his belt. He wiped his face with his cloak sleeve. He finally lifted his face to meet Jotham's. "They're gone."

"Even Jether?"

Hod nodded. "He was the first sacrificed."

Jotham fell to his knees and wept. "God have mercy!"

Hod kneeled beside him and rested his hand on his back.

When Jotham could control himself, he asked, "What did the men of Ophrah do to stop them?"

Hod coughed and cleared his throat. He couldn't look at Jotham. "I roused them to help . . . . They sacrificed."

"No one stood for right?"

Hod shook his head, "When I woke the men from the village, they thought only of the moment."

Jotham looked back the way Hod had come. "I must return with you."

"You'll be killed." Hod searched Jotham's face. "What can you do?"

But You Have Not Obeyed Me

"I'll warn of judgment."

Hod gestured toward Jotham's children. His wife had joined them. "What about your family?"

When Hod saw Jotham's face, he saw his determination and anger. He wouldn't be able to change his mind.

Discussion was over.

"Your anger will get you killed."

Jotham took the waterskin from the bag Hod had brought and attached it to his belt. "My anger will remind them that God will judge."

Jotham stood on Mount Gerizim and watched the men of Shechem. He could see Abimelech strut among the men, as if he owned them. Jotham breathed out deeply. How could the city change their loyalty so easily and forget what his father and brothers had done for them?

Jotham's anger moved him.

"Listen to me. O men of Shechem, that God may listen to you." His voice carried well down the mountain to the city below. "Once the trees anointed a king over them. They called to the olive tree, 'Reign over us!'

"But the olive tree replied, 'Shall I leave my fatness that honors God and men, and wave over the trees?'

"Then the trees spoke to the fig tree, 'You reign over us!'

"But the fig tree replied, 'Shall I leave my sweetness and good fruit, and rule over trees?'

"Then the trees said to the vine, 'Come and reign over us!'

"But the vine said, 'Shall I leave my new wine, which cheers God and men, to lord it over the trees?'

"Finally all the trees said to the bramble, 'You reign over us!'

"The bramble said to the trees, 'If you anoint me king, take refuge in my shade; but if not, may fire come from my brambles and consume the cedars of Lebanon.'

"Have you treated Jerubbaal and his house well, after my father fought, risked his life, and delivered you from the Midianites' hand? You rise against my father's house, kill his sons, and make Abimelech, son of his maidservant, king over Shechem, because he's your relative! If you have exercised truth and integrity with Gideon and his house this day, rejoice in Abimelech, your king.

"But if not, let fire come from Abimelech and consume the men of Shechem and Beth-millo. And let fire also come from the men of Shechem and Beth-millo to consume Abimelech."

When he had finished, he breathed deeply. His anger had propelled him to speak. Now his loss of all overwhelmed him. He hung his head and swallowed a sob.

He must leave before they sacrificed *him* to the gods. He fled from the place before the men of Shechem could follow and hid, living in Beer.

Abimelech milled among the men of the city as they judged. He had delegated the task to relatives. Judging taxed him. He wouldn't admit to Sable, but he didn't like making verdicts. Just listening to each case wearied him. There seemed no end to the problems people found. Surely a ruler shouldn't have to do this!

The day was a warm one. Good for the grapes ripening on the vine, but poor for him as he walked among the lines of people waiting to be heard. He loosened his belt.

He reached a table and poured himself a drink. He was wiping his mouth when a movement on the hillside caught his eye.

A man waved.

What did he want?

Abimelech shielded his eyes and squinted. Although it was too far away to see, he couldn't mistake Jotham's voice. How could he be alive?

He tried to recall the night of sacrifices. Had he killed Jotham? He scratched his beard in concentration. He couldn't remember. He assumed he had killed all his brothers.

No one said anything different.

Which group had been responsible to get him?

He couldn't remember.

As Jotham spoke, Abimelech watched the crowd. Did they believe him?

Some gawked at the sky, shaken by the words. Their faces creased, their eyes filled with fear. Panic flowed over the crowd.

Did they think fire would fall from heaven?

He scanned the crowd for Zebul. Shouldn't he be here, protecting his king? When Abimelech couldn't find him, he bit his lip to control his own indecision.

Abimelech should say something to calm their fears, to reassert his authority. But what authority did he have over God?

He gulped the rest of his drink and banged the vessel on the table. He licked his lips and raised his arms. "Notice how courageous Jotham was. He spoke, then ran before fire licked his own blood." He forced a laugh. "It took seventy brothers to rule. Now I rule as one. Didn't Moses lead our people? He didn't divide the people with many rulers."

One man from the back called, "But didn't Moses seek the counsel of elders?"

Abimelech searched for the speaker in the crowd.

There he was! That man again. He looked familiar. Who was he? Was he intentionally placing doubts?

Abimelech cleared his throat. "Just as Moses had wise counsellors to help him, so I have appointed men to help judge." He raised his eyebrows at the man. What could he say to that?

"They're your friends."

Abimelech trembled. How dare anyone question his authority! "Won't that unite us? Look around you! Your leaders work together to solve your problems!"

The people weren't listening. Their grumblings grew louder.

Abimelech's chest felt tight, like someone squeezed his heart. He clenched his fists and bowed over. What fickle disloyalty! He must regain their attention, but how? What could he say to appease them? Frantically Abimelech looked around.

His eyes rested on the temple tower that stood over everything else.

Of course, the temple.

He pointed to the temple. "We worshipped in Ophrah. Didn't Baal accept me as your leader? Tonight we will sacrifice here."

Sacrifices would appease them.

The people grew quiet.

He lowered his arms and breathed deeply. He had forestalled a mob.

Tonight's sacrifices must convince everyone of his authority. He'd replenish the temple's wasted prostitutes with his brothers' wives and daughters. And with the promised sacrifices, all would be well.

He stroked his beard. Jotham hadn't thwarted his plans. He'd enhanced them.

But even as he tried to convince himself, he studied the hillside where Jotham had stood. How had Jotham missed death? He couldn't allow Jotham to live.

Who was that hiking up Mount Gerizim?

He squinted and saw it was Zebul. He would find Jotham.

Abimelech rubbed his hands together. He felt better already. He hadn't lost control.

But the threats of fire and judgment were not soon forgotten.

Abimelech woke in a sweat. He sat to calm his rapid breathing.

Sable turned over and rubbed his back. "Another nightmare?"

Abimelech breathed deeply. "I must find Jotham."

Sable sighed. "Zebul can't find him?"

"He's searched since he appeared weeks ago."

"Is Zebul actually looking?"

Abimelech paused, thinking. "He is. He observes everything. It's almost like he can even read my thoughts."

Sable laughed. "That's not hard. You've only had one thought, and that's to remove Jotham."

"With these nightmares, I can't forget his words of doom. Nor Zebul's."

"What did Zebul say?"

"He told me I wasn't a leader. He said I just wanted to feel worthy. That eliminating my brothers wouldn't be enough." Abimelech glanced at his wife in the moonlight. He seemed to remember she had said the same thing. He waited for her response.

She pursed her lips, as if to keep from saying more.

Her hesitation prompted Abimelech to ask, "Is he right?"

She avoided answering. She continued to rub his back. "You do have only one thought."

"But is he right?"

Sable pushed his hair away from his forehead. "I think," she paused, "you are fortunate to have Zebul as your lieutenant. He will help you rise to greatness."

Abimelech nodded. "Did I tell you how quick he is?"

Sable shook her head.

"When we sacrificed, I never saw his arm move. I just saw a blur."

Sable shrugged. "It was dark with only torches for light."

Abimelech corrected her with his tone. "I saw only a blur."

Sable conceded. "Of course. He must be fast."

Abimelech was wide awake now. And irritated. He couldn't attain his brothers' standard, nor could he establish his own, just as Zebul had told him. He felt inadequate.

He rubbed his beard. But he could do one thing. One thing would solve all his problems: kill Jotham.

Several months had passed since his coronation. As king, Abimelech had taken a house overlooking the temple in the center of the city. He could watch the sacrifices without even leaving his room. He could also watch over the city. He paced his chamber now, thinking what else must be done.

Zebul entered.

Abimelech stopped pacing and evaluated Zebul from head to toe.

He was covered in dust. His cloak was torn. His hair was askew. The only thing that looked clean was his knife handle, which could be seen through a fold in his cloak.

"Did you find him?" Abimelech hated to even mention his brother's name. It angered him he had escaped.

Zebul heaved several breaths before answering. He adjusted his knife. "I searched every cave and cranny in the foothills. He's not there."

How could he have let him escape? The longer he lived, the longer his prophecy seemed to effect the city.

Men hesitated to follow him.

Zebul sighed. "It was as if someone had warned him the night we went to his home. Everyone was gone. They left just before we got there.

"I found where he had waited in a cave. But he knew you were made king. How could he without someone in your counsel telling your plans?"

Abimelech had done nothing while waiting Zebul's return. He seemed immobilized by Jotham being alive. "Who would go against me?"

Zebul shrugged. "I'll listen, maybe I can hear who's stirring up the people."

Abimelech nodded. Perhaps that was what he should do. He glanced out his window.

The merchants bartered in the streets below. Everyone lived as if nothing had happened. Didn't they realize someone was usurping his control?

He turned from the window, his face set in a hard line. "Find out who it is."

Zebul nodded and turned to leave.

When he reached the door, Abimelech stopped him. "Zebul,

But You Have Not Obeyed Me

don't come before me again looking like a dirt clod. Remember who I am."

Zebul shut his lips in a fine line. He lifted his knife partially from its sheath, then paused. He seemed to consider a long moment, before dropping it back in its sheath and nodded. Without another word, he left.

Abimelech watched him go. He had allowed his frustration to make him careless with Zebul. He must watch in the future. He trusted no one, except Zebul.

Could he lead without trust?

Weeks had passed since Zebul had returned from looking for Jotham, and still Abimelech was no closer to finding who was causing the dissention. He paced his chamber, watching from the window the activities of the people. What should he do?

He hated his caution around Zebul, but he was afraid of him. Yet without him, he'd be dead.

Zebul walked beside him in the city as his body guard.

Once, a man had bumped Abimelech in the crowded street. It seemed casual, caused by the crowds.

Before the jolt had fully registered in Abimelech, Zebul stabbed the man.

Abimelech stood over the body. He should accuse Zebul of being too hasty.

But before he could say a word, Zebul leaned over the man and pulled a knife hidden up his sleeve.

Abimelech shut his mouth. He had seen nothing, had suspected nothing. He nodded at Zebul.

He had saved his life.

Another time, Zebul had intercepted a knife thrown at Abimelech. Zebul threw his own knife as easily as someone could throw a word! His knife hit the other knife in the air.

Both knives clattered to the cobblestone street.

Holding his backup knife in his other hand, Zebul casually retrieved the two knives from the stones.

Zebul had again saved his life.

But when alone with Zebul, Zebul fingered his knife, as if one wrong word would change his support.

Abimelech watched what he said. Would this man's loyalty change by one word? Or did he even have any loyalty?

Abimelech watched out his window.

One merchant shouted above the rest that his merchandise was the finest quality.

A young man bumped into the merchant. It seemed casual enough.

But the merchant fell into his display of gold jewelry and idols.

The youth instantly helped the man up and brushed him off. It looked like he'd made amends.

But when he walked away, he tucked something into the folds of his pocket. It glittered in the sunlight.

The merchant called in alarm. "I've been robbed! Grab that boy!"

The shoppers paused in their purchases, secured their own packages and watched indifferently as the youth slipped through the crowd.

Abimelech shook his head. So quick were his movements. Like Zebul. The thought made him pause. Was Zebul doing that to him? Giving the appearance of support and loyalty, but actually robbing him?

His insides knotted into a tight ball. He felt used like the merchant, wanting to scream out his injustices. But just like the merchant, no one would listen.

CHAPTER 30

Fire fell from the clouds. Abimelech ran, but the fire chased him, burning his heels. He couldn't run fast enough. He woke, his covers drenched and wrapped around him.

"Another dream?" Sable asked. "You're consumed with finding Jotham. Forget him."

"But his prophecy—"

She laughed. "Has it come true?" She didn't allow him to answer. "Then do not be afraid."

He lay again to sleep, but his thoughts wouldn't still. "I'll send Zebul again to search for him."

She sat, pulling the covers around her chin, her voice raised in frustration, "You need Zebul here. Jotham has vanished like smoke in the clouds. You're not threatened by Jotham but you are by Zebul."

He stared at her. What did she mean?

The darkness of the room cast her face in a shadow.

"You're afraid of Zebul."

Abimelech laughed, but even he could tell it didn't sound convincing.

She pulled her knees under her chin. "You don't trust him."

He sighed. "How can I know who to trust? My supporters were

bought by seventy pieces of silver and a promise of power. After three years, they continue to demand more. If I don't provide what they want, they'll find someone else who'll give them more. How is that leading? Zebul was right when he told me I'm no leader."

"Loyalty bought is not loyalty." She shrugged. "Zebul protects you for another reason."

He shifted his anger from his own failures to her. His tone was etched with irritation, "Then how do I get loyalty?"

She leaned her head against him and rubbed his chest. "You're unapproachable. Even if someone wanted to help you, you act like you can do it alone. You can't lead by yourself."

He pulled away from her. "There you go again, telling me how I can't lead!"

She corrected, calmly. "I never said you couldn't lead, only that you wouldn't want to. But you do need others' help, especially Zebul's."

"How do I get this help? No one wants to be around me, remember!"

"Be vulnerable. At least approachable."

"You want me to be vulnerable! Vulnerable was what I was when my brothers ruled. What did I get? Ridicule! Stepped on like dung in the stables without an inheritance! I won't allow that again."

She shrugged and walked to the window. She brushed her hair from her face. The moonlight revealed her beautiful features. She softened her voice. "Being afraid to be exposed keeps you from helping your city and knowing who is loyal. It hardens you. No one wants to be around you." She turned to face him. Her eyes pled with him.

He steeled himself against her begging. He wouldn't change; he couldn't change. "I don't need people around me."

"You did when you attacked your brothers."

Abimelech's jaw hardened. "Anyone has a price for any job."

"Without loyalty, you have nothing. Someone can always pay more. But with Zebul, he helps you without payment. Do you know why?"

Abimelech hadn't considered the question before. He was irritated she asked questions he didn't know the answers to. He turned away from her.

But his silence only confirmed his lack of an answer.

She crossed her arms and leaned against the window frame. "Find out."

Abimelech walked behind her and looked at the city bathed in moonlight. "How?"

Sable seemed to have waited for this question. "Let me."

Abimelech studied her with a new appreciation. How did she know him so well? He nodded, not so much in consent, but in resignation. He had nothing else to offer. Even if he knew why Zebul stayed with him, how would that help him?

He looked at his bed. The covers were askew and torn from the bed. If he found loyalty, would the dreams stop?

Abimelech burnt his finger as he poked at the fire to burn off the morning chill. He hadn't returned to sleep but had paced until the sun had risen. Now he must focus on today's events.

He had called a meeting of the leaders of the city.

One man opened the discussion, "The merchants don't come to our city anymore. Their goods are stolen."

Another added, "The market has nothing of value to be sold. The people can't even buy food."

Abimelech remembered the merchant he had seen several weeks before. The thief had been gone before the merchant realized he was missing anything. How could anyone find him in the crowd?

But even as he remembered what he saw in the market, he pictured Jotham, running from Mount Gerizim.

He was the cause. Abimelech's thoughts took him away from the meeting.

After the meeting, Abimelech called Zebul into his chamber.

When Zebul entered, he looked the same as he had when Abimelech found him at the temple three years ago. His hair was unkempt, his cloak soiled and worn. Couldn't he dress like he represented a king? Even his manner and confidence hadn't changed. If anything, he seemed to carry more of an air of aloofness. He waited for Abimelech to speak.

"Have you found him?"

Zebul held his knife, no longer hidden in his sheath. "Your people need protection, not from Jotham's imaginary threats, but from ambushers who prevent merchants from entering the city."

Abimelech was surprised by this news. "How long has this been going on?

Zebul locked his eyes on Abimelech's. "Your people are starving."

"Who's doing this?"

"The ambusher's tracks come from the city and return to the city."

Abimelech exploded. "They're my own men?"

Zebul nodded, but kept his head down as he slid his finger along the blade of his knife. He continued as he raised his head to meet Abimelech's stare. "Your obsession with finding Jotham has caused your men to doubt your leadership."

Abimelech paced. He had called Zebul to renew his quest to find Jotham. These new developments only proved to him the truth of Jotham's prophecy and the fulfillment of his dreams. If he found Jotham—he shook his head That was the only answer. "Find Jotham. Whatever it takes, he must be found."

Zebul took a step forward. He tightened his hold on his knife and raised his voice, "Have you heard anything I'm telling you? Your men don't respect a leader who blames his problems on a cloud in the sky. They want protection. They want someone who controls."

Abimelech stepped away from Zebul toward the window. The distant hills caught his attention. "He hides in those hills, watching. I know he does. Find him."

CHAPTER 31

Zebul rushed from Abimelech's chamber. He was angry at himself for following Abimelech's orders so many times. If he had found Jotham at the beginning, he wouldn't be traipsing over the mountains these past three years for nothing. Nor would his city be in such a mess. Abimelech would know how bad the city had become. The city leaders were divided. Zebul felt pulled from all sides. They were cautious to include him because of his quick use of his knife. His aloofness kept them wondering on which side he stood. That was fine with Zebul.

Abimelech's obsession with finding Jotham above everything else had changed him. He was a maniac. Consumed with one thing. Instead of leading, he was losing his entire kingdom.

In Zebul's haste to leave the house, he barreled into Sable.

He paused to help her up. "I'm sorry."

When Sable was on her feet again, she straightened her tunic, but didn't let go of his hand. "Zebul." She said his name in a plea. She glanced down the darkened hallway toward Abimelech's room. "You've come from my husband's chamber?"

Zebul tried to withdraw his hand from hers, but she continued to hold it.

He nodded. He tried to cover his impatience at being detained by breathing slower.

Sable stepped toward him, brushing against him.

He could smell her rosemary soap and saw the intensity in her eyes. "Zebul, I need your help. I can't tell you now. There are too many listening ears. Meet me in the garden tonight." She squeezed his hand lightly and hurried down the passageway.

Zebul watched her go, her rosemary fragrance lingering to assure him she had been real. He looked at his hand, still outstretched to hold her small, dainty one. He stopped feeling the need to rush. He left wondering what had been his hurry.

The day had been long. Zebul ignored Abimelech's demand to search for Jotham. Jotham was not the problem. He sent a dispatch of men to watch the hills to find who hindered the merchants from entering. Without the merchants and farmers, their people would soon starve. Their markets were empty. Their people couldn't work their fields without being attacked. The people would revolt soon if food wasn't found.

Zebul sketched a map of the surrounding hills on a goat's hide with a piece of charcoal. He marked where he had already looked. Where else could the ambushers hide? And who were they?

A messenger returned. "Gaal, son of Ebed, has arrived."

Zebul placed his finger where he had been marking. "He's entered the city?"

The messenger nodded. "With all his relatives. He brings food."

"How was he able to enter?" Zebul studied the man.

"The ambushers didn't stop them. They seemedly escorted him into the city."

Zebul ran his hand through his hair. Perhaps this was the answer to his questions. "Watch them."

The messenger nodded and left.

Zebul searched the surrounding hillside from his window. Something was wrong. Was Gaal behind the ambushing, or was he just used by someone in the city? How could Gaal enter the city without a problem? Because he brought food, the people would listen to him. He could control the people.

Noise from the street below distracted him.

A group had definitely arrived. They attracted a following. The city hadn't been this active in a long time.

Another messenger arrived. "The city prepares for sacrifices."

Abimelech hadn't told him to prepare for any. "Who performs them?"

The messenger lowered his eyes. "Gaal and his relatives."

Zebul watched out the window. "Who is this Gaal?"

The messenger paced the floor behind him. "Rumor says he's a son of a Canaanite chief. He's known for stealing cities by first starving them, then offering them food. Any city he wants, he destroys, captures, and moves on."

This city was almost starving. Was he working with the city leaders?

Zebul turned to the messenger. "Keep me informed."

After the messenger left, Zebul continued to watch.

The people flocked toward the temple.

The temple . . . that's where Abimelech had started his reign.

Is that what Gaal had in mind?

Zebul's gaze roamed over the city. They lingered on the palace garden's fig trees that grew over the palace walls. His thoughts turned to Sable and his meeting with her tonight. He could still feel her dainty hand. Why would Sable ask for his help?

He kept away from women, except those in the temple.

His mother, a temple prostitute, had died early in his life. When no man claimed him as his son, he had fended for himself. He learned early that only those with a quick hand and a sharp knife survived. His skills had been developed by necessity.

Feelings skewed his judgement, so he guarded his thoughts, words, actions, but most of all, his feelings. They hindered survival. Only those who cared fell prey to others. His strategy worked. And he found an added bonus: people left him alone. He could do what he wanted, when he needed to. People were afraid to interfere with him.

He analyzed others. He knew why they did things. Like when Abimelech had become king. Abimelech wasn't a leader; he only wanted to feel worthy. As Zebul made him feel respected, Abimelech depended on Zebul to advise. By suggesting solutions, Zebul preserved his own freedom. He liked his autonomy, using the king's resources.

He ran his hand through his hair. All those thoughts from just a stray feeling about holding Sable's hand. He shook his head, trying to shake his feelings. He wasn't used to being distracted by those kind of thoughts. He must gain control before he met her in the garden. His feelings shouldn't influence whether he helped her. He wouldn't sacrifice his freedom, nor would he be obliged to anyone, no matter the cause. The cost was never worth it.

The sun had set while he had mused.

Torches directed the people's movements to the temple.

He could sense the spirit of people.

They hoped.

Yet a threatening cloud hovered the city. It choked him. The sensation left him feeling alone for the first time. Before, he had enjoyed being by himself, without depending upon others. No one forced him to do anything.

Tonight, the freedom he had craved strangled him. He loosened his tunic's belt and ran his hands through his hair. This isolation choked him.

Zebul grabbed his cloak and strode from his house to escape his own feelings. He followed the crowd, entering the temple. Perhaps a distraction would help.

When he entered the temple, he surveyed the room.

Torches on the pillars and around the altar cast sickly shadows over the crowd.

The drums sat quiet in the corner, waiting for the speaker to finish.

His eyes were drawn to the main altar, where someone unknown to him commanded the people, "Who is Abimelech? Where are the men of Shechem, that we should serve him? What

But You Have Not Obeyed Me

is Zebul, his lieutenant, doing to protect your streets from thieves? Why serve them? What do they do for you?"

Zebul clenched his hand over his knife, his fingers itching to throw it. He had a direct line to the man's heart. Was this man Gaal? He was turning the people.

Zebul would do well to know who followed Gaal.

Gaal continued, "He leaves you to starve.

"If I were in charge, I'd remove Abimelech."

Zebul searched the crowd for those who agreed with Gaal's claims.

The same leaders who had helped Abimelech become king, now nodded their heads at Gaal's words.

With great restraint, Zebul loosened his hold on his knife handle. For most of Zebul's work, a single stab would solve the problem. Here, there were too many people. The feeling of aloneness that had enveloped him at his house returned. Who could he trust to help?

Or could he just leave the city before it was destroyed? The thought was new to him. He had never run. He had always fought and won. But tonight . . . by fighting, he would lose. Was that giving up? What else he could do?

Zebul partook of the temple's offerings, but the memory of Sable's small hand in his, hindered his enjoyment. He left the temple frustrated, unable to participate fully.

The moon was high when he entered the side gate of the palace garden. He stepped off the stone walkway and stood a moment, allowing his eyes to adjust to the darkness under the fig leaves.

Someone grabbed his arm.

He turned, his knife ready to strike.

Sable gasped and dropped her hand. "You are quick. I've heard how fast you were, but it comforts me to see for myself."

He replaced the blade in its sheath. He hadn't heard her approach. He prided himself in his stealth. Now, a woman had not only approached him, but touched him, without him hearing. He swallowed any appearance of aggravation, though he felt his confidence shrinking. Why was it so hard to control his feelings around her?

"Zebul," her voice was a mere whisper, almost a plea. She touched his arm again. Her touch was soft as a butterfly resting on a petal.

He smelled her rosemary soap. He watched her lips form her words.

"Abimelech . . ." she hesitated.

Zebul stiffened at the name. He didn't want to hear about Abimelech now. Nothing Abimelech did helped the city. It was because of Abimelech that Gaal would soon destroy the city, if Zebul couldn't do something about it.

She didn't repeat his name. "He hasn't been right since Jotham came. He's talked about you. You've saved his life many times. Why do you stay with him?"

Zebul was frustrated with Abimelech's obsession to find Jotham. Angry at his own failure of not finding him. Each time had brought Abimelech's rebuke and depression. He doubted his own abilities.

Why did he stay with Abimelech? He didn't know. He wasn't sure.

She answered for him, "You stay, because you're loyal."

Zebul almost laughed. He had no loyalties, other than what was good for him.

She seemed to read his thoughts. "You want what's good for the city, in spite of what Abimelech does."

How did she know what he wanted? She irritated him with her insight.

"You feel it too, the tension in the city tonight. I'm afraid—" She paused, listening.

He heard someone moving on the pathway. He pulled her farther under the tree's shadows.

The shuffling passed them and continued toward the house. A door creaked open, then shut.

A servant must have returned from the temple.

Zebul's hand still rested around her waist.

But You Have Not Obeyed Me

They stood in the silence, listening for any more noise.

There was none.

Sable made no effort to move away from him; instead she leaned against him and looked into his face. "Take me with you."

Her body pressed against his. Her lips so close to his own made him lick his dry lips. He felt he couldn't breathe. The temple's offerings were never like this. They were performed under wine and drugs. This feeling of wanting and needing to protect a woman was new to him.

How did she know he was leaving? He hadn't really considered it until that night. And he wasn't sure he was leaving.

Sable sensed his hesitation. "The city is different tonight. You feel it."

He took a deep breath, trying to control these new feelings. He swallowed, unable to form any words. His thoughts to control his feelings flew from his mind. He couldn't even recall why it was so important to ignore them. He wanted to pursue these feelings.

Sable touched his face.

He covered her hand. His felt rough and calloused over her soft one. He removed her hand and held it at her side. He didn't like to be touched. It made him feel vulnerable, out of control. He couldn't make his voice respond.

Feeling his rejection, her voice shook, "I thought you'd help me." Her voice faltered at his hesitation. She stepped back. "I thought you'd protect me." She turned to leave.

Zebul blinked. He took a gulp of air. The cool air cleared his mind so he could think. What had just happened? Why wouldn't he help her?

She stirred up a longing buried deep in him.

He could move mountains with her affirmation or even save the city. Why couldn't he saying anything?

She was running to the house.

He stepped into the pathway, the moonlight lighting the way. He found his voice, "Wait!"

She paused to look back.

Zebul took several hesitant steps forward.

She was crying.

He was startled by her tears. He had trained himself not to feel sympathy for others. That was how he survived. What was happening to him?

He found himself saying, "I'll come for you."

Sable gave a half smile. Then disappeared inside.

Zebul stared at the closed door and wondered what he had just done.

Zebul paced his chamber for several hours after seeing Sable, trying to solve the city's problems. But always his mind would return to the fleeing image of Sable. Finally he knew what he would do. He returned to the palace, knocking on Abimelech's chamber. He shook, not from the coolness of the night, but from what had transpired in the garden and what he must do now. Did his face reveal his turmoil?

Abimelech held a candle when he answered his door. His hair was askew, his tunic covered in sweat.

Zebul looked past him to his bed. In the darkened room, the covers were tied in knots. What had happened here? He looked for Sable. Had he found out about her visit with him and hurt her? "What did you do to her?" He reached out to strike Abimelech.

Abimelech seemed confused. "Who?" He straightened his tunic and lifted his candle to see over the room. He seemed to be waking up.

To cover his question, Zebul pointed to his bed. "What happened?"

Abimelech scratched his head. "Just a dream."

Zebul studied Abimelech. "Must have been some dream."

Abimelech seemed unable to think of what to say. "Jotham was chasing . . ." He shook his head, his shoulders slumped. He looked pitiful and vulnerable.

Zebul couldn't speak. No wonder Abimelech was consumed with finding Jotham, if he fought like this in his dreams!

But Zebul couldn't feel sorry for him. He must implement his plan. He stared ahead as he told his news. "Gaal and his relatives have come to Shechem. They stir the city against you. Arise while it's night. Take those who support you and wait in the field outside the city. In the morning, rush upon the city. When Gaal charges out against you, do whatever you can."

The news woke Abimelech. "Who's for me? How can I tell?"

Zebul shrugged. "If they aren't worshipping at the temple with Gaal, they may be for you."

"He worships at my temple?"

"That's where he challenged your authority."

In the light of the candle, Zebul could see Abimelech's face. His jaws were clenched, but his face had paled.

Abimelech grabbed Zebul's arm. "You alone I trust."

Zebul swallowed, stepping away from him. He could feel the blood running to his face. If he was the only man he could trust—he shook his head. "What about Sable?"

"Sable?" Abimelech seemed confused.

Zebul held back his anger that he could forget her, "Your wife. If Gaal gains the city, she'll be abused."

Understanding seemed to come to Abimelech's face. "Can you take her to safety?" He looked around the room as if that helped him think. "In case things don't go well. I don't want her taken to the temple."

Maybe Zebul was assuming more than what she had asked from him. Maybe her fear had made her do things she normally wouldn't. He shouldn't assume anything. He coughed to clear his throat. "I'll look after her."

Abimelech seemed relieved by his promise. "I trust you. Thank you."

Zebul swallowed. He felt his deception. He turned away, lest Abimelech could read his face. He coughed again. "Divide your army into four companies and circle the city."

Abimelech nodded, but did his words even register with Abimelech?

Zebul left Abimelech's chamber. He called the army, preparing them to leave with Abimelech during the night.

Then he tapped lightly on Sable's room. "It's Zebul."

He heard her stirring through the door.

The door opened.

She looked as if she hadn't slept. She motioned him inside while she put on her cloak.

He shifted from one foot to the other and looked at the door as he waited. "I'll take you from the city, in case things go poorly for Abimelech."

She nodded. She grabbed a cloth sack she'd already prepared and put her hand in his arm. "I'm ready."

As they left the room, something clattered to the floor. Zebul gave a glance, but it was too dark to see.

He stepped back into the room to look better, but Sable tugged on his arm. "Hurry!"

Should he ignore the noise, something he wouldn't have done before, for Sable's safety? He looked at her face.

Her eyes were wide, her face pale. She pulled on his arm again.

He ignored the noise and led her through the darkened palace hallway.

They left the palace through the servant's door. He led her through the deserted, darkened city's streets to the gate.

She didn't speak, for which he was grateful. He wasn't sure if he could have found his voice.

Abimelech's words rang loudly through his mind. He trusted him with his kingdom, his army, and his wife. He shouldn't have trusted him with any of those things.

Zebul stopped before the city gate and knocked on the guard's door. "I must leave and return tonight. I have an urgent message to deliver."

The guard nodded. He was familiar with Zebul's requests as army's lieutenant. He unlocked a side entrance and pushed the door open for Zebul and Sable to leave.

Once out of the city, Zebul reached for Sable's hand. He felt again the traitor to Abimelech. How had he lived without acknowledging his feelings before? Now they rushed upon him in torrents. He'd have saved her from the temple even without Abimelech's request. And he'd save her from what was about to happen.

The moon was waning, its light dim. Zebul followed the road for as long as he needed until he came to the foothills where a trail veered from the main road. He followed it.

Sable finally spoke, her voice soft in the night. "Where are we going?"

Zebul realized now how much she had trusted him. He knew these hills from searching for Jotham; she knew nothing. He faced her, keeping his voice low so it wouldn't carry over the hills. "There's a cave ahead. Nothing more than a hole. I'll leave you there. I must return to the city, but I'll come back."

She shivered. Her teeth chattered a little.

"Cold?" He surprised himself at his concern.

"I don't like closed places. Or darkness."

He squeezed her hand. He thought of the contrast: he had lived in the darkness and caves while looking for Jotham. He enjoyed being away from the city and sleeping under the stars. He couldn't understand this fear. "I'll come as soon as I can. You can trust me." He held back a grimace. Abimelech had trusted him.

They veered off the trail.

A waterfall could be heard close by.

"Watch your step; the stones are slippery." He held her hand more securely to guide her over the stones. It felt cold, soft and little in his grasp.

He rubbed his other hand over his cloak where he kept his hidden knife. He couldn't feel it. He stopped and searched his garment.

It was gone.

He remembered the clattering noise in her chamber before they left. His knife must have fallen. What was wrong with him, that he would drop his knife and not even know it? He felt naked without it in his grasp.

Sable watched him. "What is it?"

He met her eyes and smiled, reassuring her. "Nothing." With his free hand, he took her sack and swung it over his back. They hiked the hillside. Tree limbs hanging low blocked their way. They crawled under them. He could hear her heavy breathing behind him as he pushed through the underbrush. He paused before a bush. Brushing its branches away, he revealed a hole. He dropped the sack into the hole. The sound of it hitting the bottom came after a moment.

He reached for Sable to follow.

Even in the dim moonlight, he could see her pale face and wide eyes. "You'll come for me?"

"I promise." He lifted her by her waist and dropped her into the hole.

When her feet touched bottom, she expelled a deep sigh.

He leaned over the hole. "I'll return for you."

The vision of her upturned, trusting face stayed on his mind as he hurried back to the city.

When he came from the foothills, back to the main road, he saw the army gathered in the fields outside the city. He counted four companies, organized. He nodded, assured Abimelech had followed his commands.

He nodded to the gate guard, and slipped into the city.

Trust was a thing not easily given. But easily lost. Two people had spoken of trusting him.

He wasn't trustworthy. But he shoved his feelings, so recently surfaced, far from him.

For the next part of his plan, he couldn't be controlled by any feelings.

He stopped at the temple. He nodded to Gaal across the room.

Gaal nodded back.

All was set for morning.

CHAPTER 32

After Zebul left his chamber, Abimelech drank from a vessel by his bed. He was exhausted from his dream. Why had Zebul asked about Sable? It seemed a strange request from him. He had certainly acted differently. Abimelech finished his drink and hurried to dress and prepare for battle. It would be his first. Was he ready? Was anyone ready for battle?

When he stepped out of the palace, he expected Zebul to be waiting for him to escort him from the city as his body guard, like he'd done before.

But when he opened the door, all that greeted him was darkness. He had never walked unprotected through the city streets as king. His mind reviewed all the times Zebul had protected him from harm. He shivered and adjusted his sword. Even with his sword, he felt exposed. Would it be too big to use in the street? He had never fought. He envied Zebul with his knife.

Louder than his own beating heart, he could hear drums from the temple. With its pounding, Abimelech's hair on the back of his neck rose. He could feel someone following him. He quickened his pace. He glanced back once and saw the temple ablaze with lights. The memory of sacrificing his brothers came to his mind. When he kicked a loose cobblestone from the road, he didn't see the stone, but a head. It wasn't Jether's head, but his own. He grimaced and closed his eyes.

His dreams were becoming real. Would he be the next sacrifice?

He began to run.

His sandals echoed on the deserted cobblestones.

He kept in the shadows, darting around corners, running faster.

Every shadow became another pursuer.

By the time he reached the city gates, he was out of breath and sweating.

Looking through the metal gates, he saw his army waiting outside the wall.

He bent over, breathing heavily.

At his command, the guards pulled the chains to allow him to leave.

When he stood outside the wall, the gate creaked and squealed shut behind him. The clank when it hit the ground gave finality to his fate.

He jumped at its loudness.

He searched for Zebul. He should be here waiting with the army.

Zebul would stand beside him and advise him.

He threw his shoulders back and stood confident, grateful he had survived the city's darkness.

But only his army stood before him.

Zebul wasn't here.

He waited.

His army grew restless.

When Zebul still didn't come, he took a deep breath and led the army into the fields. What had Zebul advised? Something about four companies . . . around the hills of the city? He found Zebul's second-in-command and ordered the troops to be organized.

Realization started to creep over Abimelech; Zebul was not coming. But still he could not believe it.

Something must have happened.
He had trusted him.
Zebul would prove true.

Morning came. Gaal stood on the roof of the temple and looked over the fields beyond the city. "Look! People are coming down from the mountains!"

Zebul stood beside him. "Those are mere shadows of the mountains that look like men."

Gaal pointed. "No, look higher on that mountain, where that oak tree the diviners use stands. Those are men armed for war!"

Zebul shrugged. He was weary of leaders who bragged of dominance, but showed no strength. "Where's your boasting now? You asked the men of the city, 'Why should we serve Abimelech? These are the people you despised and belittled. Fight them!"

He smiled to see that his words had infuriated Gaal.

But Gaal turned, leaning over the wall to see better.

As they watched, the fields grew with men, rising like the morning sun over the mountain.

Gaal swallowed once; then nodded. He commanded Zebul, "Rouse the leaders for battle."

Zebul nodded and sent for the men of Shechem who had sacrificed with Gaal the night before.

They organized as quickly as half-awake men could and marched out of the city to faced Abimelech in battle.

Zebul stayed behind and watched from the city wall.

Abimelech surrounded Gaal and his drunken men, and chased them back to the city gates.

But as Gaal and his men ran for the city's protection, Zebul called to the guard, "Shut the gates! Allow no one in."

Those who had already entered, Zebul drove from the city.

Then he returned to the wall of the city and surveyed the battle scene.

Abimelech came to the city gates. "Zebul, well done. We have routed the enemy! Let me in now!"

Zebul looked at him with pity. Abimelech still hadn't realized his trust was misplaced. Zebul spoke in a soothing voice, "Abimelech, the city's no longer yours."

Abimelech's face flushed. "What do you mean? We've won! Gaal and his relatives have fled. Open the gates!"

"The city no longer wants you." Zebul turned his back on Abimelech and left the city wall.

After Zebul left the wall, Abimelech looked around at the men with him. He couldn't understand this turn of events. They had won. They had sent Gaal away. Why wouldn't Zebul allow him inside?

He didn't notice his troops were becoming restless until his second-in-command approached him.

"The men need rest and food." The commander nodded toward the north. "Let's go to Arumah."

The city was only a half day's journey away.

Abimelech nodded. They could eat, rest, and think about what should be done next.

As Abimelech stumbled down the road away from his city, the finality of his loss fell on him. He felt betrayed, hollow, and numb. He had trusted and depended upon Zebul. He grieved like he'd lost his own arm.

They reached the city at dusk and camped outside its gates for the night.

Abimelech chewed on the figs and almonds he had found in a house outside the city. The memory of Zebul's first description of this snack returned. Abimelech spit them out, refusing to eat more. He gulped from his waterskin. The taste was bitter. He rubbed his tongue around his teeth and swished his mouth out and spit again.

He looked at the men around him.

But You Have Not Obeyed Me

They lounged around the fire, waiting for the lamb they had butchered to cook. They drank from the wine they had taken from the city's people.

They had fought bravely against Gaal and his men.

They had won.

Hadn't Gaal run from him?

Yet the victory had been taken from them.

The longer Abimelech rehearsed the fight, the more angry he became. His grief turned to anger. How dare Zebul turn him from his own city! He wouldn't bow before Zebul! He'd return and fight.

The men were finishing their meal when he stood before them. What should he say? Before his confidence had come from Zebul's strategies; now he must decide. He inhaled deeply before speaking, "Men, we will rest, gather our strength, sharpen our swords and knives, and return to our city tomorrow. And when we do," he looked around as he warmed to his subject, growing confident, "we'll attack those who leave the city to work in their fields. Another group will move behind them and enter the city. We'll kill all. For nonoe of them allowed us inside." He unsheathed his own sword and raised it to the sky. "Tomorrow, our city."

The men rose and lifted their swords and knives and repeated his charge. Their deep, full voices encouraged him.

He thought of them as he slept. But he did not forget the one whom he had trusted.

"Abimelech is gone," the guard stationed at the gate reported to Zebul after the battle.

Zebul carried only a sack filled with food and a rope over his shoulder. His full waterskin bumped his thigh as he left the city.

He followed the trail, now visible in the day. He hurried through the fields of grain, almost ready for harvest. The rains had been good this year. The people would be able to eat soon.

He took the same trail he had the night before. He surveyed

the trail ahead of him as he climbed the mountain. The thick vegetation from the trees made it hard to decide if he was followed. There could still be soldiers from both camps around that would hinder his plan.

The birds would quiet if others were near.

He listened to them.

A cote of doves flew up at his feet, startling him. He paused, checking the area for anything else.

He had enjoyed the trips to search for Jotham. Now, the freedom of the land called him. He had fulfilled his duty to Abimelech, with the exception of this final task. This task he would enjoy.

How strange his life should come to this. After ignoring his feelings for so long, to have his feelings control his actions now seemed a contradiction. And yet, the joy that bubbled up from inside him couldn't be wrong. He almost laughed out loud. Instead he hurried. He couldn't wait.

He veered off the trail as he had the night before and paused.

He heard a mourning dove cooing. The bees were buzzing under the fig trees full of blossoms. Nothing more could he hear.

He studied his back trail again. He took his time, watching. It would not do to be stopped now. Reassured that no one followed, he moved forward again. He reached the hole and surveyed the hillside for any movement. He finally brushed the limbs away from the opening, dropped to his knees, and called down the hole, "Sable."

He was relieved when she answered, "Zebul, oh please, get me out of here."

He knotted the rope in several places and dropped it down the hole. "Hold the knot. I'll bring you up."

When he had raised her from the hole, he helped her sit under a tree. "Here's water." He extended his waterskin to her.

She drank, spilling it in her haste.

He opened his sack and offered her bread and figs.

She ate hungrily, without speaking.

But You Have Not Obeyed Me

He watched her. He had never felt the contentment of providing for someone. He liked the way it felt.

When she had finished, she looked into his face. She blushed. In excuse she explained, "I was hungry."

"Ready?" His voice was tender, unusual for him. He wondered at the change.

She nodded.

He took her hand and helped her stand.

They started hiking.

She didn't ask what had happened to the city or to her husband.

Nor did he tell her.

They looked back later in the day to see a dark cloud rising in the sky. Sable pointed. "What's that?"

Zebul took his time in answering. "That's the temple."

Sable looked at him, her eyes wide.

They turned again and continued walking toward the land in the north.

As Abimelech and his army returned to the city the following day, Abimelech walked with resolution, not as he had the previous day. He had finished grieving. He now considered Zebul an enemy. He'd find as much pleasure killing him as he had his brothers.

They followed the foothills where the road was well traveled. Turning into the valley, Shechem came into view. Abimelech hesitated. Streams from spring and summer rains had watered the gardens; crops and orchards made this valley the most beautiful he had ever seen. The land overflowed with produce and beauty.

But even as he looked at the growth, his anger burned against those leaders who had betrayed him. They had starved their own people, keeping them from working their fields and harvesting their crops.

He motioned for two companies to surround the city. He didn't care who got in his way. He would slaughter any who came from the city.

Abimelech came upon one man.

He was working his fields, in spite of the threats.

Abimelech watched him harvest his wheat. His face was turned from him. But he looked familiar. When he turned, Abimelech saw his face. He knew him. "You! Stop!" Abimelech strode over to him.

The man waited. His hands resting on his scythe.

As Abimelech reached him, he remembered why his face was so familiar to him. "You traveled with the men of Shechem to Ophrah."

The man conceded, "I've traveled that road many times."

"No!" Abimelech pressed. "You came with me three years ago."

The man answered evasively, "Perhaps."

Abimelech demanded, "Who are you? Why should I know you?"

The man shrugged. "I get around."

His indifference made Abimelech more angry. Abimelech felt this man was the key to his problem these past three years. "Don't you know I have power over you? I control the city."

The man looked beyond Abimelech to the gates of the city. "No man controls what God does not allow."

Abimelech clenched his teeth. His response reminded him of Jotham's prophecy. He leaned forward, sticking his face into the man's face. "I know you. You're the brother of Jotham's wife!"

The man held his ground. "I won't deny it."

Abimelech remembered Zebul's comment that someone had warned Jotham the night of the sacrifices and had later informed him of his coronation. "You! You have caused all my problems these past three years!" He unsheathed his sword and swung it close to the man's chest. "You warned Jotham that night, didn't you?"

The man nodded.

"You told him of my coronation."

Again the man nodded.

Abimelech steadied his sword over the man's heart. "Where's Jotham?"

The man didn't flinch. "I haven't seen him."

His lack of fear and blatant disrespect infuriated Abimelech. How dare this man speak so calmly. "You lie! You and Jotham brought problems to my city."

The man looked at the sword; then at Abimelech. "If you've had problems, they are from the Hand of the Lord, giving vengeance for the lives of Gideon's sons."

Rage spilled from Abimelech as he ran his sword through the man.

He crumbled to the ground.

Abimelech struck again and again. His anger finding vent in destroying this body. "Where's Jotham?"

The second-in-command grabbed his arm. "Abimelech! He's dead."

Abimelech stopped. He looked numbly at his sword. Then at the fallen body. He stepped back and dropped his sword. His mind registered the body.

The anger was gone, and in its place was an emptiness, numbing his thoughts and feelings. He pushed back his helmet and rubbed his head. He had thought if he could kill Jotham, his problems would be solved. Killing this man who had protected him should have brought satisfaction.

He staggered backwards, putting distance between himself and the body. He seemed lost, back in the time of Jotham's prophecy. The fire coming from heaven consumed him.

He brushed his waterskin. It brought him back to the present. But still his emptiness remained. He hadn't proven his worthiness.

He gulped down the water. He licked his lips and looked at the city; then at his second-in-command. "Shall we take back the city?"

He nodded.

Abimelech directed a third company to storm the gate. They entered the open gate, killing the guards.

An alarm went out.

People fled before their swords.

Abimelech and his men fought that day with a vengeance spurred by anger caused by betrayal. He lashed at any in his way: children, women, unarmed men.

When the city was taken, he looked over the land surrounding it. Its beauty made him angry. He would show his control over these fickle people who wanted to follow another. He would control everything. He turned to his men, "Pour salt over the land."

Salt killed everything. No crops would grow. The beauty of the land would be gone.

They obeyed. Taking salt, collected from the Dead Sea, they scattered it over the land.

The people would acknowledge he was in charge.

He breathed deeply, glorying in his return to power.

But as he gazed over the city, his eyes stopped on the temple.

It's citadel had an inner chamber for special sacrifices to El-berith.

He had one more thing to do.

He returned to the streets, cleaning his sword on a fallen body.

He set his face toward the temple.

He commanded the soldiers around him, "Follow me."

The soldiers charged through the streets.

Their swords clanked at their sides.

Their armor and marching boots made the only sound in the empty streets.

Abimelech paused before a woodworker's house. He pushed the door open, stepping over the body that lay in the way and grabbed an ax. He swung it over his shoulder and continued his march to the temple.

When they reached the temple courtyard, he chopped off a fig tree branch.

The branch fell, splintering to the ground with a crash. He

But You Have Not Obeyed Me

handed the ax to the soldier beside him. "What you've seen me do, do also. Follow me." He hoisted the branch over his shoulders and strode up the stairs to the temple. He paused at the top of the stairs, catching his breath. He watched his men follow his instructions.

Would he ever trust a man without watching him?

He led the way inside the temple. He pushed his branch against the doors of the inner chamber. The leaders would have sought refuge here. They would have thought themselves safe.

"Make a wall of branches around the entire perimeter." He inspected their bundles against the wall.

He poured oil over the green branches, then grabbed a torch from the wall of the temple.

The flames caught the oil and spread over the branches around the room.

Smoke billowed from the green foliage.

Flames climbed the walls.

Others stepped back from the heat of the flames, but still Abimelech stood close, the heat warming his cheeks and singeing his hair. He watched mesmerized as the flames destroyed the room.

The walls fell inward. The roar of the flames filled his ears.

Above the fire's roar, he could hear the screams of those trapped inside.

Abimelech listened and felt calm. He stood, unable to move until the last screams were silent. He sheathed his sword. And nodded. He had sacrificed those leaders who had betrayed him.

He should have felt relief.

Instead, he remembered Jotham. He was still alive. Somewhere.

The fire spread from the temple to the city. Abimelech rushed to the palace for Sable. When he entered her chamber, he kicked something on the floor. He glanced down to see light reflect off the glint of a knife. He picked it up. This was Zebul's knife.

Why would it be in Sable's room?

He sat on her bed and remembered details of the past. They had been peculiar at the time. Zebul's question a few days ago, "What did you do to her?" Out of character for Zebul. And his nervousness. Sable's interest in Zebul's skills. She had led him to allow her to speak with Zebul. And he had granted her request.

Had he killed Zebul in the temple fire?

Or had Zebul escaped with Sable?

Had she gone willingly?

Abimelech felt betrayal of a different kind.

Not only from Zebul but from Sable.

He ripped his cloak and fell to his knees as the fire rose around his city.

Black smoke billowed around him when he came to his senses, he rose, feeling the need for revenge toward everything. The city was destroyed. But he would prove his worth.

He fled the city.

The betrayal, deceit, schemes—it all made him sick. He marched his men to Thebez, a city a day's journey north of Shechem.

When they arrived the next day, they surrounded its walls, allowing none to escape.

The people had no warning. Their leaders fled to the temple in the center of the city and bolted the doors.

Abimelech fought his way to the temple's doors, killing the people who hadn't made it inside. When he reached the barricaded doors, he paused to gain his breath. He looked for branches, as he had done the day before at Shechem.

As he leaned against the tower, a woman pushed a loose stone from the high tower's window pane above him.

It fell, crushing Abimelech's head.

He wiped the blood from his eyes with his sleeve and squinted to see the woman peering down at him.

He was bleeding heavily. His strength was leaving. He turned to the soldier beside him. "Kill me, so it won't be said, 'A woman slew him.'"

The soldier's eyes widened, but he fumbled to fulfill his master's request.

Abimelech watched the sword slide into him.

He died at the base of the temple of Baal-zebub.

He never found that his true worth came from the One Who is worthy.

God repaid the wickedness of Abimelech, which he had done to his father in killing his seventy brothers.

God returned all the wickedness of the men of Shechem on their heads and the curse of Jotham, the son of Jerubbaal came upon them.

And He proved once again, He had not forgotten.

SUMMARY REMARKS

Judges didn't judge. In most cases they became the military leader, leading a group into battle against those who oppressed them. In the case of Shamgar, he didn't bring others to follow him; he fought on his own. In the case of Deborah, she wasn't the battle leader, but did remind the people of what the Law said.

Israel, at this time, was not a united political entity with a strong leader. They operated as tribes or groups of tribes, similar to the "confederation of states" in American history. Each judge affected only a region of Israel.

The book of Judges fills the gap of Israel's history between Joshua and Samuel, setting the stage for the book of Ruth. At the time, everyone did that which was right in their own eyes. Because of this setting, Ruth's retelling of the Kinsman-Redeemer holds more significance. While everyone cared not for anyone else, the redeemer saved Ruth. The contrast brings grace and salvation to life.

God destroyed evil; He did not negotiate with it. He ordered complete annihilation of the people who lived in Israel before His people settled. The Canaanites were wicked, ripe for His judgment. By their presence, they caused God's people to sin.

God also allowed the Philistines, Canaanites, Sidonians and

Hivites to remain in the land to test Israel and teach them war (Judges 3:1-4).

Government's duty is to execute judgment upon evil-doers. Instead, the rulers rewarded injustices and favored cruelty.

Israel had no formal government to execute justice, but instead followed in the sins of those who remained in the land.

Just as God didn't permit sin in those who inhabited the land before His people, so God didn't allow it in His own people. Judges shows this cycle with God's own people. They sinned, God punished them by allowing the heathens to oppress them, and they turned to God for salvation from their suffering.

It wasn't the idea of being a foreigner that brought annihilation. God welcomed those who embraced Israel's faith: examples of this are Tamar, Rahab, and Ruth; all foreigners who became part of the Messianic line.

Many have tried to construct a time-line to explain the disjointedness of the judges. No chronology adequately explains the time required for people's fall into sin, their suffering, and their salvation as does Dr. Gerald Aardsma with his chronology. I refer you to his research at BiblicalChronology.com. But by brief explanation, if a thousand years is added to the book of Judges, the date of the Exodus becomes 2450 BC, substantiating archeological finds and radiocarbon dating without doing extensive gymnastics with the Biblical text as some scholars have tried to do to make the facts correspond to the Biblical account.

Nor do I understand exactly how Samuel fits. Does he follow the judges or reign simultaneously with the later judges?

Although I wish to be as accurate as possible in what I present, both archeologically and biblically, I do take fictitious liberties. I don't try to explain timelines of the judges.

In Chapter 11, Barak is Deborah's husband, as several sources have suggested. Deborah, "wife of Lappidoth" in Judges 4:4, may refer to her making the wicks and oil for the Tabernacle, rather than the name of her husband.

Hosea remarks on the Baal Peor event in Hosea 9:10. The Israelites defiled themselves with fornication and sexual perversion. All leading translators steer timidly clear from this name, which basically comes down to *Lord Hole*.

The people were so addicted to their pleasure and worship that it consumed all their thoughts.

Suffering was the only thing that forced them from their pleasure to look to God.

He would not be ignored.

In spite of the evil and oppression of Judges, it still offers hope, not only to Israel who floundered in their remembering, but to us as we parallel their forgetfulness. The people in judges had it bad. But time after time, we see God raising up a judge that would bring His people out of their oppression to remind them of His faithfulness. God didn't forget Israel and He hasn't forgotten us.

We see evil growing exponentially today. We wonder how bad can it get? Perhaps we wonder where God could be in all of it. God is waiting, like in the time of the judges, for us to acknowledge Him, to remember His Word and wait for His salvation.

There is great comfort in Judges, not when we look to man who keeps forgetting and falling, but to our great God who does not forget. He's still waiting for us to look to Him.

BIBLIOGRAPHY

06 Jezreel Valley Satellite Bible Atlas. June 20, 2013. https://www.youtube.com/watch?v=u0-GuClRMSU (accessed November 1, 2017).

Ancient Israel. n.d. http://www.bible-history.com/geography/ancient-israel/israel-old-testament.html (accessed October 8, 2016).

Bible History. n.d. http://bit.ly/2K2wmtV (accessed November 2016).

Abarim Publications. *Baal-Peor.* n.d. http://www.abarim-publications.com/Meaning/BaalPeor.html#.WfEq62hSwdU (accessed October 25, 2017).

"Abiezrite." *Wikipedia.* May 21, 2017. https://en.wikipedia.org/wiki/Abiezrite (accessed November 2017).

All Sinai Info: Camels. 2004. http://www.allsinai.info/sites/fauna/camel.htm (accessed October 25, 2017).

Alleman, Gayle A. "Ultimate Guide to Olive Oil." *How Stuff Works.* n.d. http://recipes.howstuffworks.com/how-olive-oil-works1.htm (accessed November 2017).

Ancient Destructions: Baalbek Temple and Human Sacrifice Worship to Baal. July 18, 2012. http://bit.ly/2MdKIEk (accessed November 4, 2017).

"Ancient Israel - Bethel." *Bible History.* n.d. http://bit.ly/2KfrIrE (accessed November 2016).

Arabian Camel. n.d. https://on.natgeo.com/2yA5DPT (accessed October 25, 2017).

"Baal worship on the Rise." *News 24.* April 26, 2013. http://www.news24.com/MyNews24/Baal-worship-on-the-rise-20130426 (accessed June 2017).

Belibtreu, Erika. "Grisly Assyrian Record of Torture and Death." *Biblical Archaeology Society.* Jan/Feb 1991 BAR 17:01. http://bit.ly/2K9HCnD (accessed July 9, 2016).

Belly Ballot: Baby Names: Hebrew, Female. n.d. http://babynames.net/all/starts-with/r female hebrew name: (accessed June 2017).

Berry, Roger. "Camel Nose Pegs, Halters, and Bosals." *Camel Photos.* March 28, 2013. http://camelphotos.com/camel_halters.html (accessed November 4, 2017).

"Bethlehem Olivewood Caring Factory." *U-Tube.* May 28, 2011. https://www.youtube.com/watch?v=7lOtqOOeVmc (accessed July 2016).

Bible Hub. *Bible Hub: Thebez.* n.d. http://biblehub.com/topical/t/thebez.htm (accessed December 9, 2017).

—. "Philistines." *Bible Hub.* n.d. http://biblehub.com/topical/p/philistines.htm (accessed July 9, 2016).

—. "The City of Palm Trees." *Bible Hub.* n.d. http://biblehub.com/topical/c/city_of_palm_trees.htm (accessed July 9, 2016).

Biblical Archaeology Society Staff. "Where Did the Philistines Come From?" *Bible History Daily.* 2012. http://www.biblicalarchaeology.org/daily/biblical-artifacts/artifacts-and-the-bible/where-did-the-philistines-come-from/ (accessed July 9, 2016).

Bowman, John S. "Crete." *Encyclopedia Britannica.* n.d. https://www.britannica.com/place/Crete (accessed July 9, 2016).

Bradford, Alina. *Live Science: Camels: Facts, Types and Pictures.* July 11, 2017. https://www.livescience.com/27503-camels.html (accessed October 25, 2017).

Bratchar, Dennis. "Israel's Codes of Conduct Compared to

Bibliography

Surrounding Nations." *The Voice: Biblical and Theological Resources for Growing Christians*. 2013. http://www.crivoice.org/lawcodes.html (accessed June 2017).

Britt, Linda. "The Camel Walk." *U-tube*. November 25, 2009. https://www.youtube.com/watch?v=L8hCFbeHFl4 (accessed November 4, 2017).

Chau, Laura. "Parts of a Spinning Wheel." *Craftsy: Spinning Blog*. April 18, 2014. https://www.craftsy.com/blog/2014/04/parts-of-a-spinning-wheel/ (accessed October 2016).

"Deborah and Jael--Women of the Bible." *The Living Word Library*. n.d. http://www.wordlibrary.co.uk/article.php?id=157 (accessed November 2017).

Deffinbaugh, Bob. *Why Study Judges*. September 16, 2009. https://bible.org/seriespage/1-why-study-judges (accessed November 26, 2016).

Dorothea. "Ashdod and the Philistines." *From Dorothea's Desktop--Articles, Letters, Thoughts*. November 8, 2013. https://fromdorothea.wordpress.com/2013/11/08/ashdod-and-the-philistines/ (accessed July 9, 2016).

Editors of Encyclopaedia Britannica. *Gaza-Strip*. n.d. https://www.britannica.com/place/Gaza-Strip (accessed October 25, 2017).

Glahn, Sandra. "Deborah: The Woman God Uses." *Bible.org*. July 21, 2011. https://bible.org/article/deborah-woman-god-uses (accessed October 2017).

Got Questions. "What is an Oxgoad in the Bible." *Got Questions*. n.d. http://www.gotquestions.org/oxgoad-Bible.html (accessed November 2016).

Got Questions: Who Were the Midianites. n.d. https://www.gotquestions.org/Midianites.html (accessed October 25, 2017).

Harry A. Hoffman, Jr. "Slavery and Slave Laws in Ancient Hatti and Israel." In *Israel: Ancient Kingdom or Late Invention?*, by Daniel Isaac Block, 129-135. Nashville, TN: B&H Publishing Group, 2008.

"Herbs That Can Cause Miscarriage." *Annies Remedy*. n.d.

Bibliography

https://www.anniesremedy.com/chart.php?prop_ID=96 (accessed June 2017).

Hitchcock, Roswell. "Baal-peor." In *Illustrated Bible Dictionary*, by M.A. D.D. M.G. Easton. NY: New York: Thomas Nelson, 1897.

"How To Make a Candle Wick." *Instructables*. August 26, 2013. http://www.instructables.com/id/How-to-Make-a-Candle-Wick (accessed November 2017).

International Dept of the Temple Institute. "The Red Heifer: The Levitical Priests: Their Function and Role in the Holy Temple." *The Temple Institute*. 1999-2017. http://bit.ly/2IhaCVe (accessed July 9, 2016).

"Jabin." *Jewish Virtual Library, Project of AICE*. n.d. http://bit.ly/2K0g7xo (accessed October 2017).

James Orr, M.A., D.D. "Day's Journey." In *International Standard Bible Encyclopedia*, by H. Porter. https://www.biblestudytools.com/encyclopedias/isbe/days-journey.html, 1915.

"Judges 4:2." *Bible Hub*. n.d. http://biblehub.com/commentaries/judges/4-2.htm (accessed October 2017).

Kadari, Tamar. "Deborah 2: Midrash and Aggadah." *Jewish Women's Archive*. n.d. http://jwa.org/encyclopedia/article/deborah-2-midrash-and-aggadah (accessed October 2017).

Kraus, Ed. *Five Tips for Using a Wine Press*. May 17, 2016. http://blog.eckraus.com/using-a-wine-press (accessed October 25, 2017).

Map of Amalekites Territory. n.d. http://www.bible-history.com/geography/maps/map_of_amalekites_territory.html (accessed October 25, 2017).

Map of Midian. n.d. http://bit.ly/2Kct9qV (accessed July 2017).

Mark, Joshua J. "Assyrian Warfare." *Ancient History Encyclopedia*. August 11, 2014. http://www.ancient.eu/Assyrian_Warfare/ (accessed July 2016).

Midnel, Nissan. "The Prophetess Deborah." *Chabad.org*. Kehot Publication Society. http://bit.ly/2ttu2kA (accessed October 2017).

"Modern Baal Worship in Theaters, Stadiums and Living

Rooms." *NCFIC.* August 5, 2014. https://ncfic.org/blog/posts/modern_baal_worship_in_theaters_stadiums_and_living_rooms (accessed June 2016).

Morri Jastrow, Jr, J. Frederic McCurdy, Marcus Jastrow, Louis Ginzberg. "Baal Berith." *Jewish Encyclopedia,* 1906: http://www.jewishencyclopedia.com/articles/2238-baal-berith .

Morris Jastrow, Jr, J. Frederic McCurdy, Duncan B. McDonald. "Baal and Baal Worship." *Jewish Encyclopedia.* n.d. http://www.jewishencyclopedia.com/articles/2236-ba-al-and-ba-al-worship (accessed November 2017).

Morris Jastrow, Jr., J. Frederic McCurdy, Duncan B. McDonald. "Ba'al and Ba'al Worship." *Jewish Encyclopedia.* n.d. http://www.jewishencyclopedia.com/articles/2236-ba-al-and-ba-al-worship (accessed October 2017).

Oriental Institute. "Ancient Mesopotamia." *The Digital Library.* n.d. http://bit.ly/2MdSWMI (accessed July 2016).

"Overview of Ancient oil Lamps ." *Bible History Online.* n.d. http://bit.ly/2yyijXF (accessed November 2016).

Oxford University Press. *Oxford Biblical Studies Online.* n.d. http://bit.ly/2yvKG8I (accessed July 9, 2016).

"Philistine Cities during Isaiah's Ministry." n.d. http://www.jesuswalk.com/isaiah/maps/philistia-1173x1800x300.jpg (accessed July 9, 2016).

Price, Dr. Nelson L. *The Philistines People of Gaza.* 2009. http://www.nelsonprice.com/the-philistine-people-of-gaza/ (accessed July 9, 2016).

Publishers of Amazing Bible Timeline. "Jabin, Canaanite King." October 4, 2014. https://amazingbibletimeline.com/blog/jabin-canaanite-king/ (accessed October 2017).

Rich, Tracey R. "Rabbis, Priests and Other Religious Functionaries." *Judaism 101.* 1995-2011. http://www.jewfaq.org/rabbi.htm (accessed July 9, 2016).

Rudd, Steve. "The Levitical Priesthood." n.d. http://www.bible.ca/archeology/archeology-exodus-route-sinai-levitical-priesthood-levi-gershomites-kohathites-merarites-

Bibliography

aaronic-zadok-asaph-heman-ethan-abiathar-eli-sadducees-annas-caiaphas-ananias.htm (accessed July 9, 2016).

"The Five Levitical Offerings." *Bible History Online*. n.d. http://www.bible-history.com/tabernacle/TAB4The_5_Levitical_Offerings.htm (accessed October 2017).

The Gale Group. "Encyclopedia Judaica: Baal Worship." *Jewish Virtual Library*. 2008. http://bit.ly/2ltxaZY (accessed June 2017).

"The Name Ramah in the Bible." *Abarim Publications*. June 11, 2011, updated November 21, 2017. http://www.abarim-publications.com/Meaning/Ramah.html#.V_9jQOArIdU (accessed December 2017).

VanderLaan, Ray. "Fertility Cults of Canaan." *That the World May Know*. n.d. https://www.thattheworldmayknow.com/fertility-cults-of-canaan (accessed October 8, 2016).

—. "Fertility Cults of Canaan." *That the World May Know*. n.d. https://www.thattheworldmayknow.com/fertility-cults-of-canaan (accessed June 2017).

"What Do You Call a Group of." In *Oxford Dictionary*. https://en.oxforddictionaries.com/explore/what-do-you-call-a-group-of, n.d.

"Where Did the Philistines Come from?" *Mysteries of the Bible: "Unanswered Questions of the Bible"*. January 6, 2010. http://bit.ly/2Kdva63 (accessed July 9, 2016).

Wight, Fred H. "Shepherd Life: The Care of Sheep and Goats." In *Manner and Customs of Bible Lands*, by Fred H. WIght, Chapter 18. http://www.baptistbiblebelievers.com/LinkClick.aspx?fileticket=qDQAYzDf0WM%3D, 1953.

Wikipedia. "Ancient Mesopotamian." *Wikipedia*. n.d. http://bit.ly/2JZhqwt (accessed July 2016).

—. "Astarte." *Wikipedia*. n.d. https://en.wikipedia.org/wiki/Astarte (accessed July 9, 2016).

—. *Baal Berith*. n.d. https://en.wikipedia.org/wiki/Baal_Berith (accessed November 30, 2017).

—. "Minoan Snake Goddess Figurines." *Wikipedia*. n.d. http://bit.ly/2yy1jR9 (accessed July 9, 2016).

Bibliography

——. "Olive Wood Carving in Palestine." *Wikipedia*. April 19, 2017. http://bit.ly/2lq3Hjy (accessed July 2017).

——. "Philistines." n.d. https://en.wikipedia.org/wiki/Philistines (accessed July 9, 2016).

——. *Priapus*. n.d. https://en.wikipedia.org/wiki/Priapus (accessed November 30, 2017).

ABOUT THE AUTHOR

Sonya Contreras grew up with five sisters. She learned not only to rise early to have the bathroom, but that emotional tension of tight quarters *could* bring harmony out of chaos—by nothing short of the work of God. Her parents provided stability and pointed her to God Who was immutable.

Her high school science teacher taught her to ask God even when she didn't like the answer. He showed her a God Who was faithful.

Studying at Cedarville University and Institute for Creation Research Graduate Program grounded her roots in God's truth from His Word *and* His world. She found God Who controls.

By God's strength and grace, she and her husband direct their sons' wanderings in truth and love. Their eight boys learn to be men with convictions, courage, and skills.

God held her hand as she learned of His steadfastness and faithfulness. But raising her boys has caused her to grab hold of His Hand and not let go. She has found God wanted her to know Him.

She writes of God Who is forgiving, faithful, and desires her friendship, in spite of her forgetfulness.

Read more at sonyacontreras.com

THERE'S MORE

Book 2 Remember Me continues the series *He Has Not Forgotten* through the book of Judges to tell of Jephthah, Ibzan, and Samson and how God helped them remember Him.

ALSO BY SONYA CONTRERAS

Tell of My Kingdom's Glory Series tells the love story between God and His people.

In **Book One:** *Until My Name Is Known,* God brings His people to see Him as He frees them from the bonds of Egypt.

In **Book Two:** *I Have Called You by Name,* God draws His people to know Him, as He provides safety through the demands of His Law and teaches dependence upon Him to reach their Land.

In **Book Three:** *I Am with You,* God reassures His people that, as He had been with Moses, so would He be with them. He brings them into the Land promised them, giving rest from their journey.

Expecting Jesus

See Jesus through the eyes of those who met Him. Most expected Him. Only a few were ready for Him.

Simeon looked for the hope of Israel. He found Him.

Herod killed to keep his throne. He sealed his own fate.

Salazar watched for the Coming One and was shown His star in the East.

James struggled to believe, until he put aside his expectations.

Judas expected to overthrow Rome, but didn't seek for power over sin.

Marinus compared Jesus's power with Rome's. He found Jesus to be stronger.

Others came with their expectations. Find them in the pages of Scripture.

Put your own expectations aside.

Know Him by the truth He reveals to you.

Our Story of His Lessons: Twenty Years of Christmas News

People ask about our boys and how we do it. The yearly letters found here give you a glimpse into those answers.

We've lived in the foothills of the Sequoias for over eighteen years. Almost half of the boys were born in the house. We've set down roots, not only in our garden and with our animals but in our hearts where the land has helped us settle. We share memories on a yearly basis of what God teaches us, thus the chronicles of the Christmas letters.

Let Her Hear: Parables from a Mom

These parables (devotionals) are not a substitute for careful, study of the Word. They give a starting point to focus on where God wants you to be all day, a help to see Him even while doing the mundane, routine, necessary, "mom" things in life. They remind you of the heavenly realm that's part of the earthly walk.

They were taken from articles previously written for my website and made into book form.

How Suffering Shows God's Love: A Paradox Explained

Pain opens the heart to search for meaning. We ask God, "Why?" and find He is silent. We question His goodness, love, and sovereignty. These questions bring us to Him.

By coming to Him, we learn the deeper answers. We find the love we crave. We discover the God Who wants us to know Him.

This collection of articles leads us to find that meaning, learn those answers, and see our God.

For a complete and current listing of books with excerpts see www.sonyacontreras.com

REMEMBER ME

But You Have Not Obeyed Me is a book about all mankind.

Man does his own thing. *"Everyone did what was right in his own eyes"* Judges 21:25. Man thinks that's good. But the Bible says, *"The heart is more deceitful than all else, and is desperately sick"* Jeremiah 17:9. *"For all have sinned and fall short of the glory of God"* Romans 3:23.

Choosing our own way brings bondage, and suffering. *"The wages of sin is death"* Romans 6:23 But, just like the Israelites, God did not leave us there. *"But God demonstrates His own love toward us, in that while we were yet sinners, Christ died for us"* Romans 5:8.

God brings us out of bondage when we repent, acknowledging Him. *"Call to Me and I will answer you"* Jeremiah 33:3.

"Cleanse me from my sin. For I know my transgressions, and my sin is ever before me. Against You (God), You only, I have sinned. . . Wash me and I shall be whiter than snow. . . Create in me a clean heart, O God, and renew a steadfast spirit within me. Do not cast me away from Your presence and do not take Your Holy Spirit from me" Psalm 51.

When we look to God, we find hope.

When we turn to Him, we are freed from our bondage.

When we remember Him, we are changed, by His Spirit working in us, to imitate Him.

Don't leave this book without remembering Him.

www.ingramcontent.com/pod-product-compliance
Lightning Source LLC
Chambersburg PA
CBHW051034160426
43193CB00010B/940